STUDY GUIDE

STUDY GUIDE

to accompany

Introducing Psychology

DANIEL L. SCHACTER
DANIEL T. GILBERT
DANIEL M. WEGNER

Russell J. Frohardt
St. Edward's University

WORTH PUBLISHERS

Study Guide
by Russell J. Frohardt
to accompany
Daniel L. Schacter, Daniel T. Gilbert, and Daniel M. Wegner: ***Introducing Psychology***

ISBN-10: 1-4292-3428-8
ISBN-13: 978-1-4292-3428-3

First Printing 2010

Worth Publishers
41 Madison Avenue
New York, NY 10010
www.worthpublishers.com

CONTENTS

Preface vii

CHAPTER 1	PSYCHOLOGY: THE EVOLUTION OF A SCIENCE	**1**
CHAPTER 2	THE METHODS OF PSYCHOLOGY	**15**
CHAPTER 3	NEUROSCIENCE AND BEHAVIOR	**27**
CHAPTER 4	SENSATION AND PERCEPTION	**39**
CHAPTER 5	MEMORY	**55**
CHAPTER 6	LEARNING	**69**
CHAPTER 7	LANGUAGE, THOUGHT, AND INTELLIGENCE	**85**
CHAPTER 8	CONSCIOUSNESS	**105**
CHAPTER 9	EMOTION AND MOTIVATION	**119**
CHAPTER 10	DEVELOPMENT	**133**
CHAPTER 11	PERSONALITY	**147**
CHAPTER 12	PSYCHOLOGICAL DISORDERS	**159**
CHAPTER 13	TREATMENT OF PSYCHOLOGICAL DISORDERS	**175**
CHAPTER 14	STRESS AND HEALTH	**189**
CHAPTER 15	SOCIAL PSYCHOLOGY	**201**

PREFACE

This **Study Guide** is designed for use with *Introducing Psychology* by Daniel L. Schacter, Daniel T. Gilbert, and Daniel M. Wegner. It offers you a chance to review and test your understanding of the textbook material on your own terms. Each chapter begins with *The Big Picture,* a real-life example of a key concept or theme from the textbook. Also included are chapter objectives, a fill-in-the-blank chapter summary, three chapter-based *Quick Quizzes,* and recommendations for further reading and Web links. The *Hey, guess what I learned in Psychology today?* feature combines essay questions and discussion topics to help you think about and discuss class material with people who are not familiar with the field. Another feature, *Things to Ponder,* is a passage that motivates you to further examine what you have learned and how it relates to other topics within the textbook.

Acknowledgments

I would like to thank Christine Burak, Laura McGinn, and Stacey Alexander of Worth Publishers for their dedication in coordinating various aspects of the editorial and production processes.

Russell J. Frohardt
St. Edward's University

STUDY GUIDE

1

Psychology: The Evolution of a Science

THE BIG PICTURE

Is psychology a science, or a practice, or both? Where did psychology originate in the first place? Who was William James, and what did he have to do with Sigmund Freud? These are all questions that prompt different degrees of understanding among the lay public. Psychology is a science, first and foremost; however, some psychologists indeed work in clinical settings to help their clients understand and resolve psychological issues. The stereotype of psychology as a stream of distressed patients divulging their troubles to an elderly Viennese therapist while lying outstretched on a comfy leather sofa is just that—a stereotype. The truth is that very few psychologists currently practice that type of psychology. Sigmund Freud's theories did influence many people and received a great deal of popular attention from nonpsychologists, but it was the greater influence of less familiar pioneers, such as William James, that nurtured the theories and principles that became the foundation of what psychology is today. Chapter 1 covers the origins of psychology in some detail, noting that it arose initially out of physiology and philosophy about 150 years ago. It is a field that has gone through many transformations over the years to embrace the broad and diverse study of the mind and behavior.

Chapter 1 lays the groundwork for all of the chapters that follow in your textbook. We're introduced to some of the key questions that led to the birth of psychology, revolutions within psychology and other academic areas, and some of the ideas that may have taken early psychologists down the wrong track for a while (e.g., phrenology). We start by understanding the desire of the original psychologists to develop a solid methodology (Chapter 2) that addresses questions about the mind without being idiosyncratic. These pioneers began by recording responses to various sensory stimuli (Chapter 4) and eventually relating those responses to the biological components that generate them (Chapter 3). Defining the mind by breaking it down to its components or by only quantifying the stimulus-response relationship was not very satisfying for some psychologists, so they took a more holistic approach, especially as they investigated complex issues such as learning and memory (Chapters 6 and 5), language (Chapter 7), social interactions (Chapter 15), and development across the lifespan (Chapter 10). The results of many of these investigations also led to practical applications, such as identifying people with psychological disorders (Chapter 12) and finding ways to treat them (Chapter 13).

Where would psychology be without the queries from ancient philosophers, quirky biologists, inquisitive surgeons, cranky physiologists, misguided writers, randy professors, daydreaming travelers, and "medicated" therapists? Like a lot of disciplines, it probably wouldn't exist, or it would be sorely lacking in scope. So the next time someone asks you, "What are you going to do with a psychology degree?" you might respond by saying, "You never know. I might just change the way the world thinks about things."

CHAPTER OBJECTIVES

After studying this chapter, you should be able to:

1. Define *psychology* and distinguish between the *mind* and *behavior.*
2. Offer several examples of the topics psychologists study, such as perception, thought, mental functioning, and the breakdown of mental functioning.
3. Explain what a "mind bug" is as described in the text, and give some examples from daily life.
4. Distinguish between *nativism* and *philosophical empiricism.*
5. Summarize the contributions of René Descartes, Franz Gall, and Paul Broca to the early development of the science of psychology.
6. Explain how the study of *physiology* contributed to the development of psychology, noting especially the work of Helmholtz on *reaction time.*
7. Define *structuralism* and describe how Wundt used the concept of *introspection* to support the basic claims of structuralism.
8. Define *functionalism* and describe how James incorporated ideas from Darwin into this school of thought.
9. Give some examples of *illusions* and discuss how errors and illusions can reveal the normal operations of mind and behavior.
10. Summarize the approach of *Gestalt psychologists* and note how it differs from the approach advocated by structuralists.
11. Discuss the development of *psychoanalytic theory* and how it formed the basis for *psychoanalysis.*
12. Describe the basic tenets of *behaviorism,* focusing on its insistence on studying objectively observable behavior.
13. Describe Watson's approach to *behaviorism,* noting how it built on the work of Pavlov.
14. Describe Skinner's approach to *behaviorism,* noting how it reflects a particular view of humankind.
15. Explain how the approach that cognitive psychologists take to the study of behavior differs from that taken by behaviorists.
16. Summarize the contributions of Frederic Bartlett, Jean Piaget, and Kurt Lewin to the early development of *cognitive psychology;* discuss the influence of computer scientists and linguists.
17. Define *behavioral neuroscience* and *cognitive neuroscience* and note some of the techniques these approaches use to studying the mind and behavior.
18. Explain how Darwin's ideas about evolution can be applied to psychology.
19. Compare *social psychology* and *cultural psychology* and describe some of the areas studied by each approach.
20. Describe how women and members of underrepresented groups developed an increasing presence in professional organizations, applied settings, and departments of psychology.
21. Discuss some of the careers available to those who have studied psychology.

CHAPTER OVERVIEW

Use the terms below to fill in the following exercises. Terms may not be used more than once. The answers can be found at the end of this chapter.

academic	Jean-Marie Charcot	postdoctoral
APA	John B. Watson	potential
Carl Rogers	Kenneth B. Clark	psychoanalysis
cognitive	Kurt Lewin	psychology
computer	laboratory	reaction time
cultural	Mary Calkins	reinforcement
evolutionary	memory	responses
Frederic Bartlett	motion	self
free will	natural selection	social
functionalism	neuroimaging	stimulus
genetics	neuroscience	structuralism
gestalt	Noam Chomsky	unconscious
humanistic	Paul Broca	Wilhelm Wundt

Psychology's Roots: The Path to a Science of Mind

The scientific study of mind and behavior is called ________________. Some of the earliest successful efforts to develop a science linking mind and behavior came from a French scientist. ________________ observed the effects of brain damage on the mental abilities and behaviors of people. Hermann von Helmholtz furthered the science by developing methods for measuring ________________. ________________ is credited with founding psychology as a scientific discipline, creating the first psychological ________________, and teaching the first course in physiological psychology. His approach, focusing on analyzing the basic elements of consciousness, was called ________________. William James pioneered the school of ________________, which emphasized the functions of consciousness, and applied Darwin's theory of ________________ to the mind.

Errors and Illusions Reveal Psychology

The errors, illusions, and foibles of mental functioning offer a glimpse into the normal operations of the mind. Max Wertheimer founded ________________ psychology by examining an illusion of ________________ that caused him to see the whole instead of its parts. ________________ and Pierre Janet studied unusual cases in which patients acted like different people while under hypnosis, raising the possibility that each of us has more than one ________________. Through his work with hysteric patients, Sigmund Freud developed the theory of ________________, which emphasized the importance of ________________ influences and childhood experiences in shaping thoughts, feelings, and behavior. Happily, ________________ psychologists, like Abraham Maslow and ________________, offered a more optimistic view of the human condition than Freud, suggesting that people are inherently disposed toward growth and can usually reach their full ________________ with a little help.

Psychology in the 20th Century: Behaviorism Takes Center Stage

Behaviorism advocated the study of observable actions and ________________, and held that inner mental processes were private events that could not be studied scientifically. ________________ launched behaviorism in 1913, focusing on the association between a ________________ and a response, and he emphasized the importance of the environment over ________________ in shaping behavior. B. F. Skinner developed the concept of ________________, demonstrating that animals will repeat behaviors that generate positive outcomes and avoid those that are associated with unpleasant events. Skinner also suggested that ________________ is an illusion, and that the principles of reinforcement should be used to benefit society.

Beyond Behaviorism: Psychology Expands

Psychologists such as ________________, Jean Piaget, and Kurt Lewin defied the behaviorist doctrine and studied the inner workings of the mind. ________________ psychology is concerned with inner mental processes such as perception, attention, ________________, and reasoning. Cognitive psychology developed as a field due to the invention of the ________________, psychologists' efforts to improve the performance of the military, and ________________'s theories about language. Cognitive ________________ attempts to link the brain with the mind through studies of both brain-damaged and healthy people using ________________ techniques that allow glimpses of the brain in action. ________________ psychology focuses on the adaptive value of the mind and behavior, and seeks to understand current psychological processes in terms of abilities and traits preserved by natural selection. Pioneered by individuals like German psychologist ________________, ________________ psychology recognizes that people exist in a network of other people and examines how individuals influence and interact with one another. ________________ psychology is concerned with the effects of the broader culture on the psychological processes of its members.

The Profession of Psychology: Past and Present

The ________________ has grown dramatically since it was formed in 1892 and now includes over 150,000 members, working in clinical, ________________, and applied settings. Psychologists are also represented nationally by the Association for Psychological Science. Through the efforts of pioneers such as the first female APA president, ________________, women have come to play an increasingly important role in psychology. Minority involvement in psychology took longer, but the pioneering efforts of Francis Cecil Sumner, ________________, and others have led to increased participation by minorities in psychology. Psychologists prepare for research careers through graduate and ________________ training and work in a variety of applied settings, including schools, clinics, and industry.

QUICK QUIZ #1

1. The early roots of psychology are firmly planted in philosophy and:
   a. anatomy.
   b. logic.
   c. dualism.
   d. physiology.
2. Historians generally credit the official emergence of psychology as a science to:
   a. Broca.
   b. Helmholtz.
   c. Wundt.
   d. Titchener.
3. William James is to ____________ as Wilhelm Wundt is to ____________.
   a. functionalism; behaviorism
   b. functionalism; structuralism
   c. structuralism; behaviorism
   d. structuralism; functionalism
4. Structuralist psychologists' beliefs were diametrically opposed to what ____________ psychologists believed.
   a. functionalist
   b. behavioral
   c. Gestalt
   d. cognitive
5. Humanistic psychologists accented the ____________, whereas Freud's view of human nature was largely ____________.
   a. constructive; prospective.
   b. negative; positive.
   c. optimistic; pessimistic.
   d. positive; negative.
6. Ivan Pavlov, a Russian physiologist, is best known for his:
   a. experiments with salivating dogs.
   b. experiments with head-bobbing pigeons.
   c. work with clinically depressed clients.
   d. experiments with rats and mazes.
7. Sue's first-grade teacher gives yellow smiley faces for good work in the hopes of encouraging the children to do their best. According to principles of reinforcement, smiley faces would be:
   a. positive reinforcement.
   b. stimuli.
   c. reactionary agents.
   d. negative reinforcement.
8. Wilhelm Wundt is to structuralism as Jean Piaget is to:
   a. functionalism.
   b. humanism.
   c. evolutionary psychology.
   d. cognitive psychology.

9. Dr. Dixon studies what makes adolescents conform to the behaviors and opinions of other adolescents. Which area of psychology does her research best represent?
   a. cognitive psychology
   b. clinical psychology
   c. social psychology
   d. cultural psychology
10. The American Psychological Association was formed in:
    a. 1892 on the campus of Clark University.
    b. 1939 at the beginning of World War II.
    c. at the turn of the century in 1900.
    d. in 1855 in conjunction with Howard University's psychology club.

QUICK QUIZ #2

1. Nurture is to nature as experience is to:
   a. nativism.
   b. adaptation.
   c. behaviorism.
   d. phrenology.
2. The first laboratory devoted exclusively to psychology as an independent field of study opened in:
   a. Berlin in 1879.
   b. Berlin in 1889.
   c. Leipzig in 1889.
   d. Leipzig in 1879.
3. Which school of psychology was most concerned with the adaptive importance of mental processes?
   a. structuralism
   b. behaviorism
   c. functionalism
   d. empiricism.
4. Edward Titchener is to Sigmund Freud as ___________ is to ___________.
   a. inner sensations; the unconscious
   b. psychoanalysis; functionalism
   c. empiricism; structuralism
   d. structuralism; functionalism
5. The branch of psychology that emphasizes the positive potential of human beings is called:
   a. humanistic psychology.
   b. Gestalt psychology.
   c. cognitive psychology.
   d. idealistic psychology.
6. Which psychologists insisted that psychology focus entirely on the study of behavior—what people do—rather than what people experience?
   a. functionalists
   b. behaviorists

c. structuralists

d. Gestalt psychologists

7. B. F. Skinner used a "conditioning chamber" in his research with:
   a. rats.
   b. sea slugs.
   c. cats.
   d. dogs.
8. The advent of ____________ in the 1950s had an enormous conceptual impact on the development of cognitive psychology.
   a. statistical programming
   b. stimulus–response
   c. conditioning
   d. computers
9. The study of the causes and consequences of interpersonal behavior is called:
   a. interpersonal psychology.
   b. cause and effect.
   c. behavioral psychology.
   d. social psychology.
10. Some psychologists believe that newborn babies turn away from noxious odors because this behavior increases their chance of survival. This perspective would be typical of ____________ psychologists.
    a. cultural
    b. psychoanalytic
    c. evolutionary
    d. social

QUICK QUIZ #3

1. Aristotle is to philosophical empiricism as Plato is to:
   a. philosophical structuralism.
   b. nativism.
   c. phrenology.
   d. physiology.
2. Which of the following people used the method of introspection to scientifically focus on basic elements of the mind?
   a. Wilhelm Wundt
   b. William James
   c. John Watson
   d. René Descartes
3. Wundt set up the first psychology research lab in Europe in 1879, but many consider ____________ to be the "father of psychology."
   a. William James.
   b. Charles Darwin.
   c. Wilhelm Wundt.
   d. Kenneth Clark.

4. When his parents put him in his car seat and start up the truck, 2-year-old Mark almost immediately goes to sleep. The sound of the truck engine is a:
   a. response.
   b. stimulus.
   c. reinforcement.
   d. reactionary agent.
5. Jean Piaget is to __________ as Edward Titchener is to __________.
   a. cognitive psychology; structuralism
   b. humanism; functionalism
   c. cognitive psychology; functionalism
   d. humanism; structuralism
6. All of the following were cognitive psychologists EXCEPT:
   a. Sir Frederic Bartlett.
   b. Jean Piaget.
   c. Kurt Lewin.
   d. William James.
7. All of the following contributed to the rise of cognitive neuroscience EXCEPT:
   a. the development of noninvasive brain-scanning techniques.
   b. increased use of introspection techniques.
   c. the advent of PET scans.
   d. the use of MRI scanners.
8. Dr. Coblentz believes that most women prefer to choose young, physically healthy men for their life partners because this boosts their chances for producing healthy offspring. This outlook illustrates the __________ perspective.
   a. cultural
   b. evolutionary
   c. behavioral
   d. developmental
9. Today about half of all members of the APA are American women, quite a contrast to the late 1800s when nearly all members were:
   a. European males.
   b. majority and minority males.
   c. European females.
   d. white males.
10. The first woman to serve as president of the American Psychological Association was:
    a. Mary Calkins.
    b. Karen Horney.
    c. Margaret Floy Washburn.
    d. Mary Clark.

"HEY, GUESS WHAT I LEARNED IN PSYCHOLOGY TODAY?" (AN ESSAY QUESTION)

We're guessing there's someone in your life who is interested in the quality of your educational experiences, is reasonably intelligent, but knows little about psychology. This might be your roommate, a previous teacher, your mom, or some other person you have access to and want to share your thoughts and feelings with. What would you tell that person about the evolution of psychology as a science? How would you explain the importance of understanding the link between the mind and behavior? Who would you say has had the most profound impact on the development of psychology as a science?

THINGS TO PONDER

You've learned a lot of information in this chapter about how psychology became a science and went through many transformations over the decades. When you put it all together, you may start to ponder how all of this relates to issues that are coming up in this textbook. For example, you may ask yourself:

- When you have a psychological question that you want to answer, how do you start your investigation?

  Think about how different psychologists developed different tests or laboratory tasks, and how that all fits into what we will refer to as "the scientific method."

  Consider the fact that there have to be statistical procedures and agreed-upon limits for other experts in the field to be convinced by your findings.

- How do we continue to discover the connection between the brain and behavior?

  Remember that the pioneers studied illusions and errors and that there are many normal and pathological behaviors that still need to be modeled and studied.

  Reflect on the fact that there is more than one way to observe bodily and behavioral changes. You can change a part of the environment and see how the nervous system responds. You could also change a part of the brain and measure changes in behaviors compared to a group of unaffected research participants.

- Is language acquisition the result of learned behavior or some innate responses?

  We saw that this was, and somewhat still is, a heated debate. Skinner believed that all behaviors are learned and based on our histories. Chomsky believed that our brains and bodies are designed to speak through the process of natural selection. Like most things in psychology, the truth contains a little bit of both.

- How can all of this research help people with mental illness?

  Understand that the knowledge gained through studying every aspect of psychology adds to the tools available for practitioners to treat social and biological pathologies of the mind.

  Subscribe to the hope of all psychologists that each one of our contributions advances our science and gets us a little closer to relieving some suffering in the world.

WEB LINKS AND SUGGESTED READING

Classics in the History of Psychology:
http://psychclassics.yorku.ca/topic.htm

- An index of many of the works throughout the history of psychology.

This Week in the History of Psychology:
http://www.yorku.ca/christo/podcasts/

- A series of podcasts hosted by Christopher Green at York University in Toronto, Canada.

Today in the History of Psychology:
http://www.cwu.edu/~warren/today.html

- Need to know *exactly* what went on *today* in the history of psychology? This is the website for you!

Society for the History of Psychology
Division 26 of the American Psychological Association: http://www.historyofpsych.org

- Official site for the APA division of the Society for the History of Psychology with information about memberships, journals, and many links to other historical resources.

VandenBos, G. R. (Ed.) (2007). *APA Dictionary of Psychology*. Washington, DC: American Psychological Association.

- Definitions of general terms, theories, philosophies, and practices in psychology.

James, William. (1890). *The Principles of Psychology*. New York: Henry Holt & Co.

- James's insights into what psychology should be. Still a great reference and an inspiring read for any psychologist.

Answers

Chapter Overview

Psychology's Roots: The Path to a Science of Mind

The scientific study of mind and behavior is called **psychology**. Some of the earliest successful efforts to develop a science linking mind and behavior came from a French scientist. **Paul Broca** observed the effects of brain damage on the mental abilities and behaviors of people. Hermann von Helmholtz furthered the science by developing methods for measuring **reaction time**. **Wilhelm Wundt** is credited with founding psychology as a scientific discipline, creating the first psychological **laboratory**, and teaching the first course in physiological psychology. His approach, focusing on analyzing the basic elements of consciousness, was called **structuralism**. William James pioneered the school of **functionalism**, which emphasized the functions of consciousness, and applied Darwin's theory of **natural selection** to the mind.

Errors and Illusions Reveal Psychology

The errors, illusions, and foibles of mental functioning offer a glimpse into the normal operations of the mind. Max Wertheimer founded **Gestalt** psychology by examining an illusion of **motion** that caused him to see the whole instead of its parts. **Jean-Marie Charcot** and Pierre Janet studied unusual cases in which patients acted like different people while under hypnosis, raising the possibility that each of us has more than one **self**. Through his work with hysteric patients, Sigmund Freud developed the theory of **psychoanalysis**, which emphasized the importance of **unconscious** influences and childhood experiences in shaping thoughts, feelings, and behavior. Happily, **humanistic** psychologists, like Abraham Maslow and **Carl Rogers**, offered a more optimistic view of the human condition than Freud, suggesting that people are inherently disposed toward growth and can usually reach their full **potential** with a little help.

Psychology in the 20th Century: Behaviorism Takes Center Stage

Behaviorism advocated the study of observable actions and **responses**, and held that inner mental processes were private events that could not be studied scientifically. **John B. Watson** launched behaviorism in 1913, focusing on the association between a **stimulus** and a response, and he emphasized the importance of the environment over **genetics** in shaping behavior. B. F. Skinner developed the concept of **reinforcement**, demonstrating that animals will repeat behaviors that generate positive outcomes and avoid those that are associated with unpleasant events. Skinner also suggested that **free will** is an illusion, and that the principles of reinforcement should be used to benefit society.

Beyond Behaviorism: Psychology Expands

Psychologists such as **Frederic Bartlett**, Jean Piaget, and Kurt Lewin defied the behaviorist doctrine and studied the inner workings of the mind. **Cognitive** psychology is concerned with inner mental processes, such as perception, attention, **memory** and reasoning. Cognitive psychology developed as a field due to the invention of the **computer**, psychologists' efforts to improve the performance of the military, and **Noam Chomsky**'s theories about language. Cognitive **neuroscience** attempts to link the brain with the mind through studies of both brain-damaged and healthy people using **neuroimaging** techniques that allow glimpses of the brain in action. **Evolutionary** psychology focuses on the adaptive value of the mind and behavior, and seeks to understand current psychological processes in terms of abilities and traits preserved by natural selection. Pioneered by individuals like German psychologist **Kurt Lewin**, **social** psychology recognizes that people exist in a network of other people and examines how individuals influence and interact with one another. **Cultural** psychology is concerned with the effects of the broader culture on the psychological processes of its members.

The Profession of Psychology: Past and Present

The **APA** has grown dramatically since it was formed in 1892 and now includes over 150,000 members, working in clinical, **academic**, and applied settings. Psychologists are also represented nationally by the Association for Psychological Science. Through the efforts of pioneers such as the first female APA president **Mary Calkins**, women have come to play and increasingly important role in psychology. Minority involvement in psychology took longer, but the pioneering efforts of Francis Cecil Sumner, **Kenneth B. Clark**, and others have led to increased participation by minorities in psychology. Psychologists prepare for research careers through graduate and **postdoctoral** training and work in a variety of applied settings, including schools, clinics, and industry.

Quick Quiz #1

1. **D.** Psychology grew out of philosophers' interests in the mind and behavior, and physiologists' interests in the body.
2. **C.** Wilhelm Wundt founded the first scientific psychology laboratory at the University of Leipzig in 1879.
3. **B.** William James advocated functionalism (focusing on the functions that consciousness serves for an individual), whereas Wilhelm Wundt advocated structuralism (focusing on the structure or "architecture" of consciousness).
4. **C.** The Gestalt psychologists adopted a position that looked at the "whole" or totality of consciousness and experience, which was in opposition to the structuralists' approach of decomposing the elements of consciousness.
5. **C.** Humanism heralds humans' striving for fulfillment and betterment, whereas psychoanalysis focuses on conflict and dark urges.
6. **A.** Pavlov studied the salivary process in dogs; his work formed the foundation for classical conditioning.
7. **A.** Smiley faces would serve as positive reinforcement for a job well done.
8. **D.** Wundt was a structuralist, whereas Piaget was a cognitive psychologist.
9. **C.** One of the topics studied by social psychologists is how and why people conform to the will or behavior of others.
10. **A.** The APA was founded in 1892 at Clark University in Massachusetts.

Quick Quiz #2

1. **A.** Nativism and nature are both shorthand ways of talking about non-environmental influences on thought and behavior.
2. **D.** Wilhelm Wundt founded the first scientific psychology laboratory at the University of Leipzig in 1879.
3. **C.** Functionalism focuses on the adaptive functions that consciousness serves for an individual.
4. **A.** Titchener advocated a kind of structuralism that examined inner feelings, whereas Freud developed psychodynamic theory, which focused on unconscious processes.
5. **A.** Humanism emphasizes human growth and fulfillment.
6. **B.** Behaviorists wanted to steer psychology away from the study of unobservable mental processes and focus only on observable behavior.
7. **A.** B. F. Skinner primarily used rats and pigeons as research subjects
8. **D.** Computer metaphors, such as input-output, information processing, and memory storage, helped inform the development of cognitive psychology.
9. **D.** Social psychologists study the causes and consequences of interpersonal behavior.
10. **C.** Evolutionary psychologists stress the adaptive significance of many human behaviors.

Quick Quiz #3

1. **B.** Aristotle adopted a position of philosophical empiricism, whereas Plato advocated nativism.
2. **A.** Wundt relied on introspection as the main methodology for his new science of psychology.
3. **A.** William James is considered the "father of psychology."
4. **B.** Mark's behavior is due to the learned connections between being in the truck and falling asleep.
5. **A.** Titchener advocated a kind of structuralism that examined inner feelings, whereas Piaget was a cognitive psychologist.

6. **D.** William James was not associated with the cognitive psychology movement; James was associated with the much earlier functionalist movement.
7. **B.** Introspection quickly fell out of favor as a primary methodology for psychology.
8. **B.** Evolutionary psychologists stress the adaptive significance of many human behaviors.
9. **D.** Like a lot of associations, the primary membership of the APA in its earliest days was mainly white males.
10. **A.** Mary Calkins was the first woman to serve as president of the American Psychological Association.

"Hey, Guess What I Learned In Psychology Today?" (An Essay Question)

What might you tell your mom about the evolution of psychology as a science?

- You could start by describing how psychology really came from several different disciplines that converged to address questions about who we are and how our physical bodies interact with the environment. You could describe how the early scientists in psychology first wanted to address the mystery of the mind, but then observable behaviors became the most important issue in psychology, although finally researchers returned to investigate many of the original questions about the mind using sophisticated cognitive and neuroimaging techniques. Flip-floppers? Probably not. As with any science, it takes some time to discover what's important to know, how best to know it, and what to pursue next. The first several decades of the science of psychology illustrate these pursuits.
- You could also discuss how ancient philosophers thought that the mind and the body were separate entities, and that one Frenchman believed that the two intersected in the pineal gland. You might continue by discussing how several early psychologists found a way to link measurable behaviors to the nervous system through some simple timing tasks and some not-so-simple brain surgeries. Maybe you could end by mentioning how many of the more subtle aspects of behavior are being investigated in the various subdisciplines of psychology (e.g., social, developmental, clinical, cognitive, cultural) now that psychology has established a firm link between the brain and behavior.
- So many pioneers with so many amazing contributions! How do you pick just one? It may be easier for you after you have gone a bit further in the textbook and found that you have an affinity for one of the schools of thought or techniques that came from one important psychologist. You may admire the early pioneers, like Wundt or James, who dared to enter unexplored territory. You may lean toward the behaviorist perspective and find Watson or Skinner to be particularly clever. Or maybe you are more of a "whole is more than the sum of the parts" person and end up being a big Max Wertheimer fan. Regardless whom you would choose, there are many people who pushed the frontiers of psychology in the past and continue to do so today.

2

The Methods of Psychology

THE BIG PICTURE

Did you have a sweetheart at home when you left for college? If you did, and you traveled a significant distance to go to school, you probably heard a couple of old proverbs before you left. Your significant other may have leaned over and whispered into your ear, as you packed that last duffle bag into your hatchback, "Absence makes the heart grow fonder." Indeed, you probably missed that person terribly those first few days, or even weeks, when you were apart. During those first weeks on campus, one of your new college friends may have been with you at a party, with lots of other attractive new students, and referenced another well-known proverb: "Out of sight, out of mind."

As you contemplated the obvious contradictions of these two wise proverbs in the context of your new life experiences, and the lessons you have learned in your introductory psychology class, maybe you began to ask yourself, "Which one of the proverbs is actually true?" You ponder the instances of other friends in similar situations, similar stories that you have heard secondhand, and even similar plots in books and movies. There seems to be plenty of evidence that both proverbs are true; then again, how good is a Hollywood movie at portraying real life? But then science comes to the rescue, and you remember some of the key concepts in describing the relationships between two things and how they affect each other. The variables have to be defined, observed, described, measured, compared, and usually manipulated in some way before you can talk about how one thing causes another. Not to mention all of the potential pitfalls that exist out there that may derail your quest to know if being away from a loved one actually makes you feel closer or more distant. Luckily, you aren't the first person to grapple with these kinds of issues, and there are methods that psychologists use to address just these kinds of questions and all of the obstacles that lie between you and the truth.

Chapter 2 describes the essential processes and tools necessary to investigate the questions that scientists (specifically, psychologists) use to answer questions about the causal nature of things in our world. Without the use of these critical methods of psychology, we wouldn't know that neurons in the occipital cortex fire when you see something (Chapters 3 and 4), or that extinguishing an operant response lays down a relatively permanent memory (Chapters 5 and 6), or that taking an Ambien pill is a sure way to end an all-night study session (Chapter 8). If we didn't have methods that allow us to describe normal distributions and averages, we would have a difficult time conceiving what being intelligent really means or when most children typically speak their first words (Chapter 7). How would we have any insight into the parts of our psychological existence that we can't see, like happiness (Chapter 9), introversion (Chapter 11), or depression (Chapter 12) without systematically asking people questions about them?

At the end of your first year of college, you may have your own personal answer to the question about which one of those relationship proverbs is true; but does that mean you are more like the majority of people in these situations, or are you one of the exceptions to the rule? Did absence make your heart "grow fonder" or "go wander"? The fact that you are interested in the answer to this question may be one of the things that drew you to psychology in the first place. Psychologists have been devising new and better methods for answering questions about behavior since the time of Wundt and James. We hope you will take advantage of their pioneering ideas and push the frontiers of psychological knowledge even further. Oh, and say "hello" to your sweetheart the next time you get a chance.

CHAPTER OBJECTIVES

After studying this chapter, students should be able to:

1. Define *empiricism* and describe how it contributes to a scientific method.
2. Explain how *complexity*, *variability*, and *reactivity* make the study of human behavior difficult; provide an example of each attribute.
3. Distinguish between *definition* and *detection* as used in the scientific process and explain what an operational definition is.
4. Explain what a *measure* is and why measures must be both valid and reliable.
5. Define *construct validity*; *predictive validity*; *reliability*; *power*.
6. Distinguish between a *population* and a *sample* and describe how the two are related by the law of large numbers.
7. Define *demand characteristics* and explain how *naturalistic observation* and *double-blind observation* may be used to diminish the problem they present.
8. Distinguish the processes of *observation* and *explanation*.
9. Explain why correlation—a pattern of variability between two things that are measured—is a valuable research technique.
10. Discuss the distinction between *correlation* and *causation* and explain how the third-variable problem limits our ability to infer causation from correlational data.
11. Describe *manipulation* and *random sampling*, the two main features that define an experiment, and discuss how experimentation allows the establishment of causal relationships between variables.
12. Explain why manipulation is critical to experimentation.
13. Define *independent variable*; *dependent variable*.
14. Explain why random sampling is critical to the conduct of an experiment.
15. Describe the characteristics of an internally valid experiment.
16. Define *external validity* and explain how it relates to representative variables used in an experiment.
17. Distinguish between a *theory* and a *hypothesis*.
18. Explain the process of *random sampling*.
19. Discuss three reasons why generalizing from nonrandom samples is not a lethal problem for psychology.
20. Explain each of the following ethical guidelines: informed consent; freedom from coercion; protection from harm; risk–benefit analysis; debriefing.
21. Discuss pros and cons of experiments involving animals.

OVERVIEW

Use the terms below to fill in the following exercises. Terms may not be used more than once. The answers can be found at the end of this chapter.

animals	error	participants
case method	ethics	power
causally	experimentation	powerful
coercion	filler items	randomly
consent	generalize	reactive
control	hypotheses	reliability
correlation	independent	Review Board
demand characteristics	internally	risk
dependent	manipulation	samples
detect	measurement	third variables
double-blind	observed	variation
empiricism	operational definition	

Empiricism: How to Know Things

__________________ involves using observation to gain knowledge about the world. Because causal observation is prone to __________________, sciences have developed methods for observation. These methods are unusually sophisticated in psychology because people are unusually complex, variable, and __________________.

The Science of Observation: Saying What

__________________ is a scientific means of observation that involves defining an abstract property in terms of some concrete condition, called an __________________, and then constructing a device, or a measure, that can __________________ the definitions specified. Measures must be valid, reliable, and __________________. __________________ refers to the consistency of a measure, and __________________ refers to the measure's ability to detect differences that do exist and not to detect differences that don't exist.

Psychologists sometimes use the __________________ to study single, exceptional individuals, but more often they use __________________ of people drawn from a population.

When people are being __________________, they may behave as they think they should. __________________ are features of a setting that suggest to people that they should behave in a particular way. Researchers use cover stories and __________________ to reduce or eliminate demand characteristics. They also use __________________ procedures so that the experimenter's expectations do not influence the participant's behavior.

The Science of Explanation: Saying Why

To determine whether two variables are __________________ related, you must first determine whether they are related at all. This can be done by measuring each variable many times and then comparing the patterns of ________________ within each series of measurements. ________________ refers to a relationship signified by synchronization in the patterns of variation of two variables.

Even when you observe a strong correlation between two variables, you can't conclude that they are *causally* related because there are an infinite number of "________________" that might be causing both. Two variables can be correlated for any one of three reasons: X→Y, Y→X, or Z→X and Y. ________________ can determine for which of these three reasons a pair of variables is correlated. It involves the manipulation of an ________________ variable, resulting in an experimental group and a ________________ group, and the measurement of a ________________ variable. It also requires that participants be ________________ assigned to groups. After comparing across groups, if statistics show that there were significant differences in the measurements across groups, then they are assumed to have been caused by the ________________.

An ________________ valid experiment establishes a causal relationship between variables as they were operationally defined and among the ________________ whom they included. When an experiment mimics the real world we may ________________ from its results. Most psychology experiments are not attempts to mimic the real world but to test ________________ and theories.

The Ethics of Science: Saying Please and Thank You

Psychologists are acutely aware of the responsibilities that come with conducting research with human and nonhuman ________________, and adhere to a strict code of ________________. People must give their informed ________________ to participate in any study, and they must do so free of ________________. The studies also must pose only minimal or no ________________ to the participant. Enforcement of these principles by federal, institutional, and professional governing agencies, such as an Institutional ________________, assures that the research process is a meaningful one that can lead to significant increases in knowledge.

QUICK QUIZ #1

1. The belief that accurate knowledge of the world can be obtained by simply trusting the views and opinions of more experienced people is called:
   a. empiricism.
   b. methodology.
   c. dogmatism.
   d. pragmatism.

2. The property of a measuring device to measure the same way each time it is used is called:
   a. accuracy.
   b. validity.
   c. infallibility.
   d. reliability.

3. Correlation is:
   a. a way of explaining observations.
   b. a pattern of covariation between two variables.
   c. an explanation for cause-and-effect relationships.
   d. the sum of observations made on a sample of participants.
4. The third-variable problem refers to:
   a. the fact that a causal relationship between two variables cannot be inferred from the correlation between two variables.
   b. the fact that correlations can only be caused by another (third) variable.
   c. the fact that each variable in a correlation exerts a causal influence on the other.
   d. the fact that third variables act causally on some other variables, but not *all* other variables.
5. The outcome that gets measured in an experiment is called the:
   a. independent variable.
   b. control variable.
   c. experimental variable.
   d. dependent variable.
6. In a study in which college students are punished (given large amounts of homework, 8:00 a.m. classes, and a steady diet of cafeteria food) to see whether this will affect their scores in their psychology course, what is the *independent variable*?
   a. whether students were punished or not
   b. students' scores on the next psychology midterm
   c. students' previous scores (or baseline) on psychology midterms
   d. students' scores on the next midterm minus the baseline score
7. Generalizability is synonymous with the concept of:
   a. internal validity.
   b. external validity.
   c. experimental manipulation.
   d. causality.
8. A hypothetical account of how and why a phenomenon occurs is called a(n):
   a. hypothesis.
   b. explanation.
   c. experimental result.
   d. theory.
9. The ethical principle of ___________ means that participants must be told the true purpose and nature of an experiment after it is over.
   a. protection from harm
   b. freedom from coercion
   c. debriefing
   d. informed consent

QUICK QUIZ #2

1. A description of a property in measurable terms is called a(n):
   a. operational definition.
   b. hypothesis.
   c. theory.
   d. rule set.

2. ___________ is a research technique that helps reduce bias due to prior expectations.
   a. The case method
   b. Double-blind observation
   c. A correlation coefficient
   d. The survey method

3. Experimentation is related to ___________, whereas observation is related to ___________.
   a. measurement of variables; manipulation of variables
   b. unobtrusiveness; correlation
   c. single variables; multiple variables
   d. manipulation of variables; measurement of variables

4. When an independent variable is manipulated, it produces an experimental group and a:
   a. reactionary group.
   b. secondary group.
   c. control group.
   d. correlational group.

5. A testable prediction derived from a hypothetical account of how and why a phenomenon occurs is called a(n):
   a. experimental result.
   b. theory.
   c. hypothesis.
   d. explanation.

6. Dr. Horton made it clear to his introductory psychology students that if they didn't participate in his research, they would receive a failing grade in his class. What ethical principle has Dr. Horton violated?
   a. freedom from coercion
   b. informed consent
   c. debriefing
   d. protection from harm

QUICK QUIZ #3

1. ___________ involves relying on assumptions and beliefs about the world, whereas ___________ involves making direct observations of the world.
   a. Methodology; dogmatism
   b. Dogmatism; empiricism
   c. Empiricism; dogmatism
   d. Empiricism; methodology

2. Ideally, a measurement process should have ___________, reliability, and power in order for scientists to use it.
   a. definition
   b. stability
   c. validity
   d. consistency
3. Simple observation can tell us *what* happened, but ___________ invokes knowing *why* an event happened.
   a. explanation
   b. statistics
   c. a population
   d. double-blind observation
4. You've noticed that there is a correlation of −.95 between talking speed and the number of questions answered by your professor. What is the most likely explanation for this correlation?
   a. Increased talking speed causes decreased question answering.
   b. Increased question answering causes decreased talking speed.
   c. A third variable causes both increased talking speed and decreased question answering.
   d. Any of these explanations could be correct.
5. The variable that gets manipulated in an experiment is called the:
   a. dependent variable.
   b. covariance variable.
   c. independent variable.
   d. experimental variable.
6. When research participants have an equal chance of ending up in the experimental group or the control group of a study, the process of ___________ has been used.
   a. self-selection
   b. matched selection
   c. correlation matching
   d. random sampling
7. A ___________ is what gets tested directly when a scientific study is conducted.
   a. hypothesis
   b. theory
   c. prediction
   d. explanation
8. The ethical principle of ___________ means that research participants are given enough information about a study to make a reasonable decision about whether they will participate.
   a. freedom from coercion
   b. informed consent
   c. debriefing
   d. protection from harm

9. Which of the following is one of the major ethical principles that psychologists must follow when conducting research?
   a. informed consent
   b. debriefing
   c. risk–benefit analysis
   d. All of these are principles a researcher must follow.

"HEY, GUESS WHAT I LEARNED IN PSYCHOLOGY TODAY?" (An Essay Question)

We're guessing there's someone in your life who is interested in the quality of your educational experiences, is reasonably intelligent, but knows little about psychology. This might be your roommate, a previous teacher, your mom, or some other person you have access to and want to share your thoughts and feelings with. What would you tell them about the methods of psychology? How would you explain that, when it comes to behavior, sometimes seeing is *not* believing? If they wanted to know the relationship between two variables, what would you tell them to do to investigate that relationship and get as close as possible to determining causality?

THINGS TO PONDER

You've learned a lot of information in this chapter about how psychologists examine the relationship between variables of interest to answer questions about behavior. When you put it all together, you may start to ponder how all of this relates to issues that are coming up in this textbook. For example, you may ask yourself:

- What kinds of things would growing up as an identical twin offer to a psychologist who is interested in studying the genetics of personality?

  Think about how many of the complications in implying causality have to do with variability between people and the fact that identical twins are genetically the same.

  Consider the fact that identical twins often share much of their environment and history, but not all of it is the same, and how that is like a natural experiment in how the environment interacts with genes.

- How do we measure intelligence?

  Note that the intelligence quotient is representative of where each individual falls on a normal frequency distribution for mental ability.

  Reflect on the fact that there might be more than one way to measure intelligence and that different groups of people (e.g., cultures) might value different mental abilities. The standard way that psychologists measure intelligence may be irrelevant to some ways of living.

- What measure would you use to determine if someone was highly motivated?

  Recall that defining your phenomenon or variable is crucial to a successful study. Because motivation is a difficult concept to operationally define, you might need to look at a combination of relatively abstract behaviors (e.g., body language, facial expressions) along with concrete measures (e.g., number of widgets produced in a day).

Remember that sometimes you can get a sense of how a phenomenon works by observing a *lack* of behavior. What do lazy people do that seemingly more motivated people don't do?

- Do clinical psychologists rely on the same kinds of methods as research psychologists?

  Understand that many of the advances in treatment techniques have come from the results of studies that were conducted using solid scientific methods. The questions in those studies were aimed at finding the causes of psychological disorders.

  Many clinicians also conduct research and teach in addition to their work as therapists.

WEB LINKS AND SUGGESTED READING

Pope, Kenneth S. – Fallacies and Pitfalls in Psychology: http://kspope.com/fallacies/fallacies.php

- An index of 18 common mistakes made doing research in psychology.

Garson, G. David – Statnotes: Topics on Multivariate Analyses (Online Research Methods Textbook): http://www2.chass.ncsu.edu/garson/pa765/statnote.htm

- A virtual book with descriptions and resources for basic and advanced methods and statistics.

Central Limit Theorem Applet: http://www.stat.sc.edu/~west/javahtml/CLT.html

- Allows you to roll dice to see how the tendency works.

Research Randomizer: http://www.randomizer.org/

- A random number generator for when you need to randomize your samples in an experiment.

Davis, Stephen F. (Ed.) (2003). *Handbook of Research Methods in Experimental Psychology*. Malden, MA: Blackwell Publishing Limited.

- Handbook of methods plus a historical foundation for the methods.

Best, Joel (2001). *Damned Lies and Statistics: Untangling Numbers from the Media, Politicians, and Activists*. Berkeley, CA: UC Press.

- A look at how statistics are often used to deceive audiences and how to cut through the numbers and the words involved in the scam.

Thomas, Jay C., and Hersen, Michel (Eds.) (2003). *Understanding Research in Clinical and Counseling Psychology*. Mahwah, NJ: Lawrence Erlbaum Associates.

- Addresses specific issues in doing research in the clinical realm.

Answers

Chapter Overview

Empiricism: How to Know Things

Empiricism involves using observation to gain knowledge about the world. Because causal observation is prone to **error**, sciences have developed methods for observation. These methods are unusually sophisticated in psychology because people are unusually complex, variable, and **reactive**.

The Science of Observation: Saying What

Measurement is a scientific means of observation that involves defining an abstract property in terms of some concrete condition, called an **operational definition**, and then constructing a device, or a measure, that can **detect** the definitions specified. Measures must be valid, reliable, and **powerful**. **Reliability** refers to the consistency of a measure, and **power** refers to the measure's ability to detect differences that do exist and not to detect differences that don't exist.

Psychologists sometimes use the **case method** to study single, exceptional individuals, but more often they use **samples** of people drawn from a population.

When people are being **observed**, they may behave as they think they should. **Demand characteristics** are features of a setting that suggest to people that they should behave in a particular way. Researchers use cover stories and **filler items** to reduce or eliminate demand characteristics. They also use **double-blind** procedures so that the experimenter's expectations do not influence the participant's behavior.

The Science of Explanation: Saying Why

To determine whether two variables are **causally** related, you must first determine whether they are related at all. This can be done by measuring each variable many times and then comparing the patterns of **variation** within each series of measurements. **Correlation** refers to a relationship signified by synchronization in the patterns of variation of two variables.

Even when you observe a strong correlation between two variables, you can't conclude that they are *causally* related because there are an infinite number of **"third variables"** that might be causing both. Two variables can be correlated for any one of three reasons: X→Y, Y→X, or Z→X and Y. **Experimentation** can determine for which of these three reasons a pair of variables is correlated. It involves the manipulation of an **independent** variable, resulting in an experimental group and a **control** group, and the measurement of a **dependent** variable. It also requires that participants be **randomly** assigned to groups. After comparing across groups, if statistics show that there were significant differences in the measurements across groups, then they are assumed to have been caused by the **manipulation**.

An **internally** valid experiment establishes a causal relationship between variables as they were operationally defined and among the **participants** whom they included. When an experiment mimics the real world we may **generalize** from its results. Most psychology experimets are not attempts to mimic the real world but to test **hypotheses** and theories.

The Ethics of Science: Saying Please and Thank You

Psychologists are acutely aware of the responsibilities that come with conducting research with human and nonhuman **animals**, and adhere to a strict code of **ethics**. People must give their informed **consent** to participate in any study, and they must do so free of **coercion**. The studies also must pose only minimal or no **risk** to the participant. Enforcement of these principles by federal, institutional, and professional governing agencies, such as an Institutional **Review Board**, assures that the research process is a meaningful one that can lead to significant increases in knowledge.

Quick Quiz #1

1. **C.** Dogmatism summarizes a view of knowledge that is based on accepted wisdom or doctrine passed down over the ages.
2. **D.** Reliability refers to the consistency of a measurement process.
3. **B.** Correlation is the pattern of covariation between two variables.

4. **A.** Correlation and causality are two separate issues; knowing correlation does not provide a solid basis for inferring causality.
5. **D.** The dependent variable is the outcome that gets measured in an experiment.
6. **A.** The independent variable is the thing that is controlled by the researcher; in this case, the presence or absence of punishment.
7. **B.** External validity refers to the generalizability of research findings.
8. **D.** A theory is a hypothetical account of how and why a phenomenon occurs.
9. **C.** Participants need to be debriefed at the end of a psychological study.

Quick Quiz #2

1. **A.** An operational definition is a description of a property in measurable terms.
2. **B.** In a double-blind procedure, neither the experimenter nor the research participant knows the true purpose of the study.
3. **D.** Experimentation involves the manipulation of an independent variable.
4. **C.** The manipulation of an independent variable results in an experimental group and a control group.
5. **C.** A hypothesis is a testable prediction derived from a theory.
6. **A.** Participants may not be coerced into taking part in a research study.

Quick Quiz #3

1. **B.** Dogmatism summarizes a view of knowledge that is based on accepted wisdom or doctrine passed down over the ages, whereas empiricism advocates taking direct measurements in the world.
2. **C.** Validity, reliability, and power are all essential aspects of a measurement process.
3. **A.** Observation is the "what" part of methodology, whereas explanation is the "why" part.
4. **D.** Correlation does not imply causality; any of these explanations might be correct.
5. **C.** The independent variable gets manipulated in an experiment.
6. **D.** Random sampling is used to make sure that participants have an equal chance of being assigned to the control group or experimental group in a study.
7. **A.** Hypotheses are tested in science, rather than the theories themselves that generate hypotheses.
8. **B.** Participants must give their informed consent before taking part in a psychological study.
9. **D.** All of these are principles that psychologists must follow when conducting a research study.

"Hey, Guess What I Learned In Psychology Today?" (An Essay Question)

What might you tell your mom about methods in psychology?

- You could start by describing how, like any other science, psychology requires systematic observation of the world in order to gain accurate knowledge of it, and the belief in that process is called empiricism. You could then explain that it is just as important to define the thing that you are interested in knowing about as it is to measure that thing. You would want to describe how to avoid some of the potential problems that arise when a person tries to examine the relationship between two things, like making sure that you are measuring what you are supposed to be measuring, getting a large and representative sample of subjects to study, and avoiding experimenter influence and bias or other variables that are not accounted for in your study.
- You might start with an example or an old proverb, like the "Big Picture" story at the beginning of this chapter of the study guide. For example, you might point out that some people say, "Birds of a feather flock together," whereas others claim the contradictory proverb, "Opposites attract," to be true. You could ask if your mom could think of instances that support either statement. Surely she would be able to come up with examples. Then you could mention that careful studies by social psychologists, using specific scientific methods, showed that opposites don't really attract as much as people who are similar do. Common sense or folk logic can be deceiving sometimes, and that is why we need to systematically test ideas about behavioral relationships and correlations.
- After these fascinating discussions, your mom is probably feeling pretty confident that she has a

handle on drawing conclusions about causality. This is when you have to put it all into context and mention some of the reasons why it is difficult to infer causality, even when studies have been performed very carefully. You would mention that it is often difficult to control all of the variables in an experiment, especially with people. Then you might go on to point out that even if you could control every variable, you can't test every single person on the planet in every conceivable circumstance in the context of every culture, making it difficult to be 100% certain that the two things you are studying are causally related. This letdown will have a silver lining when she realizes that it means you will always have a job studying these possibilities when you become a psychologist.

3

Neuroscience and Behavior

THE BIG PICTURE

Does the mind exist without the brain? This is a question that great thinkers, philosophers and scientists alike, have been contemplating for hundreds, even thousands of years. The majority of psychologists would agree that our behaviors are a product of signals from our brains. We have already learned that the science of psychology was born out of physiology and philosophy (see Chapter 1), and with the relatively recent advances in technology, we know more about how the nervous system controls behavior than ever before. Understanding the brain means knowing about thousands of brain structures, billions of neurons, complex patterns of connectivity, and sophisticated computations mediated by signals that rely on intricate molecular signaling cascades. No matter what level of the nervous system we decide to analyze, from individual synapses to neural circuits, each layer has some features that are critical for understanding development, neural plasticity, disease, and individual variability and personality.

Chapter 3 introduces us to the basic components and mechanisms that are necessary for information to be processed and actions to be taken. We start by understanding the anatomy of a neuron, how that neuron sets the stage for the possibility, or potential, for a signal to be sent to another part of the body, and then how that signal is sent, first electrically, then chemically. These basic signals result in the messages that allow us to ultimately see and hear (see Chapter 4), learn and remember (see Chapters 5 and 6), and even decide what to have for lunch (see Chapter 7).

Understanding how the brain develops and how it is eventually organized gives us the opportunity to study the functions of different areas and circuits of the brain and how they relate to our behaviors. For example, we will see that the hippocampus, a structure in the limbic system, is extremely important for forming memories, especially memories about our personal experiences. Although the hippocampus has developed to be a great structure for making memories and is connected to many other parts of the brain, it is susceptible to problems in forming those memories following damage (e.g., patient HM), ingestion of certain drugs, and even chronic stress (see Chapters 5, 9, and 14).

Chapter 3 gives us a glimpse into the unbelievably complex structures and workings of the nervous system. You will learn throughout the remainder of the textbook about a host of studies that have investigated the role of various brain structures in every facet of psychology. Although we probably won't be able to say for sure whether Descartes made an error by asserting that the mind and the body are separate, we will have a lot of fun trying to figure it out.

CHAPTER OBJECTIVES

After studying this chapter, students should be able to:

1. Identify the components of a *neuron.*
2. Distinguish among different types of neurons and support cells in the brain.
3. Define the components of a neuron's electrical properties.
4. Explain how neurons send electrical signals over long distances.
5. Describe how neurons communicate with one another through chemical signals.
6. Identify several major *neurotransmitters.*
7. Explain how some drugs mimic neurotransmitters and others block normal neurotransmission.
8. Describe the basic organization of the *nervous system.*
9. Distinguish the functional differences between major parts of the *central and peripheral nervous system.*
10. Explain how the nervous system develops from a few relatively similar cells to a complex network of differentiated cells and pathways.
11. Describe the differences between the central nervous system of an animal other than a human and that of a human.
12. Identify some of the anatomical results of the evolution of the human nervous system.
13. Discuss, in general terms, how the genes of an individual interact with the environment to produce physiology and behavior that are unique.
14. Describe some of the important findings about brain anatomy and function that have resulted from studies of people and animals with brain damage.
15. Identify some of the techniques used to monitor the nervous system.
16. Explain why it is important to measure brain function both at very basic levels (considering single neurons, neurotransmitters, and *receptors*) and holistically (considering entire areas and systems) in order to understand the connection between the brain and behavior.

CHAPTER OVERVIEW

Use the terms below to fill in the following exercises. Terms may not be used more than once. The answers can be found at the end of this chapter.

acetylcholine	forebrain	negative	refractory
action potential	gene	neurons	reticular formation
agonists	glial cells	nodes of Ranvier	reuptake
antagonists	heritability	occipital	sensory neurons
axon	hindbrain	orient	serotonin
cell body	imaging techniques	parasympathetic	spinal cord
central	interneurons	peripheral	sympathetic
cerebellum	ions	plasticity	synapse
cerebral	medulla	potassium (k^+)	temporal
dizygotic	midbrain	potential	threshold
electroencephalogram	monozygotic	presynaptic	twenty-three
enzyme deactivation	myelin	receptors	vesicles

Neurons: The Origin of Behavior

__________________ are the information-processing elements of the nervous system. They process information from the environment, communicate with one another, and send information to the rest of the body. The three main components of a neuron are the __________________ or *soma*, dendrites, and the __________________. The __________________, or small gap between neurons, is where the chemical message from the "sending" neuron travels to the "receiving" neuron. The three major types of neurons include __________________ (e.g., in the eye or ear), motor neurons, and the type of neurons that communicate between the first two types, __________________.

__________________ serve as the support team for the nervous system. One example of the support that these cells provide is the formation of an insulating sheath that improves the speed of transmission along the axon of a neuron. This insulating sheath is called __________________.

Neurons have a resting __________________ that is created by the balance of electrical forces on charged molecules, or __________________. There are more __________________ molecules inside of a neuron relative to the outside of a neuron, which leads to the __________________ charge of the inside of a neuron relative to the outside.

When the charge of a neuron breaks the __________________, as the result of depolarizing signals coming in, a(n) __________________ is initiated, which is an all-or-none signal that moves down the length of the axon. The signal travels faster in myelinated axons, jumping between the __________________. For a brief period after the action potential, the neuron is __________________, meaning that it cannot fire again.

When an action potential reaches the end of the sending, or __________________, neuron's axon, the signal turns from electrical to chemical, as a neurotransmitter is released from __________________ into the synaptic cleft. Neurotransmitters and their corresponding __________________ operate in a lock-and-key fashion on the receiving side of the synapse. After a neurotransmitter has activated the postsynaptic neuron it can be cleared from the synapse through __________________ (being taken back up into the cell), or __________________ (being broken down into smaller parts).

Some of the major neurotransmitters are __________________ of which low levels are commonly associated with Alzheimer's disease, norepinephrine, __________________, of which low levels are commonly associated with depression, dopamine, glutamate, and GABA. Drugs often affect these neurotransmitters. Drugs that enhance or mimic neurotransmitters are called __________________, whereas those that block neurotransmitters are called __________________.

The Organization of the Nervous System

The nervous system is divided into the __________________ nervous system, which is composed of the brain and spinal cord, and the __________________ nervous system, which is composed of the somatic and autonomic nervous systems. The somatic nervous system receives sensory information and controls the contractions of voluntary muscles. The autonomic nervous system automatically controls the organs of the body. The __________________ division of the autonomic nervous system prepares the body for action during times of threat, whereas the __________________ division is active during times of relaxation and rest.

In the central nervous system, the ________________ helps transmit information to and from the brain. The brain can be divided into three main sections: the ________________, the midbrain, and the ________________. In the hindbrain several structures are responsible for life-sustaining functions. For example, the ________________ coordinates breathing and heart rate, the ________________ regulates sleep and arousal, and the ________________ coordinates fine motor skills. The midbrain contains the tectum and the tegmentum, which help an organism ________________ in the environment. The forebrain coordinates high-level functions (among other things), and houses the ________________ cortex and subcortical structures. The cerebral cortex is divided into two hemispheres, each with four cortical lobes. Those lobes are the frontal lobe, parietal lobe, ________________ lobe (associated with memory), and the ________________ lobe (mostly visual). Neurons in the brain can change as a result of experience and reassign functions to other areas. This process is called ________________.

The Evolution of Nervous Systems

The three major parts of the brain differentiate as development continues, with the ________________ folding over the hindbrain, and the forebrain folding over the midbrain. Throughout development the structures of the brain continue to differentiate, migrate, and connect to one another.

The unit of hereditary transmission, or ________________, is built from strands of DNA and organized into chromosomes. Humans have ________________ pairs of chromosomes, with half coming from each parent. ________________ twins share 100% of their genes, whereas ________________ twins share 50% of their genes, just like non-twin siblings. Both genes and environmental factors exert influence on people's behaviors; however, genes do not predict a particular individual's characteristics. ________________ is a measure of the variability in behavioral traits that can be accounted for by genetic variation.

Investigating the Brain

Behavioral neuroscientists investigate the links between the brain and behavior. This chapter describes three approaches to studying these links: studying people with brain damage, electrical recording of brain activity, and ________________. The link between a brain area and language, for example, can be studied in someone who has suffered a brain injury and has difficulty producing speech. The machine that interprets the patterns of electrical activity in large brain areas from outside of the skull is called a(n) ________________. Many brain imaging techniques such as CT scans, MRI, PET, and fMRI continue to help identify the links between brain activity and specific tasks or behaviors.

QUICK QUIZ #1

Instructions: Label the following figures with the appropriate terms.

a)

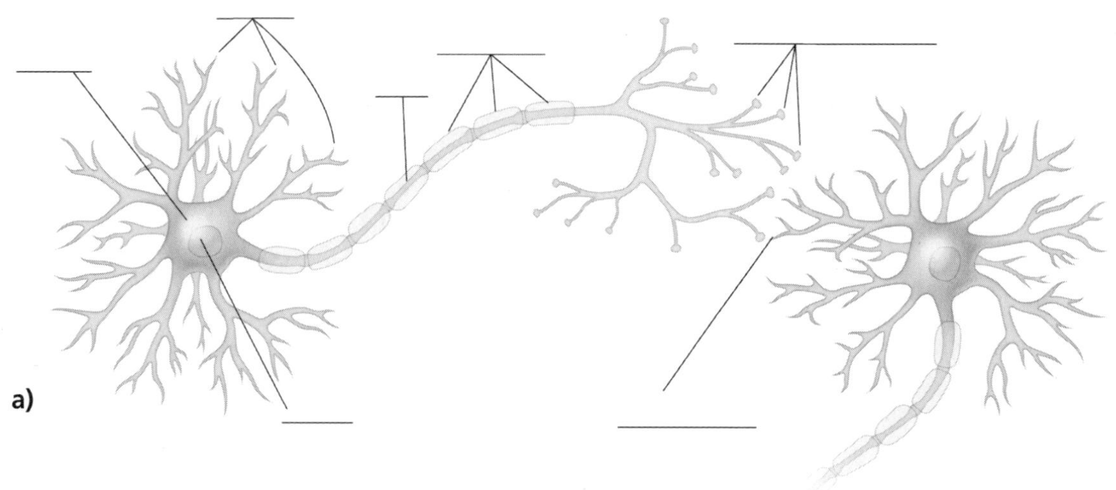

b)

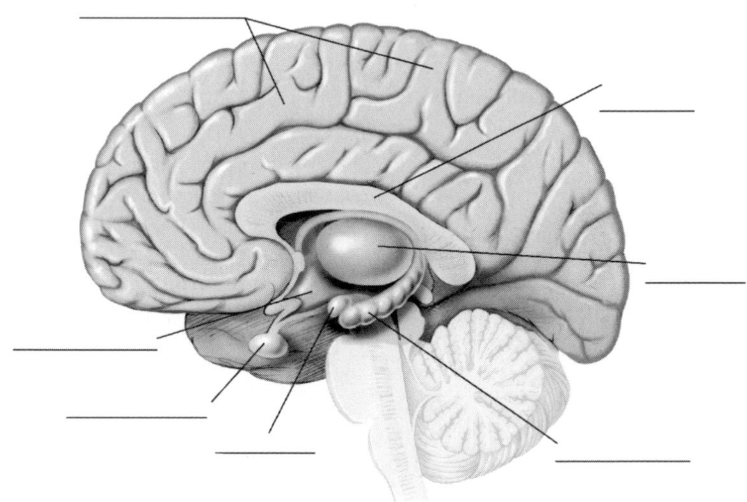

QUICK QUIZ #2

1. ____________ are cells in the nervous system that communicate with one another to perform information-processing tasks.
   a. Glia
   b. Oligodendrocytes
   c. Mitochondria
   d. Neurons

2. ___________ carry signals from the spinal cord to the muscles to produce movement.
   a. Sensory neurons
   b. Motor neurons
   c. Interneurons
   d. Cortical neurons

3. The difference in electrical charge between the inside and the outside of a neuron's cell membrane is called the:
   a. transmission.
   b. conduction.
   c. resting potential.
   d. action potential.

4. At rest, there is a higher concentration of ___________ on the inside of the cell membrane of the neuron and ___________ on the outside of the cell membrane of the neuron.
   a. Na^+; K^+
   b. K^+; Na^+
   c. Na^+; Ca^{++}
   d. Na^+; Cl^-

5. The end of a neuron contains many ___________ filled with ___________ for transmitting messages to the neuron on the other side of the synapse.
   a. vesicles; receptors
   b. transporters; neurotransmitters
   c. neurotransmitters; vesicles
   d. vesicles; neurotransmitters

6. What neurotransmitter is *most* closely associated with pleasure and motivation?
   a. Glutamate
   b. Serotonin
   c. Dopamine
   d. Acetylcholine

7. ___________ is the primary excitatory neurotransmitter in the brain, whereas ___________ is the primary inhibitory neurotransmitter in the brain.
   a. Glutamate; GABA
   b. GABA; glutamate
   c. Glutamate; serotonin
   d. GABA; dopamine

8. The central nervous system is made up of the:
   a. brain and cranial nerves.
   b. spinal nerves and cranial nerves.
   c. somatic and autonomic nervous systems.
   d. brain and spinal cord.

9. What subdivision of the autonomic nervous system would be most associated with the phrase "fight or flight?"
   a. the central nervous system
   b. the parasympathetic nervous system
   c. the sympathetic nervous system
   d. the somatic nervous system

10. The ___________ relays and filters information from the senses and transmits the information to the cerebral cortex.
    a. thalamus
    b. hypothalamus
    c. cerebellum
    d. tegmentum

QUICK QUIZ #3

1. The ___________ attaches significance to previously neutral events that are associated with fear, punishment, or reward.
    a. amygdala
    b. hippocampus
    c. hypothalamus
    d. thalamus
2. ___________ are the regions of the brain composed of neurons that help provide sense and meaning to information registered in the cortex.
    a. Occipital lobes
    b. Association areas
    c. Hippocampi
    d. Lateral ventricles
3. ___________ are strands of DNA wound around each other in a double-helix configuration.
    a. Genes
    b. Enzymes
    c. Heritables
    d. Chromosomes
4. Your biological sex would be male if you received an additional ___________ from your father.
    a. Y chromosome
    b. mustache gene
    c. X chromosome
    d. Z chromosome
5. The split-brain procedure involved severing the ___________ of patients, usually to stop the spread of debilitating seizures.
    a. anterior commissure
    b. corpus collosum
    c. pons
    d. pituitary gland
6. ___________ and ___________ are functional neuroimaging techniques.
    a. CT scans; PET
    b. PET; MRI
    c. PET; fMRI
    d. CT scans; fMRI

7. ____________ was the name of the man who had an accident that sent an iron rod through his frontal lobe, giving scientists the first clues into the role of the frontal lobes in emotion and personality.
   a. John M. Harlow
   b. Paul Broca
   c. Roger Sperry
   d. Phineas Gage

"HEY, GUESS WHAT I LEARNED IN PSYCHOLOGY TODAY?" (AN ESSAY QUESTION)

We're guessing there's someone in your life who is interested in the quality of your educational experiences, is reasonably intelligent, but knows little about psychology. This might be your roommate, a previous teacher, your mom, or some other person you have access to and want to share your thoughts and feelings with. What would you tell that person about behavioral neuroscience? How would you explain the importance of understanding the nervous system when studying behavior? How would you relate what goes on at a microscopic cellular level to the visible actions we see at a behavioral level?

THINGS TO PONDER

You've learned a lot of information in this chapter about how important the brain is for every behavior that we exhibit, whether it is a voluntary behavior or not. When you put it all together, you may start to ponder how all of this relates to issues that you have already learned about in this textbook and issues that are coming up. For example, you may ask yourself:

- How could the brain, with electrical and chemical processes, represent our complex behaviors and experiences?

  Think about how different experiences result in physical changes in the brain, or *plasticity*.

  Consider the fact that different neurons fire in different patterns and use hundreds of different neurotransmitters.

- What kind of brain activity represents consciousness?

  Think about the different parts of the brain that are used for different behaviors and the combinations that might be required to be considered consciousness.

  Reflect on the fact that much of the brain is dedicated to sensing and perceiving the world. Is that consciousness or is it something more complex?

- What parts of our brains, or neural signals, are involved in social psychology?

  We saw that there are special neurons involved in recognizing faces and registering something like empathy. Think about how those specializations might have evolved in social animals.

  Consider how males and females have evolved

slightly different parts of their brains, and other parts of their physiology and anatomy. They may have started off as sexually relevant body parts and functions that are now a part of our social signs of attraction.

- What would it be like if a specific part of your brain began to fail?

  Unfortunately, this may not be hard for you to imagine as millions of people are affected by neurological disorders and mental illness. Some of the pathologies involve multiple systems, whereas others are the result of one simple step of a process gone wrong.

  Put yourself in the shoes of someone with depression, Alzheimer's disease, epilepsy, or multiple sclerosis. Imagining the loss of many of the behaviors and functions that we take for granted may make you stop and smell the roses a bit more often.

WEB LINKS AND SUGGESTED READINGS

Milestones in Neuroscience Research: http://faculty.washington.edu/chudler/hist.html

- A history of the important discoveries in neuroscience.

Interactive Atlases: Digital Anatomist Project: http://www9.biostr.washington.edu/da.html

- Features several illustrated and photographic maps of the brain and other parts of the body.

The online edition of Gray's *Anatomy of the Human Body*: http://education.yahoo.com/reference/gray/

- Links pictures and descriptions of all different parts of the body, including the brain and peripheral nerves.

Genetics Home Reference: Your Guide to Understanding Genetic Conditions: http://ghr.nlm.nih.gov/

- Descriptions of genetic conditions that can affect the nervous system and links for other genetically related questions.

Neuroscience for Kids: http://faculty.washington.edu/chudler/neurok.html

- Great resources for teaching younger children about the brain.

Brain Facts: http://www.sfn.org/index.cfm?pagename=brainfacts

- A 64-page primer on the brain and nervous system, and a starting point for a lay audience interested in neuroscience, published by the Society for Neuroscience.

Brain Briefings: http://www.sfn.org/index.cfm?pagename=brainBriefings_main

- A series of topical, short articles written for the lay public, published by the Society for Neuroscience.

WebMD: http://www.webmd.com/

- A great searchable resource for the description of illnesses and medications.

Armond, Stephen J., Fusco, Madeline M., and Dewey, Maynard M. (1989). *Structure of the Human Brain: A Photographic Atlas, 3rd Edition*. New York: Oxford University Press.

- Pictures of the human brain in a spiral atlas.

Blumenfeld, Hal. (2002). *Neuroanatomy through Clinical Cases*. Sunderland, CT: Sinauer Associates.

- Case presentations lay the framework for patient care, and this text provides cases that allow insight into the regions of the brain that are affiliated with particular afflictions or behavioral symptoms.

Defries, John C., McGuffin, Peter, McClearn, Gerald E., and Plomin, Robert (2000). *Behavioral Genetics, 4th* Edition. New York: Worth Publishers.

- An in-depth coverage of the complex interactions between genes, behavior, and the environment.

Kandel, Eric R., Schwartz, James H., and Jessell, Thomas M. (2000). *Principles of Neural Science*. New York: McGraw Hill.

- An all-encompassing text on the different parts of the brain and the research associated with it by a Nobel laureate and his colleagues.

Answers

Chapter Overview

Neurons: The Origin of Behavior

Neurons are the information-processing elements of the nervous system. They process information from the environment, communicate with one another, and send information to the rest of the body. The three main components of a neuron are the **cell body** or soma, dendrites, and the **axon**. The **synapse**, or small gap between neurons, is where the chemical message from the "sending" neuron travels to the "receiving" neuron. The three major types of neurons include **sensory neurons** (e.g., in the eye or ear), motor neurons, and the type of neurons that communicate between the first two types, **interneurons**.

Glial cells serve as the support team for the nervous system. One example of the support that these cells serve is the formation of an insulating sheath that speeds the speed of transmission along the axon of a neuron. This insulating sheath is called **myelin**.

Neurons have a resting **potential** that is created by the balance of electrical forces on charged molecules, or **ions**. There are more **potassium (K^+)** molecules inside of a neuron relative to the outside of a neuron, which leads to the **negative** charge of the inside of a neuron relative to the outside.

When the charge of a neuron breaks the **threshold**, as the result of depolarizing signals coming in, an **action potential** is initiated, which is an all-or-none signal that moves down the length of the axon. The signal travels faster in myelinated axons, jumping between the **nodes of Ranvier**. For a brief period after the action potential, the neuron is **refractory**, meaning that it cannot fire again.

When an action potential reaches the end of the sending, or **presynaptic**, neuron's axon, the signal turns from electrical to chemical, as neurotransmitter is released from **vesicles** into the synaptic cleft. Neurotransmitters and their corresponding **receptors** operate in a lock-and-key fashion on the receiving side of the synapse. After a neurotransmitter has activated the postsynaptic neuron it can be cleared from the synapse through **reuptake** (being taken back up into the cell), or **enzyme deactivation** (being broken down into smaller parts).

Some of the major neurotransmitters are **acetylcholine**, of which low levels are commonly associated with Alzheimer's disease, norepinephrine, **serotonin**, of which low levels are commonly associated with depression, dopamine, glutamate, and GABA. Drugs often affect these neurotransmitters. Drugs that enhance or mimic neurotransmitters are called **agonists**, whereas those that block neurotransmitters are called **antagonists**.

The Organization of the Nervous System

The nervous system is divided into the **central** nervous system, which is composed of the brain and spinal cord, and the **peripheral** nervous system, which is composed of the somatic and autonomic nervous systems. The somatic nervous system receives sensory information and controls the contractions of voluntary muscles. The autonomic nervous system automatically controls the organs of the body. The **sympathetic** division of the autonomic nervous system prepares the body for action during times of threat, whereas the **parasympathetic** division is active during times of relaxation and rest.

In the central nervous system, the **spinal cord** helps transmit information to and from the brain. The brain can be divided into three main sections: the **hindbrain**, the midbrain, and the **forebrain**. In the hindbrain several structures are responsible for life-sustaining functions. For example, the **medulla** coordinates breathing and heart rate, the **reticular formation** regulates sleep and arousal, and the **cerebellum** coordinates fine motor skills. The midbrain contains the tectum and the tegmentum, which help an organism **orient** in the environment. The forebrain coordinates high-level functions (among other things), and houses the **cerebral** cortex and subcortical structures. The cerebral cortex is divided into two hemispheres, each with four cortical lobes. Those lobes are the frontal lobe, parietal lobe, **temporal** lobe (associated with memory), and the **occipital** lobe (mostly visual). Neurons in the brain can change as a result of experience and reassign functions to other areas. This process is called **plasticity**.

The Evolution of Nervous Systems

The three major parts of the brain differentiate as development continues, with the **midbrain** folding over the hindbrain, and the forebrain folding over the midbrain. Throughout development the structures of the brain continue to differentiate, migrate, and connect to one another.

The unit of hereditary transmission, or **gene**, is built from strands of DNA and organized into chromosomes. Humans have **twenty-three** pairs of chromosomes, with half coming from each parent. **Monozygotic** twins share 100% of their genes, whereas **dyzygotic** twins share 50% of their genes, just like non-twin siblings. Both genes and environmental factors exert influence on people's behaviors; however, genes do not predict a particular individual's characteristics. **Heritability** is a measure of the variability in behavioral traits that can be accounted for by genetic variation.

Investigating the Brain

Behavioral neuroscientists investigate the links between the brain and behavior. This chapter describes three approaches to studying these links: studying people with brain damage, electrical recording of brain activity, and **imaging techniques**. The link between a brain area and language, for example, can be studied in someone who has suffered a brain injury and has difficulty producing speech. The machine that interprets the patterns of electrical activity in large brain areas from outside of the skull is called an **electroencephalograph**. Many brain imaging techniques such as CT scans, MRI, PET, and fMRI continue to help identify the links between brain activity and specific tasks or behaviors.

Quick Quiz #1

a)

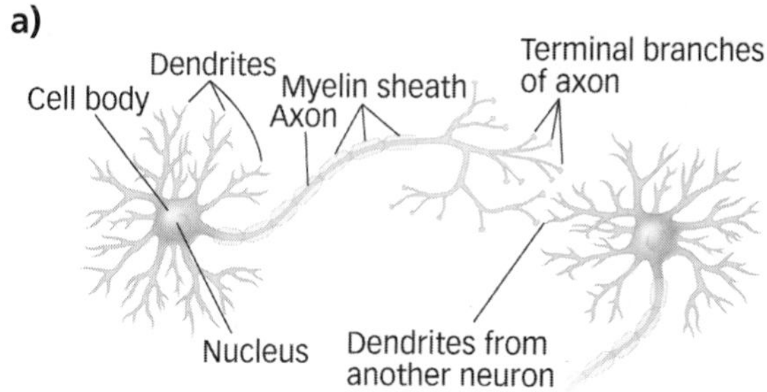

b)

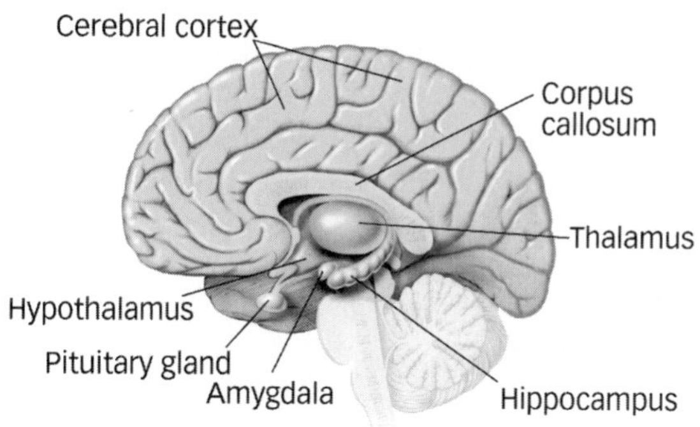

Quick Quiz #2

1. **D.** Neurons are the only cells in the nervous system that send signals of communication.
2. **B.** Motor neurons carry signals out to voluntary muscles in order for them to contract or expand.
3. **C.** The difference in electrical charge between the inside and the outside of a neuron's cell membrane is called the resting potential.
4. **B.** There is more K^+ on the inside of a neuron and more Na^+ on the outside when it is at rest.
5. **D.** Vesicles contain neurotransmitters before they are released into the synapse and are bound, or received by, receptors on the postsynaptic cell.
6. **C.** Dopamine has been identified in the "reward circuit" to play a role in motivation for drugs, food, and sex.
7. **A.** Gutamate and GABA are the most common excitatory and inhibitory neurotransmitters in the brain, respectively. They are both amino acid neurotransmitters.
8. **D.** The brain and the spinal cord make up the central nervous system.
9. **C.** The sympathetic nervous system is the division of the autonomic nervous system that prepares the body to respond when a person is threatened.
10. **A.** The thalamus is the brain's "relay station," sending sensory information to be processed in other regions of the brain, particularly the cerebral cortex.

Quick Quiz #3

1. **A.** The amygdala is implicated in many emotionally mediated functions in the brain.
2. **B.** Association areas help provide sense and meaning to information registered in the cortex.
3. **D.** Chromosomes are strands of DNA wound around each other in a double-helix configuration.
4. **A.** The extra Y chromosome from the father determines male sex. Females have two X chromosomes.
5. **B.** The corpus collosum is the large commissure that connects the cerebral hemispheres. Surgeons would sometimes cut the corpus collosum to reduce seizure activity.
6. **C.** PET and fMRI are *functional* neuroimaging techniques. CT and MRI do not examine function, just anatomy only.
7. **D.** Phineas Gage was the famous brain damage patient who had the accident on the Burlington and Rutland railroad.

"Hey, Guess What I Learned In Psychology Today?" (An Essay Question)

What might you tell your Mom about behavioral neuroscience?

- You could start by asking her what she thinks life would be like if she had to consciously think about breathing or her heart beating. She will most likely come to the conclusion that it would be horribly intrusive to think about these automatic processes all the time. You could then explain that not only are all those automatic processes the result of neurons firing and different chemicals initiating signals, but the same processes are involved in every behavior from voluntary movement to deciding which pair of shoes goes best with that trendy new jacket.
- You could also discuss how various parts of the brain are important for different kinds of behaviors. One example would be the sympathetic response to a car backfiring on the street next to you. Your heart rate would increase, you would breathe faster, and you would orient to the noise (that's the job of the tectum). You might also remember the conversation that you were having with your friend while standing in front of the Gap several days later because the amygdala tagged the events with emotional significance, even though it turned out that you weren't really in any danger.
- You might also mention that the reason Uncle Chad, who has Parkinson's disease, is able to still get around is because of our understanding of how drugs work in the brain through studying people with damaged brains, and imaging the brains of those people with normal function. Uncle Chad is probably taking L-dopa, or another dopamine agonist, to accommodate for the loss of dopamine function due to damaged cells in his substantia nigra. You might mention that much of the progress in understanding the mechanism of that damage was sparked by some people who were trying to create a designer drug and ended up creating a drug that acts similar to the process that results in Parkinson's disease. You could talk about how hundreds of discoveries in medicine have come about in this way and that understanding the brain better helps us fight diseases and pathologies, as well as giving us insight on how to perform better and more efficiently on some tasks.

4

Sensation and Perception

THE BIG PICTURE

Or is it "THE SMALL PICTURE" that just looks big from your perspective? Maybe the picture is tiny and it is just taped to the inside of your eyeglasses, so that it appears to you to be a grandiose scene. Maybe the picture is huge but you are too far away to really appreciate the details. So get to sprinting! Okay, okay, you understand the analogy. You took the SAT. The point is that the way the world appears to you is often *NOT* the way that it actually is. You have several elaborate systems of sensors in your body that feed information to your brain from the environment around you (e.g., eyes, ears, skin, nose, tongue), and inside you (e.g., inner ear, stretch receptors). Your brain does the best it can with that information to represent your unique world and select options for responding to that information. What we frequently forget is that each of us has a slightly different set of sensors and a unique personal history that changes the way sensations are ultimately perceived. Add to that the fact that we can all be "tricked" by some common misperceptions, or illusions, because of the way our brains try to make sense of the world (e.g., the Ames room and moon illusion) as we have learned to experience it. With all this in mind, you start to see the wisdom of the old adage "seeing is believing."

Research on sensation and perception is the basis for much of psychology, a pathway toward understanding more complex cognition and behavior such as memory (Chapter 5), emotion and motivation (Chapter 9), and decision making (Chapter 7). How would we begin to understand the processes that are responsible for learning (Chapter 6) without first understanding the fundamentals of how information from the outside world gets registered in our brains (Chapter 3)? We discover in Chapter 4 that the process of aging (Chapter 10) can change how we perceive things (e.g., taste buds disappear and the shape of the eye can change), and those differences, in combination with our unique experiences of the world, contribute to some of the differences in our personalities (Chapter 11) and the way that we interact with one another (Chapter 15). We also learn that illness (Chapter 14), as simple as a head cold, can change the perception of the flavor of food because of the combined components of taste and smell that contribute to flavors. We will also find out in Chapters 12 and 13 that several psychological disorders can severely alter the way people perceive the world around them, or even their own bodies.

Chapter 4 introduces you to a variety of complex mechanisms that have evolved to represent the "outer world" of your environment to the "inner world" that you perceive. In the end, you are caught between a rock and a hard place: the only way to get the information from the outside world into your brain is through the systems that sense and perceive the world, but that perception sometimes can be deceiving and tricky. You can take comfort in knowing that just about everyone is susceptible to errors in perception, and even a little cross-wiring, like the kind that leads to synesthesia, can result in brilliant music and science. So don't take the lyrics of a couple of synesthetes (Duke Ellington and Stevie Wonder) too much to heart regarding your less-than-perfect representation of the world and "Do nothin' till you hear from me," or you might end up being "Superstitious."

CHAPTER OBJECTIVES

After studying this chapter, you should be able to:

1. Define *synesthesia* and discuss how the phenomenon may reveal different, and otherwise normal, ways of brain organization of *sensation* and *perception.*
2. Distinguish between *sensation* and *perception,* noting where in the body each process occurs, and explain why these processes are separable.
3. Discuss how *psychophysics* laid the foundation for the psychological study of *sensation* and *perception.*
4. Describe the relationships between the *absolute threshold, just noticeable difference,* and *Weber's law.*
5. Describe the principles of *signal detection theory.*
6. Discuss why *sensory adaptation* is a good thing for humans, focusing on how and why it is beneficial for us to reduce our level of response to a stimulus over time.
7. Compare the physical dimensions of wavelength, amplitude, and purity with their psychological counterparts, hue, brightness, and saturation.
8. Describe the path that light follows through the human eye from the pupil to the optic nerve.
9. Distinguish between *rods* and *cones* and discuss how their relative concentrations around the *fovea* contribute to vision.
10. Describe how *receptive fields* work in vision.
11. Discuss how color vision takes place and compare additive and subtractive color mixing.
12. Discuss visual processing in the brain, noting how *area V1* contributes.
13. Compare the modular view and the distributed representation view of object recognition. How do these explanations apply to the perception of faces?
14. Outline the basic principles of Gestalt perception, including simplicity, closure, continuity, similarity, proximity, common fate, and the figure–ground distinction.
15. Compare *monocular depth cues* and *binocular disparity* in vision and discuss how illusions of depth and size illustrate the otherwise typical process of perceiving depth or size.
16. Compare the physical dimensions of sound wave frequency, amplitude, and complexity with their psychological counterparts, *pitch, loudness,* and *timbre.*
17. Describe the path that sound follows through the human ear from the pinna to the auditory nerve.
18. Describe the components of the inner ear and discuss how the *cochlea, basilar membrane,* and *hair cells* work together in hearing.
19. Discuss how auditory processing takes place in the brain, noting how *area A1, place codes,* and *temporal codes* all contribute.
20. Describe the basic operations of the body senses, discussing how touch, pain, and the senses of balance and movement occur.
21. Outline the principles of *gate-control theory.*
22. Describe the components of the olfactory system and discuss how the *olfactory bulb* and *ORNs* work together in olfaction.
23. Describe the components of the taste system and discuss how *taste buds,* papillae, and microvilli work together in taste.

CHAPTER OVERVIEW

Use the terms below to fill in the following exercises. Terms may not be used more than once. The answers can be found at the end of this chapter.

absolute threshold	ganglion	perception
adaptation	gate-control	pheromones
A-delta fibers	gestalt	pitch
amplitude	haptic	place
apparent	hearing	psychophysics
auditory nerve	high	pupil
balance	illusions	retina
basilar	interprets	rods
binocular	joints	sensation
bipolar	just noticeable difference	sensitive
bitter	lateral geniculate nucleus	sensitivity
canals	light	short
central	location	signal detection
C fibers	long	smell
changes	loudness	somatosensory
closure	medium	subtractive
cochlea	memories	sweet
color	middle	taste
cones	modular	temporal
constancy	mouth	texture
criteria	neural	timbre
depth	occipital	transduction
distant	opposite	trichromatic
distributed representation	optic nerve	V1
figures	organ	vibration
fingertips	ossicles	
flavor	papillae	

The Doorway to Psychology

__________________ and __________________ are critical to survival, and are separate events that, from the vantage point of the perceiver, feel like one single process. Sensation is the simple awareness that results from stimulation of a sense __________________, whereas perception organizes, identifies, and __________________ sensation at the level of the brain in order to form a mental representation. All sensory modalities depend on the process of __________________, which converts physical signals from the environment into __________________ signals carried by sensory neurons into the __________________ nervous system.

In the 19th century, researchers developed __________________, an approach to studying percepion that measures the strength of a stimulus and an observer's __________________ to that stimulus. These researchers developed procedures for measuring an observer's ________________, or the smallest intensity needed to just barely detect a stimulus, and the ________________, or the smallest change in a stimulus that can just barely be detected. ________________ theory represents a refinement of these basic approaches and allows researchers to distinguish between an observer's perceptual sensitivity to a stimulus and ________________ for making decisions about the stimulus. Sensory ________________ occurs because sensitivity to lengthy stimulation tends to decline over time. This process illustrates that the perceptual system is more sensitive to ________________ in stimulation than to constant levels of stimulation.

Vision: More Than Meets the Eye

Light waves have the properties of length, ________________, and frequency. These properties are perceived as ________________, brightness, and saturation (or purity), respectively. ________________ initially passes through the cornea and ________________ of the eye, with the ________________ linking the world of light outside and the world of visual perception inside the central nervous system. Two types of photoreceptor cells in the retina transduce light into neural impulses: ________________, which operate under normal daylight conditions and sense color, and ________________, which are active only under low-light conditions for night vision. There are three layers that make up the retina, with the outermost layer consisting of retinal ________________ cells that collect signals from the middle layer, containing ________________ cells that receive signals from the photoreceptor layer, and send them to the brain. The point where the axons that make up the ________________ leave the back of the eyeball is called the blind spot because it doesn't have any photoreceptors. Information from the eye travels to the ________________ of the thalamus, and then on to the primary visual cortex, area ________________, in the ________________ lobe.

Light striking the retina causes a specific pattern of response in each of three cone types that are critical to color perception: ____________-wavelength (bluish) light, ________________-wavelength (greenish) light, and ________________-wavelength (reddish) light. The overall pattern of response across the three types results in a unique code for each color, known as its ________________ color representation. Both additive and ________________ color mixing determine how shades of color can be produced.

Both the ________________ view and the ________________ view offer explanations of how we perceive and recognize objects in the world. At a minimum, humans show a great deal of perceptual ________________: Even as aspects of sensory signals change, perception remains consistent. We are rarely led to believe that ________________ objects are actually tiny. ________________ principles of perceptual grouping, such as simplicity, ________________, and continuity, govern how the features and regions of things fit together. We also tend to perceive ________________ against some sort of background. Many visual ________________ capitalize on the perceptual ambiguities related to these principles. ________________ perception depends on monocular cues, such as familiar size and linear perspective; ________________

cues, such as retinal disparity; and motion-based cues. Depth and motion processes can give rise to illusions such as ____________________ motion.

Audition: More Than Meets the Ear

____________________ takes place when sound waves are transduced by receptors in the ear. Perceiving sound depends on three physical dimensions of a sound wave: The frequency of the sound wave determines the ________________; the amplitude determines the ________________; and differences in the complexity, or mix, of frequencies determines the sound quality or ____________________. Auditory perception begins in the outer ear, which funnels sound waves toward the ______________ ear, where tiny bones called ____________________ mechanically transmit the vibrations to the inner ear, which contains the ____________________. Stimulation of thousands of tiny hair cells, embedded in the ____________________ membrane, initiates neurotransmitter release that results in a neural signal sent to the brain via the ____________________. Both a ________________________ code, which is better for ______________________________ -frequency sounds, and a temporal code, which is better for low-frequency sounds, are involved in transducing sound frequencies. Auditory signals travel to area A1, the primary auditory cortex, located in the ____________________ lobe. Our ability to localize sound sources depends critically on the placement of our ears on ____________________ sides of the head.

The Body Senses: More Than Skin Deep

____________________ perception involves the active exploration of the environment through touching and grasping. Four types of specialized receptor cells are located under the surface of the skin to transduce pressure, ____________________, pattern, and ____________________. Touch is represented in the brain according to a topographic scheme in which locations on the body project sensory signals to locations in the ____________________ cortex, a part of the parietal lobe. Areas of the body that are more ____________________ occupy a greater area in this strip of cortex. For example, the ____________________ have a greater representation than do the trunk or legs.

________________ transmit the initial sharp pain from sudden injury, and ________________ transmit the duller lasting pain that persists after an injury. The experience of pain depends on signals that travel along two distinct pathways. One sends signals to the somatosensory cortex to indicate the ____________________ and type of pain, and another sends signals to the emotional centers of the brain to initiate escape. The experience of pain varies across individuals, which is explained by bottom-up and top-down aspects of ____________________ theory.

Body position and movement are regulated by receptors located in the muscles, ______________, and tendons. ____________________ is regulated by the semicircular ____________________ in the inner ear and to some extent by visual cues.

The Chemical Senses: Adding Flavor

Smell and taste are both chemical senses; ____________________ occurs when molecules enter the nose, and ____________________ occurs when molecules are dissolved in saliva. Smell and taste combine to produce the experience of ____________________. Olfaction is the result of odorant molecules binding to sites on specialized olfactory receptors. The olfactory bulb in turn sends signals to parts of the brain that control drives, emotions, and ________________, which helps to explain why smells can have immediate and powerful effects on us. ________________ are biochemical odorants that affect behavior, including some sexual behavior, and physiology.

The tongue is covered with ________________, which contain taste buds, the organs of taste transduction. Each taste bud contains taste receptor cells that respond to a taste sensation; salty, ________________, ________________, sour, and umami. Odorants from food enter the nasal cavity both through the nose and through the back of the ________________ and upper throat.

QUICK QUIZ #1

1. A person who hears musical notes in specific colors is a(n):
   a. synesthete.
   b. kinetic perceptor.
   c. easily hypnotizable individual.
   d. drug addict.
2. Sensation and perception:
   a. are two words for the same event.
   b. are separate events.
   c. take place solely in the brain.
   d. were originally studied by biologists.
3. Psychophysics was an approach to studying perception that:
   a. focused primarily on transduction.
   b. incorporated the physics of movement with sensory modalities.
   c. measured the strength of a stimulus and an observer's sensitivity to that stimulus.
   d. was essential to the understanding of gate-control theory.
4. Adjusting to the subfreezing temperatures of winters in the Midwest is a good example of:
   a. the just noticeable difference.
   b. an absolute threshold.
   c. transduction.
   d. sensory adaptation.
5. Light initially passes through the ____________ and ____________ of the eye before visual information progresses to the brain.
   a. cornea; pupil
   b. retina; lateral geniculate nucleus
   c. pupil; optic nerve
   d. cornea; lateral geniculate nucleus
6. Similarity, a perceptual organizational principle, helps us:
   a. identify images on the television.
   b. distinguish between figure and ground.
   c. sort our socks into blue and brown piles.
   d. recognize our favorite restaurant.

7. Amplitude is to our perception of loudness as ____________ is to our perception of pitch.
   a. timbre
   b. sound wave length
   c. complexity
   d. sound wave frequency
8. The hammer, anvil, and stirrup are tiny bones called ____________ that are located in the middle ear.
   a. ossicles
   b. cochleas
   c. basilars
   d. auditory transducers
9. Smell occurs when molecules enter the nose, and taste occurs when molecules:
   a. respond to a taste sensation.
   b. are dissolved in saliva.
   c. combine with smell.
   d. combine with pheromones.

QUICK QUIZ #2

1. All sensory modalities depend on the process of ____________, which converts physical signals from the environment into neural signals that are carried to the brain.
   a. transduction
   b. psychophysics
   c. signal detection
   d. sensory adaptation
2. Absolute threshold refers to:
   a. the point where the increasing intensity of a stimulus enables an individual to detect it 50% of the time.
   b. the intensity needed to just barely detect a stimulus.
   c. a measurement devised by 19th-century psychophysics researchers.
   d. All of these statements are true.
3. The researcher who developed an approach to measuring sensation and perception called psychophysics was:
   a. Wilhelm Wundt.
   b. Ernst Weber
   c. Gustav Fechner.
   d. Edward Titchener.
4. Length, amplitude, and purity are:
   a. physical properties of sound waves.
   b. words associated with haptic perception.
   c. words associated with the chemical senses.
   d. physical properties of light waves.

5. When the ophthalmologist shines a bright light into your eye, your iris reacts by:
   a. constricting.
   b. dilating.
   c. accommodating.
   d. defecting.
6. If you have trouble seeing well enough to read the newspaper, you are probably:
   a. nearsighted.
   b. farsighted.
   c. myopic.
   d. developing retinal disparity.
7. Two types of photoreceptor cells in the retina that transduce light into neural impulses are:
   a. cones and retinal ganglion cells.
   b. rods and fovea.
   c. cones and rods.
   d. retinal ganglion cells and bipolar cells.
8. The ___________ that leads from the eye to the brain contains axons from retinal ganglion cells that code information in the right and left visual fields.
   a. ganglion nerve
   b. fovea
   c. retinal nerve
   d. optic nerve
9. When Freddie listened to the choir director give each section a different pitch, he was actually perceiving changes in the:
   a. physical frequency of the sound waves.
   b. amplitude.
   c. complexity of the frequencies.
   d. loudness of the various pitches.
10. Lamaze techniques enable expectant mothers to relax and focus on their breathing during painful labor contractions. This is a good example of:
   a. haptic perception.
   b. the gate-control theory.
   c. the referred pain theory.
   d. bottom-up control.

QUICK QUIZ #3

1. Some people experience letters of the alphabet as having specific colors, a phenomenon that is known as:
   a. synesthesia.
   b. color perception.
   c. color hypnosis.
   d. cognitive aphasia.
2. You are not bothered by the constant pressure of your shoes against the skin on your feet because of:
   a. haptic accommodation.
   b. sensory adaptation.

c. perceptual assimilation.
d. thermoreception.

3. Your iris:
a. is located directly underneath the retina.
b. bends the light wave as it enters your eye.
c. controls how much light can enter your eye.
d. is a hole in the colored part of your eye.

4. The eye contains ____________ rods than cones.
a. a few less
b. a few more
c. many less
d. many more

5. When you listen to your friend play her guitar, the ossicles in the ____________ pick up the eardrum vibrations.
a. pinna
b. middle ear
c. inner ear
d. outer ear

6. The primary auditory cortex is located in the ____________ beneath the lateral fissure in each hemisphere of the brain.
a. frontal lobe
b. parietal lobe
c. temporal lobe
d. occipital lobe

7. ____________ transmit sudden stinging pain, whereas ____________ transmit throbbing, dull pain that lingers long after the injury.
a. A-delta fibers; D fibers
b. D fibers; A-delta fibers
c. C fibers; A-delta fibers
d. A-delta fibers; C fibers

8. Taste and smell combine to cause you to experience:
a. flavor.
b. gustation.
c. olfaction.
d. taste transduction.

9. One reason dogs are often used to sniff out drugs or track down suspects is that they have many times more ____________ than humans.
a. olfactory epithelium cells
b. olfactory receptor neurons
c. hair cells
d. pheromones

"HEY, GUESS WHAT I LEARNED IN PSYCHOLOGY TODAY?" (An Essay Question)

We're guessing there's someone in your life who is interested in the quality of your educational experiences, is reasonably intelligent, but knows little about psychology. This might be your roommate, a previous teacher, your mom, or some other person you have access to and want to share your thoughts and feelings with. What would you tell that person about sensation and perception? How would you explain the key processes for translating the outside world of experience to the inside world of your mind and body? What would you say to reassure this person, after explaining some of the mind bugs of perception, that the bright red Christmas sweater he or she is wearing looks red to you too?

THINGS TO PONDER

You've learned a lot of information in this chapter about how sensation and perception are the basis for many questions about behavior. When you put it all together, you may start to ponder how all of this relates to issues that are coming up in this textbook. For example, you may ask yourself:

- Why do taste and smell have such a powerful impact on learning and memory, relative to your other senses?

  Think about how the information from those senses gets into the brain and the pathways that they take to emotional centers that have the capability of tagging memories with extra importance.

  Consider the fact that you see and hear a lot more things in the world than you smell and touch, generally speaking. What's more, assigning importance to things is often a bit of a numbers game; you physically *can't* give equal weight or equal importance to all of the sensations to impinge on your body at any given time, so some of them must take precedence over others.

- Why do people choose to alter their conscious perception with drugs?

  Note that some people tend to be less averse to risk, whereas others enjoy pushing the boundaries of socially acceptable behavior.

  Reflect on the fact that some people face issues in their lives that they may not want to perceive fully, and turn to drugs in an attempt to dull or escape their daily perceptions.

- Does perceiving the world differently than most other people make you a genius or a freak?

  Remember that many of the synesthetes in the opening vignette ended up being famous and well respected in their crafts. That is not to say that they didn't have to endure the hardships of being outside the norm during their lives.

People have often said that there is a fine line between genius and madness. Maybe substantial changes in perception put you a little closer to both.

- What kind of sensory and perceptive alterations would classify someone as having a psychological disorder?

  Luckily, the majority of symptoms for classification of psychological disorders are spelled out in the *Diagnostic and Statistical Manual* that clinicians use to diagnose patients, including anomalies in sensation and perception.

  Unfortunately, dramatic changes in sensation and perception are often indicators of relatively serious psychological disorders such as *psychosis*, or a break from reality.

WEB LINKS AND SUGGESTED READING

YouTube—Hubel Weisel Visual Cortex Cell Recording Line Stimulus: http://www.youtube.com/watch?v=IOHayh06LJ4

- An interview and demonstration of the groundbreaking visual experiments with a Nobel Prize winning scientist.

Krantz, John H. (2005). Sensation and Perception Tutorials from Hanover College: http://psych.hanover.edu/KRANTZ/sen_tut.html

- Several illusions and principles of perception illustrated through animations and activities.

Landrigan, David T.—Illusions Gallery, UMass, Lowell: http://dragon.uml.edu/psych/illusion.html

- Excellent source for many common and not so common visual illusions.

Sachs, Oliver (1985). *The man who mistook his wife for a hat: And other clinical tales.* New York: Touchstone.

- The famous book that recounts the stories of individuals afflicted with fantastic perceptual and intellectual aberrations.

Ramachandran, V.S., and Blakeslee, Sandra (1998). *Phantoms in the brain: Probing the mysteries of the human mind.* New York: HarperCollins Publishers.

- More stories about odd perceptual cases by one of the foremost experts in perceptual neuropsychology.

Peynaud, Emily (1996). *The taste of wine: The art and science of wine appreciation.* Hoboken, NJ: John Wiley and Sons.

- Information about your senses and how they result in the perception of flavor related to wines.

ANSWERS

Chapter Overview

The Doorway to Psychology

Sensation and **perception** are critical to survival, and are separate events that, from the vantage point of the perceiver, feel like one single process. Sensation is the simple awareness that results from stimulation of a sense **organ**, whereas perception organizes, identifies, and **interprets** sensation at the level of the brain in order to form a mental representation. All sensory modalities depend on the process of **transduction**, which converts physical signals from the environment into **neural** signals carried by sensory neurons into the **central** nervous system.

In the 19th century, researchers developed **psychophysics**, an approach to studying perception that measures the strength of a stimulus and an observer's **sensitivity** to that stimulus. These researchers developed procedures for measuring an observer's **absolute threshold**, or the smallest intensity needed to just barely detect a stimulus, and the **just noticeable difference**, or the smallest change in a stimulus that can just barely be detected. **Signal detection** theory represents a refinement of these basic approaches and allows researchers to distinguish between an observer's perceptual sensitivity to a stimulus and **criteria** for making decisions about the stimulus. Sensory **adaptation** occurs because sensitivity to lengthy stimulation tends to decline over time. This process illustrates that the perceptual system is more sensitive to **changes** in stimulation than to constant levels of stimulation.

Vision: More Than Meets the Eye

Light waves have the properties of length, **amplitude**, and frequency. These properties are perceived as **color**, brightness, and saturation (or purity), respectively. **Light** initially passes through the cornea and **pupil** of the eye, with the **retina** linking the world of light outside and the world of visual perception inside the central nervous system. Two types of photoreceptor cells in the retina transduce light into neural impulses: **cones**, which operate under normal daylight conditions and sense color, and **rods**, which are active only under low-light conditions for night vision. There are three layers that make up the retina, with the outermost layer consisting of retinal **ganglion** cells that collect signals from the middle layer, containing **bipolar** cells that receive signals from the photoreceptor layer, and send them to the brain. The point where the axons that make up the **optic nerve** leave the back of the eyeball is called the blind spot because it doesn't have any photoreceptors. Information from the eye travels to the **lateral geniculate nucleus** of the thalamus, and then on to the primary visual cortex, area **V1**, in the **occipital** lobe.

Light striking the retina causes a specific pattern of response in each of three cone types that are critical to color perception: **short**-wavelength (bluish) light, **long**-wavelength (greenish) light, and **medium**-wavelength (reddish) light. The overall pattern of response across the three types results in a unique code for each color, known as its **trichromatic** color representation. Both additive and **subtractive** color mixing determine how shades of color can be produced.

Both the **modular** view and the **distributed representation** view offer explanations of how we perceive and recognize objects in the world. At a minimum, humans show a great deal of perceptual **constancy**: Even as aspects of sensory signals change, perception remains consistent. We are rarely led to believe that **distant** objects are actually tiny. **Gestalt** principles of perceptual grouping, such as simplicity, **closure**, and continuity, govern how the features and regions of things fit together. We also tend to perceive **figures** against some sort of background. Many visual **illusions** capitalize on the perceptual ambiguities related to these principles. **Depth** perception depends on monocular cues, such as familiar size and linear perspective; **binocular** cues, such as retinal disparity; and motion-based cues. Depth and motion processes can give rise to illusions such as **apparent** motion.

Audition: More Than Meets the Ear

Hearing takes place when sound waves are transduced by receptors in the ear. Perceiving sound depends on three physical dimensions of a sound wave:

The frequency of the sound wave determines the **pitch**; the amplitude determines the **loudness**; and differences in the complexity, or mix, of frequencies determines the sound quality or **timbre**. Auditory perception begins in the outer ear, which funnels sound waves toward the **middle** ear, where tiny bones called **ossicles** mechanically transmit the vibrations to the inner ear, which contains the **cochlea**. Stimulation of thousands of tiny hair cells, embedded in the **basilar** membrane, initiates neurotransmitter release that results in a neural signal sent to the brain via the **auditory nerve**. Both a **place** code, which is better for **high**-frequency sounds, and a temporal code, which is better for low-frequency sounds, are involved in transducing sound frequencies. Auditory signals travel to area A1, the primary auditory cortex, located in the **temporal** lobe. Our abillity to localize sound sources depends critically on the placement of our ears on **opposite** sides of the head.

The Body Senses: More Than Skin Deep

Haptic perception involves the active exploration of the environment through touching and grasping. Four types of specialized receptor cells are located under the surface of the skin to transduce pressure, **texture**, pattern, and **vibration**. Touch is represented in the brain according to a topographic scheme in which locations on the body project sensory signals to locations in the **somatosensory** cortex, a part of the parietal lobe. Areas of the body that are more **sensitive** occupy a greater area in this strip of cortex. For example, the **fingertips** have a greater representation than do the trunk or legs.

A-delta fibers transmit the initial sharp pain from sudden injury, and **C fibers** transmit the duller lasting pain that persists after an injury. The experience of pain depends on signals that travel along two distinct pathways. One sends signals to the somatosensory cortex to indicate the **location** and type of pain, and another sends signals to the emotional centers of the brain to initiate escape. The experience of pain varies across individuals, which is explained by bottom-up and top-down aspects of **gate-control** theory.

Body position and movement are regulated by receptors located in the muscles, **joints**, and tendons. **Balance** is regulated by the semicircular **canals** in the inner ear and to some extent by visual cues.

The Chemical Senses: Adding Flavor

Smell and taste are both chemical senses; **smell** occurs when molecules enter the nose, and **taste** occurs when molecules are dissolved in saliva. Smell and taste combine to produce the experience of **flavor**. Olfaction is the result of odorant molecules binding to sites on specialized olfactory receptors. The olfactory bulb in turn sends signals to parts of the brain that control drives, emotions, and **memories**, which helps to explain why smells can have immediate and powerful effects on us. **Pheromones** are biochemical odorants that affect behavior, including some sexual behavior, and physiology.

The tongue is covered with **papillae**, which contain taste buds, the organs of taste transduction. Each taste bud contains taste receptor cells that respond to a taste sensation; salty, **sweet, bitter**, sour, and umami. Odorants from food enter the nasal cavity both through the nose and through the back of the **mouth** and upper throat.

Quick Quiz #1

1. **A.** The perceptual experience of one sense that is evoked by another sense is known as synesthesia.
2. **B.** Although sensation and perception may *feel* like one single process to the individual, they are separate events.
3. **C.** Psychophysics was developed by Gustav Fechner as a way to measure sensation and perception by focusing on the strength of a stimulus and an individual's sensitivity to that stimulus.
4. **D.** Individuals are able to adapt to sensory stimulation, whether it involves extreme temperatures, noxious odors, or other sensations.
5. **A.** The cornea is a clear, smooth outer tissue which bends the light and sends it through the pupil, where it proceeds to the retina and then to the brain.
6. **C.** Similarity is the principle of perceptual organization that helps us group together those things that are similar in color, lightness, or texture.
7. **D.** In audition, sound wave frequency determines pitch.
8. **A.** Ossicles are located in the middle ear and are composed of these tiny bones.
9. **B.** It takes molecules dissolving in saliva to produce taste. Flavor is a combination of smell and taste.

Quick Quiz #2

1. **A.** Transduction is the process that changes physical signals in the environment to neural signals that go to the brain.
2. **B.** This was the original definition of absolute threshold, the intensity level necessary for an individual to detect a stimulus.
3. **C.** Gustav Fechner was influenced by Ernst Weber, but Fechner himself developed the approach called psychophysics.
4. **D.** These terms refer only to vision, not audition or haptic perception.
5. **A.** When you are exposed to a bright light, your iris automatically constricts in order to limit the amount of light that enters the eye.
6. **B.** A person who can see well at a distance is said to be farsighted, whereas a person who can see well to read is said to be nearsighted.
7. **C.** Cones and rods are the photoreceptor cells responsible for transduction in the eye.
8. **D.** It is the optic nerve that leads from the eye to the brain.
9. **A.** Sound wave frequency determines pitch.
10. **B.** When the mother focuses on her breathing, she is attempting to gate the pain pathway to the brain.

Quick Quiz #3

1. **A.** The perceptual experience of one sense that is evoked by another sense is known as synesthesia.
2. **B.** Individuals are able to adapt to sensory stimulation, whether it involves extreme temperatures, noxious odors, or other sensations.
3. **C.** The iris is responsible for determining how much light is allowed into the eye. The hole in the colored part of the eye is the pupil, and the cornea bends the light wave as it enters the eye.
4. **D.** The eye contains approximately 120 million rods but only about 6 million cones.
5. **B.** Ossicles are located in the middle ear. See the diagram of the ear on p. 112 of your textbook.
6. **C.** The primary auditory cortex is located in the temporal lobe of the brain.
7. **D.** Tissue damage is transduced by pain receptors (free nerve endings), fast-acting A-delta fibers (initial pain), and slower C fibers, which transmit longer-lasting, duller pain.
8. **A.** Flavor is experienced when taste and smell are combined.
9. **B.** Dogs have up to 100 times more ORNs than humans, making them good at detecting and discriminating among millions of odors.

"Hey, Guess What I Learned In Psychology Today?" (An Essay Question)

What might you tell your mom about sensation and perception?

- You could start by describing how sensation and perception are really separate, yet related, processes. Pause briefly to let this sink in. After the glaze has cleared from her eyes, you could use a simple example of taste, where you pick a common food (let's say a strawberry); have her close her eyes, taste it, and then tell you what she ate without looking at the bowl of strawberries in your hand. After she has successfully identified the strawberry taste you can explain how the molecules from the strawberry have to be *sensed* first by the taste and olfactory receptors of the tongue and mouth, then that information has to be *perceived* by the parts of the brain that are responsible for putting the pieces of the puzzle together. Voilà, sensation and perception!
- After the demonstration, a natural follow-up question might be, "How do the molecules in my mouth end up as me saying 'strawberry'?" This is when you can talk a little bit about transduction, the process that is necessary to turn any energy or stimulus to be sensed into the stuff that makes sense in your brain. You will probably want to avoid words like *glomerulus*, but you can describe how the molecules in strawberry juice and the light waves that are reflecting off her sweater (at roughly 700 nanometers) get turned into action potentials that travel from sense organs to your brain. Then you could explain that your brain has a few tricks and calculations that result in the perception of flavor and color.
- In the end it might be a bit of a trippy conversation, especially if you are having it with your

mom. She might reflect on similar conversations that she had with friends when she was younger and contemplating the meaning of things. A natural logical road to go down would be that everything you perceive is different than what she perceives. Again, you can reassure her that most things register fairly consistently with most people. Red is red in the visible spectrum. You might have slightly different experiences with red in your life than she has, and maybe your younger eyes are a bit more acute, but you are both taking in much of the world around you in much the same way. You might end with a tidbit about how synesthetes do experience things quite differently than most other people, but they seem to do okay in the end too. Maybe she is a Duke Ellington or Eddie Van Halen fan. Use that to your advantage to win Mom over to the wonders of sensation and perception.

5

Memory

THE BIG PICTURE

Is amnesia the ultimate mind bug? If you have seen films such as *Memento* or *50 First Dates*, you have glimpsed the frightening and frustrating world of an amnesic, or at least someone with severe anterograde amnesia. If you can't store new memories for more than a minute or two, how do you know what is going on around you or whom you should trust? In the words of another famous amnesic, Clive Wearing, a former symphony director and composer who lost much of his temporal lobes to viral encephalitis, "It is as if I have just awakened for the first time." Could you imagine feeling as though you just "woke up" at every moment during your conscious life, except instead of rolling out of bed to get a cup of coffee, you find that you are in the middle of a conversation?

Chapter 5 describes what we know about the various aspects of memory through many key studies on the topic, from Ebbinghaus' own recall of lists of nonsense syllables to sophisticated fMRI scans of people while they are remembering specific words and events. Memory is the result of mechanisms explored in previous chapters; that is, the firing of neurons in specific patterns (Chapter 3) give rise to the sensations and perceptions that culminate in our experiences (Chapter 4), ultimately resulting in memories.

Understanding memory also sets the stage for all of the chapters that follow. It would be extremely difficult to learn new things, communicate effectively, interact with others, or begin to contemplate consciousness without memory. For example, in Chapter 15 we will learn that *social cognition*, or the processes by which people come to understand others, relies on the ability to group together previous experiences, refer to known categories, and attribute a host of characteristics to someone after only a brief observation or interaction. How would any of those processes be possible without being able to refer to previous experiences or being able to hold information in mind for more than a few seconds?

In Chapter 5 we learn that the three key processes involved in memory—encoding, storage, and retrieval—each have their own little quirks that help us to remember. We also learn that there are multiple forms of memory, some that are easy to describe and others that are not. Finally, we learn that there are more ways for our memories to fail than we would probably like, but those same failures are key to the way that our memory normally functions. In the end, memory is a lot like that cheesy 1988 rock ballad from the "hair band" Cinderella: "Don't Know What You Got Till It's Gone."

CHAPTER OBJECTIVES

After studying this chapter, you should be able to:

1. Provide an accurate and appropriate definition of *memory, encoding, storage,* and *retrieval.*
2. Identify areas of the brain that are associated with various aspects of memory.
3. Discuss the distinctions between *elaborative encoding, visual imagery encoding,* and *organizational encoding.*
4. Describe the *sensory memory store* and distinguish *iconic memory* and *echoic memory.*
5. Distinguish the *short-term memory store* from *working memory.*
6. Describe how *rehearsal* and *chunking* contribute to the success of retaining information in short-term memory.
7. Define the *long-term memory store.*
8. Contrast *anterograde amnesia* and *retrograde amnesia.*
9. Describe the process of *long-term potentiation* (LTP) and how it contributes to the formation of memories.
10. Discuss why and how the *encoding specificity principle, state-dependent retrieval,* and *transfer-appropriate processing* are all aspects of retrieving information from memory.
11. Compare *implicit memory* and *explicit memory,* and provide an example of each.
12. Compare *semantic memory* and *episodic memory,* and provide an example of each.
13. Describe how the memory "sins" of *transience, absentmindedness,* and *blocking* all involve elements of forgetting.
14. Discuss the *curve of forgetting,* and how *retroactive interference* and *proactive interference* each contribute to the loss of information over time.
15. Describe how the memory "sins" of *misattribution, suggestibility,* and *bias* all involve elements of distorting remembered information.
16. Discuss how *source memory* and false recognition might contribute to faulty eyewitness accuracy.
17. Compare the *consistency bias, change bias,* and *egocentric bias* in memory distortion.
18. Explain why *persistence* is considered a failure of memory, when it involves an enhanced memory for some events.
19. Discuss whether the *seven sins of memory* are virtues or vices.

CHAPTER OVERVIEW

Use the terms below to fill in the following exercises. Terms may not be used more than once. The answers can be found at the end of this chapter.

absentmindedness	implicit memory	retrieval cues
amygdala	long-term memory	semantic memory
bias	long-term memory	sensory memory
blocking	long-term potentiation (LTP)	short-term memory
elaborative encoding	memory misattribution	suggestibility
encoding	organizational encoding	temporal lobe
episodic memory	persistence	transience
experiences	priming	visual imagery encoding
explicit memory	procedural memory	
hippocampal region	recovery	

Encoding: Transforming Perceptions into Memories

Memories are not passive recordings of the world, but instead result from combining incoming information with previous experiences. ________________ is the process of linking new and old information together and turning that information into lasting memories. Memory is influenced by the type of encoding we perform regardless of whether we consciously intend to remember an event, fact, or experience. Three types of encoding are ________________ (actively linking incoming information to existing associations and knowledge), ________________ (converting incoming information into mental pictures), and ________________ (noticing relationships among items you want to encode), and they all enhance memory. Different regions within the frontal lobes play important roles in elaborative encoding and organizational encoding, whereas the occipital lobes are important for visual imagery encoding.

Storage: Maintaining Memories over Time

Three major forms of memory storage hold information for different amounts of time. These three forms are ________________ (which holds information for a second or two), ________________ (which holds information for less than a minute), and ________________ (which holds information for several minutes to several years). At the cellular level, memory storage depends on changes in synapses, and ________________ is a process that increases the strength of a synaptic connection.

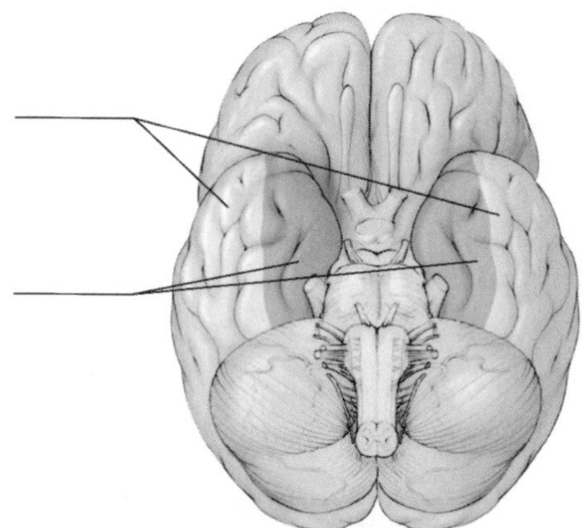

The ________________ and surrounding structures in the ________________ are critical for transferring information into long-term storage, as shown by the severe anterograde amnesia of patients such as HM.

Retrieval: Bringing Memories to Mind

Recall of past ________________ depends critically on retrieval cues, which trigger recall by reinstating what we thought or how we felt during the encoding of an experience. Information or an experience we can't recall on our own is sometimes only temporarily inaccessible and can be brought to mind with appropriate retrieval cues. Moods and inner states can serve as powerful

________________. Retrieval can be separated into the effort we make while trying to remember what happened in the past and the successful ________________ of stored information. Several studies suggest that trying to remember something activates the right frontal lobe, whereas successful recovery of stored information activates the hippocampus and the sensory regions of the brain associated with the aspects of the experience being remembered.

Multiple Forms of Memory: How the Past Returns

One of the three forms of memory, ________________, can be broadly divided into ________________, involving conscious, intentional retrieval of previous experiences, and ________________, which is the nonconscious influence of past experiences on later behavior and performance, such as procedural memory and priming. ________________ involves the acquisition of skills as a result of practice, and ________________ is a change in the ability to recognize or identify an object or word as the result of past exposure to it. People who have amnesia often retain implicit memory, including procedural memory and priming, but often lack explicit memory, particularly episodic memory. ________________ is the collection of personal experiences from a particular place and time, whereas ________________ is a networked, general, impersonal knowledge of facts, associations, and concepts. Nonhuman animals possess extensive memory abilities, but it is still debatable whether they can engage in the kind of "mental time travel" that is characteristic of human episodic memory.

Memory Failures: The Seven Sins of Memory

There are seven major ways that memory can be problematic: transience, absentmindedness, blocking, memory misattribution, suggestibility, bias, and persistence.

________________ is reflected by a rapid decline in memory followed by more gradual forgetting. With the passing of time, memory switches from being detailed to being more general. Both decay and interference contribute to transience. ________________ results from failures of attention, shallow encoding, and the influence of automatic behaviors, and it is often associated with forgetting to do things in the future. ________________ occurs when stored information is temporarily inaccessible.

________________ happens when we experience a sense of familiarity but don't recall, or mistakenly recall, the specifics of when and where an event occurred. Misattribution can result in eyewitness misidentification or false recognition. ________________ gives rise to implanted (false) memories of small details or entire episodes. Suggestive techniques such as hypnosis or visualization can promote vivid recall of suggested events, and therapists' use of suggestive techniques may be responsible for the "recovered memories" of childhood traumas that some patients recall during therapy. ________________ reflects the influence of current knowledge, beliefs, and feelings on memory or past experiences. Bias can lead us to make the past consistent with the present, exaggerate changes between past and present, or remember the past in a way that makes us look good.

________________ is often the result of enhanced memories for emotionally charged events, which leads to obtrusive thoughts related to those memories. Persistence is partly attributable to the activation of hormonal systems via the ________________.

Each of the seven "sins" has adaptive features, so it is useful to think of these memory failures as prices we pay for the benefits of a memory system that usually serves us well. Examining these memory mind bugs helps psychologists better understand the normal operations of memory.

QUICK QUIZ #1

1. The process by which we transform what we perceive, think or feel into an enduring memory is called:
   a. encoding.
   b. remembering.
   c. recalling.
   d. storing.
2. Visual imagery encoding works effectively because:
   a. the lobes of your brain are able to more easily communicate.
   b. your brain stores the information directly into short-term memory.
   c. the eyes are the windows to the soul.
   d. you can more easily relate new information to knowledge already in memory.
3. In this list of words (peach, umbrella, orange, apple, tomato, potato, strawberry), the word ____________ is the one likely to be most easily remembered because of ____________.
   a. tomato; rhyme differences
   b. umbrella; memory storage
   c. strawberry; visual differences
   d. umbrella; organizational differences
4. Short-term memory can hold:
   a. a 7-digit telephone number but not a list of seven words.
   b. approximately 7 meaningful items.
   c. information for no more than 3 minutes.
   d. an unlimited amount of information.
5. Active maintenance of information in short-term memory is referred to as:
   a. working memory.
   b. dynamic storage.
   c. active memory.
   d. labor storage.
6. The process of bringing to mind information that has been previously encoded and stored is called:
   a. revival.
   b. recall.
   c. rehearsal.
   d. retrieval.

7. When taking a final exam in physics, Arturo was unable to remember the answers for several of the questions, even though he was certain that he knew the answers before he sat down to take the test. What advice might you give to him?
   a. Arturo, you were hungry last night when you were studying, so you should not have eaten such a big breakfast the morning of the test.
   b. Arturo, you should have studied longer the night before.
   c. Arturo, you would have retrieved more information if you had read the chapter aloud.
   d. Arturo, no offense intended, but your hippocampus must have been asleep.
8. Emily said that she vividly remembered the day she turned twenty-one. This would be an example of a(n):
   a. explicit memory.
   b. procedural memory.
   c. implicit memory.
   d. iconic memory.
9. Absentmindedness is often a failure of:
   a. blocking.
   b. prospective memory.
   c. transience.
   d. persistence.
10. When asked if she remembers meeting Joe at the café last week, Hana says, "Sure, he plays on the lacrosse team." Although Joe does play on the lacrosse team, Hana really met Frank at the café last week. This failure of memory is the result of:
   a. suggestibility.
   b. bias.
   c. persistence.
   d. memory misattribution.

QUICK QUIZ #2

1. ____________ is the ability to store and retrieve information over time.
   a. Learning
   b. Memory
   c. Recall
   d. Encoding
2. The main reason Markus, who is thirty-five years old, remembers his sixteenth birthday so clearly is because:
   a. sixteen is a magical birthday.
   b. that was the day he was able to get his driver's license.
   c. he had a birthday party.
   d. he was able to sleep late.
3. The term for where sensory information is kept for only a few seconds or less is:
   a. rehearsal memory storage.
   b. extra-short-term memory storage.
   c. sensory memory storage.
   d. retrieval memory storage.

4. The process of keeping information in short-term memory by mentally repeating it is called:
   a. rehearsal.
   b. chunking.
   c. memorizing.
   d. mnemonic storage.
5. A term for where information can be kept for hours, days, weeks, or years is:
   a. retrieval terminal.
   b. the hippocampus.
   c. remembrance database.
   d. long-term memory store.
6. HM, a severe epileptic, had his hippocampus and adjacent structures in the medial temporal lobe surgically removed to stop his seizures. As a result, he:
   a. cannot remember anything that happened in his past.
   b. no longer has use of his short-term memory.
   c. cannot remember his twenties in great detail.
   d. cannot make new long-term memories.
7. Enhanced neural processing that results from the strengthening of synaptic connections is known as:
   a. explicit memory booster.
   b. long-term potentiation.
   c. synaptic enhancement.
   d. PTL.
8. The best example of a procedural memory common to most college students in the United States is:
   a. how to drive a standard transmission car.
   b. how to ride a bull.
   c. how to surf the Internet.
   d. identifying the capital of the United States.
9. The three sins of memory that are mostly associated with forgetting are:
   a. transience, absentmindedness, blocking.
   b. memory misattribution, bias, suggestibility.
   c. persistence, blocking, bias.
   d. transience, suggestibility, absentmindedness.
10. Automatic behaviors have been closely linked to activation of the ____________ through PET scanning studies.
    a. hippocampus
    b. amygdala
    c. frontal cortex
    d. parietal cortex

QUICK QUIZ #3

1. The three steps in memory information processing are:
   a. input, processing, output.
   b. encoding, storage, retrieval.
   c. encoding, processing, retrieval.
   d. input, storage, output.

2. Which of the following is a process for keeping information in short-term memory?
   a. rehearsal
   b. recall
   c. redundancy
   d. recounting
3. Memory for skills is called:
   a. declarative memory.
   b. prime memory.
   c. implicit memory.
   d. explicit memory.
4. Studies have demonstrated that the process of encoding a memory causes permanent neural changes in the ___________ of the organism's neurons.
   a. myelin
   b. soma
   c. synapses
   d. mitochondria
5. Studies of amnesia victims suggest that:
   a. long-term memory is a single, unified system.
   b. there are two distinct types of long-term memory.
   c. there are dozens of distinct types of long-term memory.
   d. amnesia is always the result of traumatic brain injury.
6. The disruptive effect of earlier learning on memory for information acquired later is known as:
   a. proactive interference.
   b. retroactive interference.
   c. regressive interference.
   d. absentmindedness.
7. The two parts of the brain identified as being critical for processing emotional memories are the:
   a. hippocampus and hypothalamus.
   b. thalamus and occipital cortex.
   c. hippocamps and amygdala.
   d. amygdala and cerebellum.
8. The contents of textbook chapters are often organized into ___________ in order to facilitate information processing.
   a. mnemonics
   b. chunks
   c. algorithms
   d. cliques
9. Walking through the center of the university campus 15 years after his graduation, Arnie experienced a flood of old memories. Arnie's experience exemplifies:
   a. context effects.
   b. retroactive interference.
   c. state-dependent memory.
   d. semantic recall.

"HEY, GUESS WHAT I LEARNED IN PSYCHOLOGY TODAY?" (AN ESSAY QUESTION)

We're guessing there's someone in your life who is interested in the quality of your educational experiences, is reasonably intelligent, but knows little about psychology or the study of memory. This might be your roommate, your chemistry teacher, your mom, or some other person you have access to and want to share your thoughts and feelings with. What would you tell that person about the psychology of memory? What are the main points or crucial findings that you could summarize? How would you explain some of these memory concepts without getting too technical or boring this person to tears? Imagine you're telling your mom what you learned in psychology today.

THINGS TO PONDER

You've learned a lot of information in this chapter about how important memory is for getting through our everyday lives. When you put it all together, you may start to ponder how all this relates to issues that you have already learned about in this textbook and issues that are coming up. For example, you may ask yourself:

- How could the hippocampus, such a relatively small part of the human brain, be so critical for building new memories?

  Think about the relative size of this structure in other animals.

  Consider the five divisions of the brain and how they have evolved in humans.

- Is LTP the elusive *"engram,"* or physical representation of memory, that Karl Lashley and other scientists have been trying to identify for so long?

  Think about the fact that there must be a physical representation of every memory that you have and how flexible one mechanism would have to be to form and differentiate each one of those memories.

  Reflect on the fact that LTP is not a simple process; rather, it involves multiple processes (e.g., protein synthesis, concurrent activation, specific frequencies of stimulation).

- Is all memory the same?

  Ask yourself these questions: *"What did I have for breakfast? Where is the capital of Montana? How do you ride a bike? What did my friend just say?"* and then think about how these are all slightly different forms of memory (episodic, semantic, procedural, working memory, respectively).

- Are there really people who have a *"photographic"* memory?

  Imagine if you didn't ever forget anything. Sounds great, doesn't it? Now imagine that you couldn't assign any greater importance to your memory of graduating from high school than to your memory of what kind of bagel you had for breakfast thirty-seven days ago.

  Remember that, for the most part, memory is not video playback, or rarely even a snapshot of a moment in time. Instead, we forget certain things and remember others for many different reasons.

WEB LINKS AND SUGGESTED READINGS

About Memory: Exploratorium: http://www.exploratorium.edu/memory/index.html

- Features, exhibits, articles, lectures and additional memory links.

Memory Expansion Channel: http://www.brainchannels.com/Memory/memory2.html

- History, trivia, and tips for improving memory.

Improving Memory (Intelegen Inc.): http://web-us.com/memory/improving_memory.htm

- Theories and tips for improving memory.

Neuroscience for Kids – Memory Experiments: http://faculty.washington.edu/chudler/chmemory.html

- Great resources for teaching younger children about memory and the role of neuroscience in memory (the games are fun for adults too).

Baddeley, A. (2004). *Your Memory: A User's Guide.* Buffalo, NY: Firefly Books.

- Illustrated guide to your memory and how to improve it.

Loftus, Elizabeth F., and Katherine Ketcham (1996). *The Myth of Repressed Memory: False Memories and Allegations of Sexual Abuse.* New York: St. Martin's Griffin.

- A memory expert shows that many "repressed" memories are false.

Noll, Richard, and Carol Turkington (2001). *The Encyclopedia of Memory and Memory Disorders.* New York: Facts on File.

- An overview for general readers as well as professionals.

Schacter, D.L. (1996). *Searching for Memory: The Brain, the Mind, and the Past.* New York: Basic Books.

- Reviews of false memory, Alzheimer's disease, recovered memories, and amnesia, with first-hand accounts from patients with brain injury or psychological trauma.

Tulving, E., and Craik, F. I. M. (Eds.). (2000). *The Oxford Handbook of Memory.* New York: Oxford University Press.

- Several of the world's leading memory scientists review the field in this accessible overview of recent research. Topics such as memory development in childhood and old age, memory impairment in brain injury and disease, and the emergence of memory functions from brain activity are addressed. Reviews of current behavioral, neuroimaging, and computer simulation theories of memory are also considered.

ANSWERS

Chapter Overview

Encoding: Transforming Perceptions into Memories

Memories are not passive recordings of the world, but instead result from combining incoming information with previous experiences. **Encoding** is the process of linking new and old information together and turning that information into lasting memories. Memory is influenced by the type of encoding we perform regardless of whether we consciously intend to remember an event, fact, or experience. Three types of encoding are **elaborative encoding** (actively linking incoming information to existing associations and knowledge), **visual imagery encoding** (converting incoming information into mental pictures), and **organizational encoding** (noticing relationships among items you want to encode), and they all enhance memory. Different regions within the frontal lobes play important roles in elaborative encoding and organizational encoding, whereas the occipital lobes are important for visual imagery encoding.

Storage: Maintaining Memories over Time

Three major forms of memory storage hold information for different amounts of time. These three forms are **sensory memory** (which holds information for a second or two), **short-term memory** (which holds information for less than a minute), and **long-term memory** (which holds information for several minutes to several years). At the cellular level, memory storage depends on changes in synapses, and **long-term potentiation (LTP)** is a process that increases the strength of a synaptic connection.

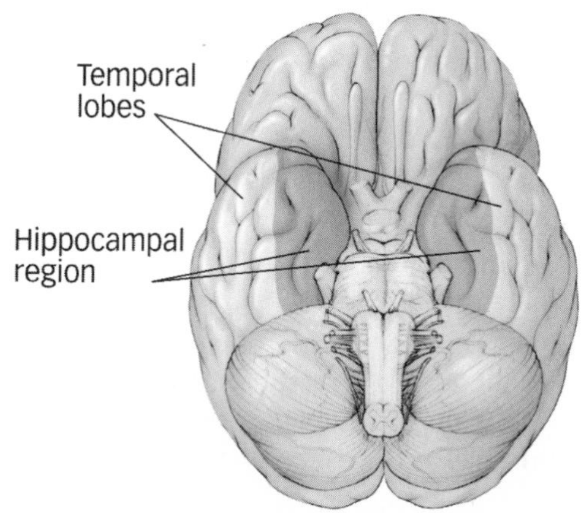

The **hippocampal region** and surrounding structures in the **temporal lobes** are critical for transferring information into long-term storage, as shown by the severe anterograde amnesia of patients such as HM.

Retrieval: Bringing Memories to Mind

Recall of past **experiences** depends critically on retrieval cues, which trigger recall by reinstating what we thought or how we felt during the encoding of an experience. Information or an experience we can't recall on our own is sometimes only temporarily inaccessible and can be brought to mind with appropriate retrieval cues. Moods and inner states can serve as powerful **retrieval cues**. Retrieval can be separated into the effort we make while trying to remember what happened in the past and the successful **recovery** of stored information. Several studies suggest that trying to remember something activates the right frontal lobe, whereas successful recovery of stored information activates the hippocampus and the sensory regions of the brain associated with the aspects of the experience being remembered.

Multiple Forms of Memory: How the Past Returns

One of the three forms of memory, **long-term memory**, can be broadly divided into **explicit memory**, involving conscious, intentional retrieval of previous experiences, and **implicit memory**, which is the nonconscious influences of past experiences on later behavior and performance, such as procedural memory and priming. **Procedural memory** involves the acquisition of skills as a result of practice, and **priming** is a change in the ability to recognize or identify an object or word as the result of past exposure to it. People who have amnesia often retain implicit memory, including procedural memory and priming, but often lack explicit memory, particularly episodic memory. **Episodic memory** is the collection of personal experiences from a particular place and time, whereas **semantic memory** is a networked, general, impersonal knowledge of facts, associations, and concepts. Nonhuman animals possess extensive memory abilities, but it is still debatable whether they can engage in the kind of "mental time travel" that is characteristic of human episodic memory.

Memory Failures: The Seven Sins of Memory

There are seven major ways that memory can be problematic: transience, absentmindedness, blocking, memory misattribution, suggestibility, bias, and persistence.

Transience is reflected by a rapid decline in memory followed by more gradual forgetting. With the passing of time, memory switches from being detailed to being more general. Both decay and interference contribute to transience. **Absentmindedness** results from failures of attention, shallow encoding, and the influence of automatic behaviors, and it is often associated with forgetting to do things in the future. **Blocking** occurs when stored information is temporarily inaccessible.

Memory misattribution happens when we experience a sense of familiarity but don't recall, or mistakenly recall, the specifics of when and where an event occurred. Misattribution can result in eyewitness misidentification or false recognition. **Suggestibility** gives rise to implanted (false) memories of small details or entire episodes. Suggestive techniques such as hypnosis or visualization can promote vivid recall of suggested events, and therapists' use of suggestive techniques may be responsible for the "recovered memories" of childhood traumas that some patients recall during therapy. **Bias** reflects the influence of current knowledge, beliefs, and feelings on memory or past experiences. Bias can lead us to make the past consistent with the present, exaggerate changes between past and present, or remember the past in a way that makes us look good.

Persistence is often the result of enhanced memories for emotionally charged events, which leads to obtrusive thoughts related to those memories. Persistence is partly attributable to the activation of hormonal systems via the **amygdala**.

Each of the seven "sins" has adaptive features, so it is useful to think of these memory failures as prices we pay for the benefits of a memory system that usually serves us well. Examining these memory mind bugs helps psychologists better understand the normal operations of memory.

Quick Quiz #1

1. **A.** "Encoding" is the term used to refer to how information is transformed into a memory.
2. **D.** Visual imagery encoding relies on forming a "mental picture" of the information to be remembered.
3. **D.** The word that is unlike the others ("umbrella") is easier to remember.
4. **B.** Seven chunks of information can be held in short-term memory. The size of each chunk can vary, however.
5. **A.** Working memory refers to short-term memory and all of the operations and processes that accompany it.
6. **D.** Retrieval involves bringing previously-stored information to mind.
7. **A.** Arturo would have benefited from state-dependent retrieval. This occurs when the state in which information is retrieved matches the state in which information was encoded.
8. **A.** Explicit memory involves consciously or intentionally retrieving past experiences from memory.
9. **B.** Absentmindedness results from a lapse in attention. It represents a failure of prospective memory.
10. **D.** Hana has misattributed the origin of her memory for that event.

Quick Quiz #2

1. **A.** Memory is the ability to store and retrieve information over time.
2. **B.** Markus probably remembers his 16th birthday because of elaborative encoding. This is the process of relating an event (his birthday) to other information in memory (learning to drive).
3. **C.** Sensory memory holds information for a few seconds or less.
4. **A.** Rehearsal can be an effective strategy for maintaining information in short-term memory.
5. **B.** The case of HM and others have shown that there are two distinct types of long-term memory, implicit and explicit, that are controlled by different parts of the brain.

6. **D.** A side effect of HM's surgery was the inability to form new long-term memories. The hippocampus plays a fundamental role in this ability.
7. **B.** Long-term potentiation is the term used for enhanced neural processing that occurs when synaptic connections are strengthened.
8. **C.** Procedural memory refers to our knowledge of how to do things. Most current college students in the United States have a well-established procedural memory for surfing the Internet.
9. **A.** The seven sins of memory refer to different ways in which our memory can fail us. Some of these—transience, absentmindedness, and blocking—are instances of forgetting.
10. **C.** The frontal cortex plays a role in the activation of automatic behaviors. These automatic behaviors, in turn, are often associated with the experience of absentmindedness.

Quick Quiz #3

1. **B.** Information must be encoded first, stored (retained over time), and then retrieved, or brought back to mind, when the information is needed.
2. **A.** Rehearsal is a process for keeping information in short-term memory by mentally repeating it.
3. **C.** Implicit memory is the kind of memory that is used for skills, such as riding a bike. You can access the memory, but it is difficult to describe or declare.
4. **C.** The changes that result in long-term potentiation that are related to memory storage happen at the level of the synapse.
5. **B.** There are different systems for storing long-term implicit and explicit memories.
6. **A.** Proactive interference is the disruptive effect of earlier learning on memory for information acquired later. Retroactive interference is essentially the reverse: information acquired later interferes with information acquired earlier.
7. **C.** Patients with amygdala damage are unable to remember emotional events any better than nonemotional events. The hippocampus and amygdala are heavily interconnected, particularly for processing the cues involved in emotionally charged events.
8. **B.** Chunks of information can be remembered later better than the individual pieces of information by themselves.
9. **C.** Returning to a particular context can serve as a retrieval cue for experiences that occurred in that context previously. For example, Arnie may have met a particularly interesting person in a classroom several years earlier, and he remembers that meeting as he walks by the room on his way through campus.

"Hey, Guess What I Learned In Psychology Today?" (An Essay Question)

What might you tell your mom about memory?

- You could start by asking her what she thinks life would be like without memory. She will most likely assume that life would be like "soap opera" amnesia, the one where people can't remember who they are or what they've done. Then you can tell her about Greg and HM, and how they can't retain new information, but they know who they are, what the capital of France is called, and how to ride a bike.
- You could also segue to the topic of memory the next time your mom can't remember where she left her keys: "Mom, you know that I learned that there are several possible reasons why you can't remember where you left your keys, and none of them have to do with early-onset Alzheimer's disease!" You can talk about increasing her recall by using a couple of simple memory tricks (deepen the level of processing, use retrieval cues, or be aware of some of the seven sins of memory failure). She'll be happy to learn the new memory aid, proud that you are learning so much in college, and relieved that she doesn't have Alzheimer's disease.
- The next time you are at your family's house and everyone is startled by a sudden knock at the door or the dog barking at a passerby, you could tell your mom that you will all probably remember that moment better than other parts of the day because of the sudden arousal that you all briefly experienced. If you really want to dazzle her, you could mention that there is an almond-shaped structure in the brain that initiates the release of stress hormones that are responsible for that effect.

6

Learning

THE BIG PICTURE

Christy hears a knock on the door. As she answers the door her friends, Crystal and Shay, shrill with excitement. Shay says, "Girl, you look fabulous!" Christy replies, "Well, I learned from the best." The three friends head downtown to celebrate Christy's 21st birthday. On their way to the shuttle stop they wander through campus and wave to shouts of "Happy Birthday!" coming from other friends as they pass by. They stop for Christy's favorite, Szechuan chicken, at her favorite restaurant, The Peking Duck, before they head out to the clubs. Shay orders hot sake for the table and they toast Christy's special day. On their way to the dance club, they stop in at O. Henry's, where they run into Danny and Carlos, who each buy Christy a different birthday shot. The whole gang makes their way to a 70s-themed club and dance under the disco ball all night long. As the night draws to a close, Sylvester, the slick prankster and Christy's biology lab partner, notices the group at the club and buys Christy a shot of tequila. As she tips up the shot glass she notices the strong smell and the little worm that Sylvester paid the bartender to drop in, but it was too late to stop. The smoky liquor and the rubbery bug were on their way to Christy's stomach, which sent her running to the ladies' room. Shay and Crystal hailed a cab, after shooting dagger stares at Sylvester, and returned Christy to her room. As they were laying her down, Christy muttered, "I don't think I'll be having the Szechuan chicken for a while." In the following weeks, Christy joked with her good friends about that night and thanked them for taking care of her. She also noticed that the smell of Chinese food or anything smoked made her a bit queasy, as did the sight of Sylvester, particularly when they had to do an earthworm dissection together.

How does all of this relate to learning? Well, we see examples of several different types of learning that are described in Chapter 6 at work in this scenario. When Christy hears a knock on the door, she goes over to answer it. As she operates the doorknob—that is, as she turns it—she has an expectation that someone, in this case her friends, will be on the other side when the door is open. Her friends serve as a reinforcer for door-opening behavior. If there were an annoying salesperson there every time Christy answered the door, she would be a lot less likely to open the door when people knock. This is an example of operant conditioning. Christy also had learned some fashion tips from Shay. This may have been through observational learning, just watching Shay's style of dress and noting the compliments she receives, or through instruction from Shay and repeated advice, or from direct experience with dressing fabulously. The rest of the story has to do with the complexities of classical conditioning. There are several examples of possible conditioned stimuli, from the smell and taste of food and drink to the sights of buildings on campus and flashing lights. These things were relatively neutral for Christy before the evening began, but they took on a special meaning for her when they were associated with an unconditioned stimulus—feeling sick. After Christy got sick, which was an unconditioned response, she noticed that a similar response has been conditioned to some of the initially neutral stimuli, such as the smell of Szechuan chicken. In this case, the learning even generalizes to other similar stimuli, such as other Chinese food, because of the strength of the conditioned taste aversion, which is arguably the result of biological preparedness.

Understanding how organisms learn has been at the heart of psychology since its inception. Chapter 6 describes the approaches that scientists have taken to study the mechanisms of learning and how they affect all the other realms of psychology. It would be very difficult to talk about concepts such as memory (Chapter 5), intelligence, or thought and decision making (Chapter 7) without invoking the learning process. Of course, it is critical to understand sensation and perception (Chapter 4) as they relate to the stimuli that are being learned. Learning also lays the foundation for many of the things that make us who we are. How did you learn to speak (Chapters 7 and 10)? Do your learning styles and preferences affect how you interact with others (Chapters 11 and 15)? Do you learn while you sleep (Chapter 8)? We will also see in Chapters 12 and 13 that people with psychological disorders learn in very different ways from those without those disorders.

Chapter 6 introduces the terms, concepts, and procedures that researchers use to study and understand how we learn. One thing to keep in mind is that there are usually several different types of learning occurring all of the time in our daily life. Maybe they aren't as obvious as Christy's birthday story, but we are constantly taking in information and processing it to determine whether or not it is useful, meaningful, good, bad, scary, or something that should be ignored. On top of all of that, these things are happening in different and changing environments. Now that you are aware of some of the mechanisms responsible for learning you can focus on some of the things that facilitate learning, like consistency and reinforcement, and avoid some of the things that get in the way of learning, like distractions and randomness. And no doubt you will steer clear of the little worm.

CHAPTER OBJECTIVES

After studying this chapter, you should be able to:

1. Define *learning* and discuss how learning can take a variety of forms, including *habituation.*
2. Make connections between the overall behaviorist approach and specific research on learning processes.
3. Describe *classical conditioning.*
4. Distinguish between an *unconditioned stimulus (US), unconditioned response (UR), conditioned stimulus (CS), and conditioned response (CR)* in classical conditioning.
5. Compare *acquisition, extinction,* and *spontaneous recovery.*
6. Discuss how stimulus *generalization* and stimulus *discrimination* occur in classical conditioning.
7. Describe the events surrounding the experience of Little Albert, noting in particular how this case appeared to bolster the behaviorist view of conditioned emotional responses.
8. Identify the neural elements of classical conditioning, with focus on the involvement of the amygdala.
9. Identify the cognitive elements of classical conditioning, with focus on the principles identified in the Rescorla-Wagner model.
10. Identify the evolutionary elements of classical conditioning, with focus on conditioned food aversions and preferences and the concept of *biological preparedness.*
11. State the *law of effect* and explain how it contributes to *operant conditioning.*
12. Distinguish between *reinforcers* and *punishers* in operant conditioning and explain how the presentation or removal of a stimulus affects the likelihood of a given subsequent behavior.
13. Describe types of primary and secondary reinforcers and punishers.
14. Discuss how *extinction,* stimulus *generalization,* and stimulus *discrimination* occur in *operant conditioning.*

15. Explain how schedules of reinforcement affect learning; include examples of *fixed interval, fixed ratio, variable interval,* and *variable ratio schedules.*
16. Explain how the *shaping* of successive approximations to a desired behavior can eventually produce that behavior.
17. Identify the neural elements of operant conditioning, with focus on the involvement of structures in the "pleasure center" of the brain.
18. Identify the cognitive elements of operant conditioning, especially the concepts of *latent learning* and *cognitive maps* identified by Edward Chace Tolman.
19. Identify the evolutionary elements of operant conditioning, especially the "misbehavior" of organisms that was first identified by Marion and Kellar Breland.
20. Explain how *observational learning* can occur in humans, noting especially the research on learning aggressive responses; explain how observational learning can occur in animals.
21. Define *implicit learning* and provide examples of ways in which it differs from explicit learning; discuss whether or not different neural mechanisms are implicated in these different types of learning.

CHAPTER OVERVIEW

Use the terms below to fill in the following exercises. Terms may not be used more than once. The answers can be found at the end of this chapter.

acquisition	explicit	neural
adaptive	extinction	performed
amygdala	generalization	prepared
awareness	habituation	psychosis
awareness	implicit	punishment
B. F. Skinner	increase	reinforcement
conditioned response	infants	resistant
conditioned stimulus	Ivan Pavlov	schedule
contingencies	John B. Watson	shaping
creative	latent	spontaneous recovery
CS	learning	unconditioned stimulus
discrimination	maps	US
emitted	mirror	variety
errors	model	
expectation	more	

Defining Learning: Experience That Causes a Permanent Change

__________________ refers to any of several processes that produce relatively permanent changes in an organism's behavior. __________________ is a process by which an organism changes the way it reacts to external stimuli.

Classical Conditioning: One Thing Leads to Another

Classical conditioning is a kind of learning in which a neutral stimulus, or ______________, is paired with a meaningful event, or ________________. In his initial work, ________________, the founder of classical conditioning, paired a neutral tone with the presentation of food. The pairing of these stimuli repeatedly during the ________________ phase of classical conditioning eventually allowed the presentation of the previously meaningless tone to elicit a response called a ________________. ________________ of a learned response will occur if the CS is presented repeatedly without being followed by the US; ________________ will occur if an organism is allowed a rest period following extinction. Stimulus ________________ occurs if a CS that is similar to the one used in the original training is introduced; however, stimulus ________________ is important for learning how to tell the difference between relatively similar stimuli.

Behaviorists, including ________________, viewed classical conditioning as an automatic and mechanical process, believing that no higher-level functions, such as thinking and ________________, were needed to understand behavior. It turned out that the underlying mechanisms of classical conditioning are more complex than the simple association between a ________________ and a ________________. The brain is involved in many types of conditioning, as in the case of fear conditioning and the action of the ________________. The evolutionary aspects of classical conditioning show that each species is biologically ________________ to acquire particular CS–US associations based on its evolutionary history. In short, classical conditioning is a sophisticated mechanism that evolved precisely because it has ________________ value.

Operant Conditioning: Reinforcements from the Environment

Operant conditioning, as developed by ________________, is a kind of learning in which behaviors are shaped by ________________. Behaviors in operant conditioning that are reinforced are ________________ likely to occur, and the ________________ between actions and outcomes are critical in determining how an organism's behavior will be displayed. Whereas classical conditioning involves behaviors that are elicited from an organism, operant conditioning deals with overt and ________________ behaviors. ________________ by successive approximations is a procedure that encourages organisms to manipulate the environment in a way that may not be natural for them to do. Reinforcement is defined as any operation that functions to ________________ the likelihood of the behavior that led to it, unlike ________________, which functions to decrease the likelihood of a behavior.

Like classical conditioning, operant conditioning shows acquisition, generalization, discrimination, and extinction. The ________________ with which reinforcements are delivered has a dramatic effect on how well an operant behavior is learned and how ________________ it is to extinction. Also like classical conditioning, operant conditioning is better understood when taking into account underlying ________________, cognitive, and evolutionary components. ________________ learning and the development of cognitive ________________ in animals clearly implicate cognitive factors underlying operant learning.

Observational Learning: Look at Me

Learning can take place through the observation of others and does not necessarily require that the acquired behaviors be ________________ and reinforced. Observational learning does not simply result in imitation; it can also show ________________ elements. A child who sees an adult behave in a gentle manner with a toy will often show a ________________ of gentle reactions, including ones that were not exhibited by the adult ________________. When one organism patterns its actions on another organism's successful behaviors, learning is speeded up and potentially dangerous ________________ are prevented. These behavioral advantages can save an organism from considerable pain. At a neural level, ________________ neurons possibly provide an additional advantage related to imitation and ________________, which is why they are implicated in the process of empathy.

Implicit Learning: Under the Wires

Implicit learning takes place largely in the absence of ________________ of either the actual learning or the knowledge of what was learned. Complex behaviors, such as language use or socialization, can be learned through this ________________ process. ________________ show intact implicit learning long before they develop conscious awareness. Even those with severe neurological disorders or ________________ show virtually normal implicit learning.

Implicit learning is mediated by areas in the brain that are distinct from those activated by ________________ learning.

QUICK QUIZ #1

1. When you moved from the family farm into the city, you found that the traffic noises initially kept you awake at night, but after a while, you slept right through the honks and backfires. You benefited from a process called:
   a. implicit learning.
   b. explicit learning.
   c. habituation.
   d. classical conditioning.

2. Pavlov was also able to teach his dogs to salivate to the sound of a buzzer or the tick of a metronome, as long as he:
   a. rewarded the dogs with a pat on the back every time they salivated to the tone.
   b. withheld food so that the dogs were always hungry.
   c. made sure the odor of food was in the air when he sounded the tone.
   d. paired the tone over time with the presentation of food.

3. During ____________, typically there is a gradual increase in learning, which starts low, rises rapidly, and then slowly tapers off.
   a. habituation
   b. generalization
   c. discrimination
   d. acquisition

4. After the acquisition phase, the presentation of the white rat was enough to cause Little Albert to cry. The white rat was the:
   a. CS.
   b. CR.
   c. US.
   d. UR.

5. The part of the brain that is essential to fear conditioning is the:
   a. reticular formation.
   b. amygdala.
   c. thalamus.
   d. hippocampus.
6. Behavior that requires an organism to act, solve a problem, or otherwise manipulate elements of its environment is called:
   a. instrumental behavior.
   b. latent behavior.
   c. unconscious behavior.
   d. unconditional behavior.
7. In a research study on ___________, pigeons were trained to discriminate between art by Picasso (a Cubist) and Monet (an Impressionist).
   a. classical conditioning
   b. second-order conditioning
   c. stimulus control
   d. primary reinforcement
8. All the following are pleasure centers in the brain except the:
   a. nucleus accumbens.
   b. medial forebrain bundle.
   c. reticular formation.
   d. hypothalamus.
9. Learning that takes place by watching the actions of others is called:
   a. surveillance learning.
   b. duplicative learning
   c. imitative learning.
   d. observational learning.
10. Most children have learned not to eat with their feet, an accomplishment that is likely a result of:
    a. cognitive mapping.
    b. shaping.
    c. implicit learning.
    d. explicit learning.

QUICK QUIZ #2

1. The period in the history of psychology during which most of the fundamental work on learning theory was taking place overlapped primarily with:
   a. structuralism.
   b. behaviorism.
   c. functionalism.
   d. cognition.

2. When Pavlov had taught his dogs to salivate to the sound of a buzzer, salivation beame the:
   a. CS.
   b. CR.
   c. US.
   d. UR.

3. Watson's goals in his controversial study on Little Albert included all the following except:
   a. wanting to demonstrate that a relatively complex reaction could be conditioned by Pavlov's techniques.
   b. wanting to show that emotional responses such as fear and anxiety could be produced by classical conditioning.
   c. wanting to demonstrate that all animals, even children, have strong emotions.
   d. wanting to confirm that conditioning could be applied to humans as well as to other animals.

4. Introducing cognitive components into classical conditioning, Robert Rescorla and Allan Wagner (1972) theorized that classical conditioning occurs only when:
   a. the amygdala is involved.
   b. the acquisition phase is complete.
   c. the UR and CR are the same.
   d. an animal has learned to set up an expectation.

5. According to B. F. Skinner, a reinforcer ____________ the likelihood of the behavior that led to it, whereas a punisher ____________ the likelihood of the behavior that led to it.
   a. decreases; increases
   b. increases; decreases
   c. changes; stabilizes
   d. promotes; increases

6. Workers who receive their paycheck at the post office every two weeks will visit the post office much more frequently toward the end of each two-week pay period. These workers are on a ____________ schedule of reinforcement.
   a. variable interval
   b. fixed interval
   c. variable ratio
   d. fixed ratio

7. Much of Tolman's research focused on latent learning and:
   a. pigeons.
   b. cognitive maps.
   c. shaping the behavior of human subjects.
   d. the pleasure centers of the brain.

8. The classic study on observational learning, which involved a Bobo doll, was done by:
   a. Edward L. Thorndike.
   b. Albert Einstein.
   c. Albert Bandura.
   d. Edward Titchener.

9. Most likely you have gathered that clipping your toenails in class is not considered advantageous behavior. It is very likely that this is an example of:
   a. mirror learning.
   b. behavior that was shaped.
   c. explicit learning.
   d. implicit learning.

QUICK QUIZ #3

1. Because your roommate insists on having the television on while she studies, you have begun to adjust to the noise and hardly notice it anymore. This is a result of:
   a. habituation.
   b. acquisition.
   c. generalization.
   d. discrimination.
2. When your cat runs to his food dish every time he hears the sound of the can opener, it is likely that the noise of the can opener has become a(n) ____________ for the cat.
   a. CS
   b. CR
   c. US
   d. UR
3. Even if a sufficient number of extinction trials are conducted so that there is no longer any evidence of spontaneous recovery, can we still conclude that any residual associations have been completely eliminated?
   a. no, not completely
   b. yes, in 99% of cases
   c. yes, except in extreme circumstances
   d. no, 50% of the time spontaneous recovery will occur
4. In Watson's experiment with Little Albert, the ____________ and the ____________ were the same.
   a. UR; CR
   b. US; CS
   c. UR; US
   d. CS; CR
5. Last year you ate some tainted chili at the Red Hot Chili Cook-Off and got very sick. Now you no longer want to eat chili. You have developed a(n):
   a. food adaptation.
   b. evolutionary reaction to beef.
   c. food aversion.
   d. unconditioned response.
6. Most children love to use crayons and colored pencils, but research has shown that rewarding people for doing what they love will, in the case of these children:
   a. undermine their love of coloring.
   b. increase the pleasure they derive from coloring.

c. produce an underjustification effect.
d. make them angry when they are not able to use the crayons.

7. How would a behaviorist explain why some baseball players refuse to shower on the morning of a big game?
   a. They prefer to focus on the big game, not on other activities of daily living.
   b. Their coach has rewarded them with a steak dinner after a winning game.
   c. Their winning games have been reinforced on an intermittent schedule.
   d. They previously had a good game on a day when they happened not to have showered.

8. An evolutionary perspective would suggest that, when placed in a multi-option maze:
   a. rats will repeatedly travel down the same arm in which they initially were reinforced with food.
   b. rats will not explore a maze unless they are reinforced on a continuous reinforcement schedule.
   c. rats will systematically travel from arm to arm in search of food.
   d. rats are not likely to search for food pellets in a maze.

9. Cecilia is very afraid of snakes and yet she has never seen one. How might she have developed this fear?
   a. classical conditioning
   b. observational learning
   c. cognitive mapping
   d. operant conditioning

10. What is the best advice you can give a friend who has a big vocabulary test in Spanish tomorrow morning?
   a. Study and then get a good night's sleep.
   b. Recite the vocabulary words into a tape recorder and play it while you sleep.
   c. A reminder that research has shown that a minimum of four hours of sleep is necessary for alertness.
   d. It's okay to pull an all-nighter if it gets you the grade.

"HEY, GUESS WHAT I LEARNED IN PSYCHOLOGY TODAY?" (AN ESSAY QUESTION)

We're guessing there's someone in your life who is interested in the quality of your educational experiences, is reasonably intelligent, but knows little about psychology. This might be your roommate, a previous teacher, your mom, or some other person you have access to and want to share your thoughts and feelings with. What would you tell that person about learning? How would you explain the differences between classical and operant conditioning? What advice would you give to your mom about training her miniature schnauzer to stop jumping up on the sofa?

THINGS TO PONDER

You've been provided a lot of information in this chapter about how learning is the foundation for many questions about behavior. When you put it all together, you may start to ponder how it all relates to other issues in this textbook. For example, you may ask yourself:

- Are different parts of the brain active during explicit and implicit learning?

  Think about the case of HM. After the removal of his medial temporal lobes he could not learn or remember new information about his life, but he could acquire new skills on a procedural task. So implicit learning must occur outside the hippocampus and medial temporal lobes.

  Consider that there are also cases such as Korsakoff's syndrome and Alzheimer's disease that result in learning deficits similar to those that HM experienced, but the damage is in different parts of the brain. So there must be multiple systems that are responsible for explicit memory.

- Is learning involved in drug addiction, or is it purely a physiological phenomenon?

  Note that all learning happens within a context, and although the CSs related to the drug are being paired with the direct effects of the drug, the environment in which the drug is taken is also being paired with those drug effects.

  Reflect on the idea that the development of tolerance to a drug is physiological in part, but there is also a learned, or conditioned, tolerance that develops simultaneously with the physiological tolerance.

- Did you learn language as a young child through reinforcement or were you biologically prepared to develop language?

  Consider the pure behaviorist perspective: Changes in behavior are the result of outcomes. This would indicate that you would need to be reinforced for every word that you tried to produce and every grammar rule that you discovered. On the flip side, you don't wake up one day with a complete grasp of language or a ready-to-go vocabulary. Reinforcement almost certainly plays a role in the development and shaping of language.

  B. F. Skinner and Noam Chomsky argued publicly about these issues at length. The answer probably lies somewhere in between. Parts of our brain are dedicated specifically to language, but we wouldn't learn language if we weren't around language and being reinforced for using it.

- How do we learn the complex rules of social interaction in a given culture?

As with language, we most likely fashion our early social interactions after the models that are available to us (parents, siblings, friends). However, we most certainly modify our behaviors on the basis of their success—whether they work out for us or not. If that pickup line gets you the date, you're more likely to use it again, if not, you may resort to a different strategy.

WEB LINKS AND SUGGESTED READING

emTech (Emerging Technologies)—Learning Theories: http://www.emtech.net/learning_theories.htm

- A list of dozens of links to information about influential learning theorists, theories, games, and so forth.

Stufflebeam, Robert—The MindProject—Connectionism: http://www.mind.ilstu.edu/curriculum/modOverview.php?modGUI=76

- A description of how connectionism works and how it attempts to model learning.

Pavlov, Ivan (1927). *Conditioned reflexes*. New York: Dover Publications.

- Pavlov's original work on classical conditioning.

Bandura, Albert (1977). *Social learning theory*. New York: Prentice-Hall.

- An overview of theoretical and experimental advances in the field of social learning, exploring the origins of behavior, antecedent and consequent determinants, and cognitive control.

Schmajuk, Nestor, and Holland, Peter (Eds.) (1998). *Occasion setting: Associative learning and cognition in animals*. Washington, DC: American Psychological Association.

- Over 60 years ago, B. F. Skinner proposed that a discriminative stimulus in an operant conditioning paradigm does not elicit a response but simply "sets the occasion" for the response to occur. The eminent group of experimental psychologists and theoreticians who wrote the chapters of this book discuss the current status of the data and theories concerning simple classical conditioning and occasion setting.

Skinner, B. F. (1957). *Verbal behavior*. Acton, MA: Copely Publishing Group.

- Skinner's ideas about how language is learned and maintained.

ANSWERS

Chapter Overview

Defining Learning: Experience That Causes a Permanent Change

Learning refers to any of several processes that produce relatively permanent changes in an organism's behavior. **Habituation** is a process by which an organism changes the way it reacts to external stimuli.

Classical Conditioning: One Thing Leads to Another

Classical conditioning is a kind of learning in which a neutral stimulus, or **conditioned stimulus**, is paired with a meaningful event, or **unconditioned stimulus**. In his initial work, **Ivan Pavlov**, the founder of classical conditioning, paired a neutral tone with the presentation of food. The pairing of these stimuli repeatedly during the **acquisition** phase of classical conditioning eventually allowed the presentation of the previously meaningless tone to elicit a response called a **conditioned response. Extinction** of a learned response will occur if the CS is presented repeatedly without being followed by the US; **spontaneous recovery** will occur if an organism is allowed a rest period following extinction. Stimulus **generalization** occurs if a CS that is similar to the one used in the original training is introduced; however, stimulus **discrimination** is important for learning how to tell the difference between relatively similar stimuli.

Behaviorists, including **John B. Watson**, viewed classical conditioning as an automatic and mechanical process, believing that no higher-level functions, such as thinking and **awareness**, were needed to understand behavior. It turned out that the underlying mechanisms of classical conditioning are more complex than the simple association between a **CS** and a **US**. The brain is involved in many types of conditioning, as in the case of fear conditioning and the action of the **amygdala**. The evolutionary aspects of classical conditioning show that each species is biologically **prepared** to acquire particular CS–US associations based on its evolutionary history. In short, classical conditioning is a sophisticated mechanism that evolved precisely because it has **adaptive** value.

Operant Conditioning: Reinforcements from the Environment

Operant conditioning, as developed by **B. F. Skinner**, is a kind of learning in which behaviors are shaped by **reinforcement**. Behaviors in operant conditioning that are reinforced are **more** likely to occur, and the **contingencies** between actions and outcomes are critical in determining how an organism's behavior will be displayed. Whereas classical conditioning involves behaviors that are elicited from an organism, operant conditioning deals with overt and **emitted** behaviors. **Shaping** by successive approximations is a procedure that encourages organisms to manipulate the environment in a way that may not be natural for them to do. Reinforcement is defined as any operation that functions to **increase** the likelihood of the behavior that led to it, unlike **punishment**, which functions to decrease the likelihood of a behavior.

Like classical conditioning, operant conditioning shows acquisition, generalization, discrimination, and extinction. The **schedule** with which reinforcements are delivered has a dramatic effect on how well an operant behavior is learned and how **resistant** it is to extinction. Also like classical conditioning, operant conditioning is better understood when taking into account underlying **neural**, cognitive, and evolutionary components. **Latent** learning and the development of cognitive **maps** in animals clearly implicate cognitive factors underlying operant learning.

Observational Learning: Look at Me

Learning can take place through the observation of others and does not necessarily require that the acquired behaviors be **performed** and reinforced. Observational learning does not simply result in imitation; it can also show **creative** elements. A child who sees an adult behave in a gentle manner with a toy will often show a **variety** of gentle reactions, including ones that were not exhibited by the adult **model**. When one organism patterns its actions on another organism's successful behaviors, learning is speeded up and potentially dangerous **errors** are prevented. These behavioral advantages can save an organism from considerable pain. At a neural level, **mirror** neuons possibly provide an additional advantage related to imitation and **expectation**, which is why they are implicated in the process of empathy.

Implicit Learning: Under the Wires

Implicit learning takes place largely in the absence of **awareness** of either the actual learning or the knowledge of what was learned. Complex behaviors, such as language use or socialization, can be learned through this **implicit** process. **Infants** show intact implicit learning long before they develop conscious awareness. Even those with severe neurological disorders or **psychosis** show virtually normal implicit learning.

Implicit learning is mediated by areas in the brain that are distinct from those activated by **explicit** learning.

Quick Quiz #1

1. **C.** "Habituation" refers to the gradual reduction in response after repeated or prolonged exposure to a stimulus.
2. **D.** The tone, which when paired over time with the presentation of food, became a CS, and eventually could alone produce salivation, the CR.
3. **D.** The period of acquisition is a period of training, in which the association of the CS and the US is learned over time.
4. **A.** The white rat was a conditioned stimulus because Albert had learned by its earlier pairing with an unpleasant sound (an unconditioned stimulus) to be fearful when he saw it.
5. **B.** The amygdala, which is important in the experience of emotion, is critical in conditioning various emotional responses.
6. **A.** Instrumental behavior is behavior in which the organism performs like an "instrument," or tool, to accomplish some end.
7. **C.** Stimulus control takes place when a particular response occurs only when a particular stimulus is presented; in this case, the presentation of one artist's work versus another's.
8. **C.** The reticular formation is located in the medulla and regulates sleep, wakefulness, and levels of arousal.
9. **D.** Observational learning, which takes place without reinforcement, plays a large role in the transmission of culture.
10. **C.** Implicit learning is a result of our unconscious internalizations of patterns of various sorts in the world that surrounds us.

Quick Quiz #2

1. **B.** Behaviorism, including the work of classical conditioning theorists such as John B. Watson and operant conditioning theorists such as B. F. Skinner, is closely associated with the study of learning.
2. **B.** Salivation is now the conditioned response because it occurs with the buzzer alone only after earlier training with paired stimuli—the buzzer and food.
3. **C.** As a strict behaviorist, Watson sought to demonstrate that virtually all behavior—emotional and physical—can be elicited by use of the principles of classical conditioning.
4. **D.** Rescorla and Wagner proposed that the function of a learned and reliable expectation—a cognitive state—facilitates the association of the US and CS by eliminating other possible associations.
5. **B.** Skinner viewed reinforcers and punishers neutrally, simply in terms of their effect on behavior; one person's punishment is another person's reinforcer.
6. **B.** There's no point in looking for a check in the mail before you know it's due; but in other contexts, the behavior produced by a fixed interval schedule is typical of a procrastinator—little response immediately after a reinforcer, and a burst of activity immediately before the next one.
7. **B.** Latent learning—which is not immediately manifested—contributes to the development of cognitive maps, which are

mental representations of the features of a physical environment.

8. **C.** Edward L. Thorndike formulated the law of effect; Albert Einstein is known for the theory of relativity; Edward Titchener brought structuralism to the United States from Germany.
9. **D.** Implicit learning—learning that occurs without awareness of the process or the result—has been studied with the use of artificial grammars and serial reaction time tasks.

Quick Quiz #3

1. **A.** Habituation is adaptive; without it daily life—for example, in a noisy city—could be unbearable.
2. **A.** The can opener is not food—it has been conditioned to signify food to your cat.
3. **A.** Some neural changes apparently remain; if after extinction, and no evidence of spontaneous recovery, the same CS and US are again paired, the acquisition phase is much faster than in the earlier training.
4. **A.** The noise alone produced fear, a UR; after conditioning, the white rat alone, previously paired with the noise, produced a CR—also fear.
5. **C.** Food aversions were undoubtedly adaptive for our evolutionary ancestors.
6. **A.** This finding contradicts strict behaviorist views, which propose that reward for a behavior should increase the likelihood of that behavior occurring again in the future.
7. **D.** Skinner believed that superstitious behavior results from accidental reinforcement of some trivial behavior.
8. **C.** This behavior on the part of the rats is the best guarantee of finding food in an environment.
9. **B.** Observational learning can take place even in the absence of direct experience with an object or situation.
10. **A.** Sleep has practical effects on learning (as it does on efficient performance in general).

"Hey, Guess What I Learned In Psychology Today?" (An Essay Question)

What might you tell your mom about learning?

- You could start by talking about the mealtime behavior of Sammy the mini schnauzer, how he runs to the kitchen when you turn on the can opener or shake the bag of dog food. You could point out to your mom that Sammy, like most pets, didn't run to the kitchen the first time that this ritual took place. Initially, something more salient, like the smell or sight of the actual food, an unconditioned stimulus, led to the approach behavior. As the sounds of preparation became associated with the food, they became conditioned stimuli, and elicited the same, or similar, responses as the actual food did. You could then point out that people do similar things, and extend your conversation one step further, to talk about second-order conditioning, whereby we work for the money that has no intrinsic value but represents the things that we can buy that might make us happier. Most people can relate to the concept of working for a paycheck, but most don't stop to think that it isn't really the paycheck that they are excited about at the end of the month, it is the possibility of buying something exciting or keeping the bill collectors at bay.
- The difference between classical and operant conditioning is a subtle but important difference that is often difficult to explain. The key difference is that the subject in classical conditioning is a passive recipient of the associations occurring, whereas the subject in operant conditioning is affecting and manipulating the environment in some way that affects the way that the associations are occurring. Classical conditioning is reactive; operant conditioning is active. According to classical conditioning theories, behavior is the result of antecedents, while operant conditioning theories claim "behavior is a function of its consequences" (Thorndike's law of effect). Both versions of conditioning have similar properties—acquisition, extinction, discrimination, generalization—and both are heavily influenced by the contexts in which

they occur. In general, if you are flipping a switch, pulling a lever, or opening a door, there is some operant conditioning that is involved. If you are slobbering, trembling, or getting goose bumps, it is more likely that classical conditioning is involved.

- You could advise your mom to buy a taller sofa, or get rid of Sammy. Back to reality. It shouldn't be that hard to break Sammy of the annoying habit of jumping up on the couch. In fact, you could tell your mom that she could pick either version of conditioning to get the little pooch to stop. The key is associating the desired behavior, not jumping, with something good, praise or little treats. Most people tend to think that punishment is more effective at controlling undesirable behavior than reinforcement. Although punishment reduces behavior, it typically takes longer and is not as robust as reinforcement. So you could have your mom classically condition Sammy to sit somewhere else by associating a comfy dog bed with treats, or she could shape Sammy's behavior by rewarding him when he approaches the edge of the couch, then when he jumps down, then for sitting in the dog bed, shaking her hand, and fetching her slippers and the paper.

7

Language, Thought, and Intelligence

THE BIG PICTURE

Jeannetta and Sara are enjoying a breakfast burrito and coffee at the student union while recapping their psychology class earlier in the morning, when Liam saunters by their table and says, "Top of the morning, ladies." They reply, "Wussup?" and "Hola, Liam." He asks if they are still enjoying their eight o'clock introductory psychology class. "It doesn't seem so bad to get up early when you are learning so many interesting things about people," Jeannetta tells Liam, before she takes a long drink from her double latte. "Do you remember where the loo is in this building?" asks Liam, looking like his mind is starting to stray from the conversation. After pausing for a second, Sara points toward the end of the hallway and exclaims, "Yeah, the men's room is down there on the left." Liam nods in appreciation and starts down the hall as he says, "Right. Cheers!"

Once Liam is out of earshot, Sara asks Jeannetta, "Where do you think he is from?" "Well, he has a British accent, refers to the bathroom as the 'loo,' and sounds kind of like my friend Justin from London. I'm guessing he is from England," replies Jeannetta. Sara scratches her head and explains her guess, "Yeah, he does use some Britishisms, but he doesn't fit the mold of the typical Londoner. His accent is similar to Justin's, yet it also sounds kind of like Crocodile Dundee or that Steve Irwin guy. He is also a lot taller than most of the Brits I've met, and he is blonde. I'll bet he is from Australia." "Do you think he'll hate us if we ask him?" Jeannetta asks. Sara quips back, "Maybe he'll think we're hitting on him. Besides, he is kind of cute." So, they decide that they will just ask Liam where he is from if he comes back by.

A few minutes pass and they catch Liam on his way back through the student union. "Could you settle a debate for us, Liam?" asks Jeannetta. "Sure thing," replies Liam. "Are you from England or Australia?" Jeannetta inquires. "Neither," he answers, "I'm a Kiwi. Americans always get the accent confused, so I won't take offense," he chuckles and winks at them. "The simple difference is that New Zealanders are much better looking than Brits or Aussies," he adds as he continues on his way. "Yankees," he mumbles to himself and shakes his head as he walks out the door to his next class.

What does this story have to do with language, thought, and intelligence? We see examples of the way that we learn and distinguish differences in language and some of the processes that are involved in the way that we categorize, compare, and make decisions about things and people that we encounter that are described in Chapter 6 at work in this scenario. When Liam first speaks to Jeannetta and Sara, he greets them with a phrase that is not very typical of a young adult who grew up in the U.S. Similarly, the responses offered to Liam are both colloquial, and one is even in Spanish. Because both are common greetings in American culture, Liam continues on without missing a beat. The request for directions to the 'loo' causes Sara to engage in extra cognitive work even though it is a simple noun, or object reference, because the term is more specific to British culture than American culture, but she manages to help Liam out because of her adaptability and possibly her attraction to Liam. As the ladies try to decide where Liam is from they engage in two forms of category comparison: prototype theory (Justin is the prototype of a British gentleman and is similar to Liam) and exemplar theory (several other people look and speak like Liam who are from Australia). Last, the two women engage in the prospect theory of decision making when they choose to take on risk after evaluating the potential losses that may occur. Sadly, they both fell prey to some minor mind bugs and were wrong about Liam's accent and origin.

What about Liam's level of intelligence? Do you associate a British gentleman with intelligence and refinement? Who is the smartest person you have ever met? How did you decide whether or not that person was smart? It probably didn't take you very long. Was that person well-read? Highly educated? Have an occupation or profession that smart people tend to have? Or maybe your smartest person is someone wise in the ways of the world, possessing "street smarts" rather than academic or professional achievement. When asked, "Who is the smartest person you have ever met," why don't we all think of the same kind of person?

Language and cognition are arguably the things that make us uniquely human and what many would consider intelligent. Language and thought are clearly involved in the other aspects of psychology. Our brains have evolved to process language and calculate gains and losses relative to our decisions (Chapter 3). The process of language acquisition is clearly entrenched in the learning (Chapter 6) and developmental (Chapter 10) aspects of psychology. There is also evidence that emotions and motivation (Chapter 9) play an important role in gauging whether or not to engage in risky behavior. Our development and use of language and various thought processes also make us unique as individuals (Chapter 11) and set the stage for how we interact with one another (Chapter 15) to a certain extent.

Chapter 7 introduces you to some of the terms and concepts that psychologists use to study and describe language, thought, and intelligence. Even before you could remember, you were acquiring the rules that govern the way that you now speak, write, and think. These principles are now constantly at work as you interact with other people and your surroundings. We all have our unique ways of expressing ourselves; however, in a lot of ways we communicate and think alike. Most of us get caught in the same mindbug traps as everyone else. So the next time you think you are being witty and say to your new friend with the accent from down under, "Crikey! Let's throw some shrimp on the barbie," make sure he isn't from Dunedin, because some of those Kiwis don't like to be confused with Australians and they do tend to like tackling people.

CHAPTER OBJECTIVES

After studying this chapter, you should be able to:

1. Describe how *phonemes*, *morphemes*, and grammatical rules interact with one another to form a system of human *language*.
2. Compare the *deep structure* and *surface structure* of language, and note how language milestones are achieved over the course of development.
3. Compare the behaviorist, *nativist*, and interactionist explanations of language development.
4. Discuss the neurological specializations that allow language to develop.
5. Describe what a *category-specific deficit* is, and provide an example.
6. Discuss the *family resemblance theory* of category formation, and describe how it led to the *prototype* theory of categorization.
7. Describe the *prototype* theory of categorization, noting the main points and providing examples of how it works.
8. Discuss the *exemplar theory* of categorization, noting the main points and providing examples of how it works.
9. Compare *rational choice theory* with how most real-world decisions actually get made.
10. Describe the *conjunction fallacy*, and provide an example.
11. Discuss *framing effects*, especially the *sunk-cost effect.*
12. Describe the basic tenets of *prospect theory*.
13. Discuss some of the reasons why humans may have evolved to do better at judging frequency rather than probability.

14. Describe the origins of intelligence testing in the French school system, noting the contributions of Alfred Binet and Theodore Simon to the development of the *ratio IQ*, and explain how the *deviation IQ* was eventually adopted.
15. Explain how responses, consequential behaviors, and hypothetical properties interact with one another in the logic of intelligence testing.
16. Summarize the research evidence showing that intelligence test scores predict a range of outcomes, such as educational level, job performance, and life experiences such as divorce, incarceration, or unemployment.
17. Describe the evidence that led Charles Spearman to conclude that a *two-factor theory of intelligence* was appropriate for describing the nature of intellectual performance.
18. Describe the evidence that led Louis Thurstone to conclude that a multiple-factor theory of intelligence was appropriate for describing the nature of intellectual performance.
19. Describe how a three-level hierarchy offers the most compelling account of intelligence test data.
20. Contrast the bottom-up and top-down approaches to determining middle-level intellectual abilities.
21. Give a brief description of the eight independent middle-level intellectual abilities developed in the bottom-up approach taken by John Carroll.
22. Compare *fluid intelligence* and *crystallized intelligence*.
23. Discuss the three factors of analytic intelligence, creative intelligence, and practical intelligence identified by Robert Sternberg's top-down approach to intellectual performance.
24. Discuss the eight factors suggested by Howard Gardner's top-down approach to intellectual performance.
25. Offer a definition of *intelligence* that results from considering multiple approaches to intelligence testing and multiple approaches to understanding levels of intellectual performance.
26. Distinguish between *identical twins* and *fraternal twins* on the basis of their respective genetic makeups.
27. Explain what a *heritability coefficient* is and discuss how it contributes to our understanding of the genetic basis of intelligence.
28. Distinguish between group differences in intelligence test scores and group differences in intelligence, and discuss why differences in test scores may not necessarily indicate differences in intellectual ability.
29. Explain why relative intelligence is likely to remain stable over time, but absolute intelligence typically changes over the course of a lifetime.
30. Define the Flynn effect.
31. Describe research evidence that indicates that education enhances IQ.
32. Describe the current state of research on drugs to enhance intelligence.

CHAPTER OVERVIEW

Use the terms below to fill in the following exercises. Terms may not be used more than once. The answers can be found at the end of this chapter.

abstractly	experiences	prototypes
academic	family	quotient
acquisition device	framing	rational
attributable	frequencies	responses
average	general	rules
avoiding	genes	scholastic
behaviors	grammatical	sentences
biases	heritability	socioeconomic
bottom-up	inferences	Spearman
Broca's	intelligence	specialized
categories	language	specific
cognitive	mental	statistic
cultures	middle	top-down
difference	mind	thought
education	narrower	time
emotional	neurological	typical
environments	outcomes	wealth
evidence	phonemes	Wernicke's
exemplar	probability	
experience	prospect	

Language and Communication: Nothing's More Personal

Human language is characterized by a complex organization, from ____________________, the smallest units of sound recognizable as speech, to morphemes to phrases and finally ____________________. Each level of human language is constructed and understood according to ____________________ rules, none of which are taught explicitly. Children appear to be biologically predisposed to process ____________________ in ways that allow them to extract grammatical rules from the language that they hear. This language ____________________ emerges as a child matures. The biological predisposition is represented by ____________________ specialization. Our abilities to produce and comprehend language depend on distinct regions of the brain, with ____________________ area critical for language production and ____________________ area critical for comprehension. Recent studies on color processing and ____________________ judgments point to an influence of language on thought. However, it is also clear that language and ____________________ are separate to some extent.

Concepts and Categories: How We Think

We store our knowledge in three main ways: our ____________________ in terms of individual memories, generalizations that take the form of ____________________, and factual information that is codified in terms of ____________________. The brain organizes concepts into distinct ____________________, such as living things and human-made things. We acquire concepts differently according to three theories: ____________________ resemblance theory, which states that items in the same category share certain features, if not all; prototype theory, which uses the most "____________________" member of a category to assess new items; and ____________________ theory, which states that we compare new items with stored memories of other members of the category. We use concepts and categories to solve problems, make ____________________, and guide judgments.

Judging, Valuing, and Deciding: Sometimes We're Logical, Sometimes Not

Human decision making often departs from a completely ____________________ process, and the mindbugs that accompany this departure tell us a lot about how the human ____________________ works. The values we place on ____________________ weigh so heavily in our judgments that they sometimes overshadow objective ____________________. We excel at estimating ____________________, defining categories, and making similarity judgments, but we do not make ____________________ judgments very well. Errors in decision making often take the form of ____________________. Because we feel that ____________________ losses is more important than achieving gains, ____________________ effects can affect our choices. ____________________ theory was developed in part to account for these tendencies. ____________________ information also strongly influences our decision making, even when we are not aware of it.

Intelligence

Early intelligence tests were designed to predict a child's ____________________ performance but were eventually used to calculate an intelligence ____________________ either as a ratio of mental to physical age or as a deviation of a test score from the average score of those in the same age group. ____________________ is a hypothetical property that cannot be directly measured, so intelligence tests measure ____________________ to questions and tasks that are known to be correlated with consequential ____________________ that are thought to be made possible by intelligence. These consequential behaviors include ____________________ performance, job performance, health, and ____________________, all of which are enhanced by intelligence.

A person's score on one test of ____________________ ability is likely to be highly correlated with his or her score on another. This pattern led Charles ____________________ to suggest that performances require *g* (____________________ intelligence) and *s* (____________________ abilities). Modern research reveals that *g* and *s* are ____________________-level abilities. The ____________________ approach suggests that there are eight of these, but the ____________________ approach suggests that there may be middle-level abilities that intelligence tests don't measure. ____________________ may disagree about what constitutes intelligence, but Western scientists agree that it involves reasoning, solving problems, thinking ____________________, comprehending complex ideas, and learning quickly from ____________________.

The Origins of Intelligence: From SES to DNA

________________ exert a significant influence on intelligence. The ________________ coefficient (h^2) tells us what percentage of the difference between the intelligence scores of different people is attributable to differences in their genes, and this ________________ changes depending on the ________________ level and the age of the people being measured. Genes may directly influence intelligence, and they may also influence it indirectly by determining the ________________ to which people are drawn and by which they are shaped. Some groups of people have lower ________________ intelligence test scores than others. Part of the ________________ between groups is clearly attributable to environmental factors, and it is not yet determined whether or not some of the difference is also ________________ to genetic factors.

________________ increases intelligence, but its impact is smaller, ________________, and more short-lived than we might wish. ________________ enhancers can also increase intelligence, though it is not clear by how much. People who are extremely intelligent are not necessarily happier, and their gifts tend to be highly ________________.

QUICK QUIZ #1

1. Language is defined as:
   a. the speech sounds produced when humans reach a certain point of evolution.
   b. a system for communicating with others using signals and rules of grammar.
   c. a symbolic system characterized by increasing levels of complexity.
   d. an abstract ability unique to humans and their ancestors.
2. ____________ refers to the meaning of a sentence, whereas ____________ refers to how a sentence is worded.
   a. Surface structure; deep structure
   b. Semantics; grammatics
   c. Phonological structure; morphological structure
   d. Deep structure; surface structure
3. Which view of language development holds that it is an innate, biological capacity that all humans possess?
   a. the nativist view
   b. the biobehaviorist view
   c. the behavioral view
   d. the totalitarian view
4. The prototype theory of categorization holds that:
   a. members of a category are derived from a single prototypical instance of that category.
   b. only the best examples of a category will be included for membership in that category.
   c. "best examples" of a category are fundamentally different from "good examples" of that same category.
   d. potential members of a category are assigned to that category after being compared to a prototype or "best example" of that category.

5. The probability of two events co-occurring simultaneously is always ____________ the probability of either event occurring separately.
   a. more than
   b. less than
   c. the same as
   d. less specific than

6. ____________ and ____________ are responsible for developing the first intelligence test.
   a. John Watson; B. F. Skinner
   b. Alfred Binet; Theodore Simon
   c. William Stern; Lewis Terman
   d. Charles Spearman; Louis Thurstone

7. Ten-year-old Ian has an IQ of 102; this score means that his IQ is:
   a. a little below average when compared with that of other children his age.
   b. about average when compared with that of other 10-year-old children.
   c. well above average for his age group.
   d. in the top 2% for children of his age.

8. Which of the following statements about ratio IQ and deviation IQ is NOT true?
   a. Ratio IQ is most often used to describe the intelligence of children.
   b. Deviation IQ is most often used to describe the intelligence of adults.
   c. Ratio IQ is most often used to describe the intelligence of adults.
   d. Both have an average score of 100.

9. The intelligence tests most widely used today are the Wechsler Adult Intelligence Scale and the ____________ test.
   a. Stanford-Binet
   b. Binet-Simon
   c. Simon-Binet
   d. Stanford-Terman

10. The two-factor theory of intelligence is important because it suggests that:
    a. individuals can be tested for their two primary abilities.
    b. a primary intelligence area can be matched with one at the other end of the cognitive spectrum.
    c. both heredity and environment play a role in intelligence testing.
    d. intelligence is not a single, general ability.

11. Louis Thurstone challenged Charles Spearman's:
    a. Adult/Adolescent Intelligence Scale.
    b. idea that there are eight primary mental abilities.
    c. two-factor theory of intelligence.
    d. idea of deviation IQ.

12. A savant typically has a ____________ intelligence than a prodigy.
    a. higher
    b. lower
    c. much higher
    d. more variable

13. Bryan and Sam are 8-year-old brothers who are genetic copies of each other. They are:
    a. monozygotic twins.
    b. dizygotic twins.
    c. fraternal twins.
    d. maternal twins.
14. Who of the following would likely score highest on a test of transformations in spatial memory?
    a. Maria, a young adult who likes to work out.
    b. Anna, a young mother of twins.
    c. Lucas, who just graduated from college.
    d. Winnie, the twenty-something daughter of an engineer.
15. Intelligence test performance has ____________ over the past century.
    a. remained steady
    b. steadily decreased
    c. increased dramatically
    d. steadily increased

QUICK QUIZ #2

1. The smallest unit of sound that is recognizable as speech is called a:
    a. phonoun.
    b. morpheme.
    c. phoneme.
    d. proneme.
2. Between the ages of 1 and 4 years, approximately how many words does an average child acquire?
    a. 1,000
    b. 5,000
    c. 10,000
    d. 100,000
3. Difficulty in producing or comprehending language is called:
    a. asynomy.
    b. apraxia.
    c. aphasia.
    d. dystaxia.
4. Most of the Smiths' boxers have white feet, docked ears, and a white blaze between their eyes. Kudra has white feet and a blaze, but her ears are not docked, yet she is still considered part of the group, Smith's boxers. The theory that best describes this categorization is:
    a. prototype theory.
    b. examplar theory.
    c. family resemblance theory.
    d. selective breeding theory.
5. Generally speaking, humans excel on cognitive tasks that involve ____________, but perform poorly on cognitive tasks that involve ____________.
    a. estimation; accuracy
    b. frequency; probability

c. accuracy; estimation
d. probability; frequency

6. One assumption of prospect theory is called the *certainty effect*. This means that:
   a. when making decisions, people give greater weight to outcomes that are a sure thing.
   b. people are certain that they want to avoid risk, but are unsure that they want to maximize gains.
   c. when making decisions, people rely more on past outcomes than on future speculations.
   d. people are certain that they want to maximize gains, but are unsure that they want to avoid risks.
7. The first intelligence test was created to:
   a. identify children who were early achievers.
   b. identify children who needed to wait a year before starting first grade.
   c. identify children who qualified for programs for the gifted and talented.
   d. identify children who needed remedial educational programs.
8. If 10-year-old Jeannetta has the mental age of an 11-year-old, her ratio IQ is approximately:
   a. 110.
   b. 90.
   c. 100.
   d. 80.
9. If your aunt's intelligence was tested today, her IQ score would be a(n):
   a. aptitude score.
   b. achievement score.
   c. deviation IQ.
   d. ratio IQ.
10. Aaron, a teenager whose intelligence score of 101 is considered average, plays the violin extraordinarily well and studies with some of the best violin teachers in the world. Aaron can be considered a(n):
   a. prodigy.
   b. savant.
   c. aspiring musician.
   d. music fanatic.
11. Initially only expecting a girl, Deana and Tom were surprised and delighted to learn she was carrying twins; she ultimately delivered a girl and a boy. The two infants are:
   a. monozygotic twins.
   b. dizygotic twins.
   c. identical twins.
   d. supernal twins.
12. The heritability factor among wealthy children is .72; the heritability factor among poor children is:
   a. similar.
   b. slightly lower.
   c. substantially lower.
   d. slightly higher.

13. According to current research on intelligence, which of the following statements is NOT correct?
    a. Intelligence is influenced by environment.
    b. Intelligence is influenced by genes.
    c. Average IQ score is 100.
    d. Some groups are innately more intelligent than others.
14. On tests that measure such items as vocabulary, general information, and verbal reasoning, people show ___________ from age 18 to age 70.
    a. very little change
    b. a steady decline
    c. a slight improvement
    d. a dramatic decline
15. Dana is a second-grade teacher returning to the classroom after summer vacation. She is probably aware that children's test scores tend to:
    a. fall over the course of the school year.
    b. remain stable over the summer months.
    c. fall when they are away from school over the summer months.
    d. rise over the summer months.

QUICK QUIZ #3

1. A set of rules that specify how units of language can be combined to produce meaningful messages is called:
    a. syntax.
    b. morphology.
    c. grammar.
    d. deep structure.
2. During language development, children often match a word sound to an underlying concept after only a single exposure. This phenomenon is known as:
    a. concept development.
    b. fast mapping.
    c. telesis.
    d. phonemic invariance.
3. Broca's area is located in the:
    a. left frontal cortex.
    b. right frontal cortex.
    c. posterior cingulate gyrus.
    d. left posterior temporal cortex.
4. Brett can easily recognize fruits, trees, and mammals, but he cannot recognize bottles, cars, or tools. Brett's unusual affliction is an example of:
    a. production blocking.
    b. category-specific deficit.
    c. amnesia.
    d. category enhancement.
5. ___________ is a syndrome characterized by an inability to learn the grammatical structure of language despite having otherwise normal intelligence.
    a. Genetic agnosia
    b. Apraxia

c. Genetic dysphasia
d. Tardive dyskenesia

6. The developers of the Concorde jet went horribly over budget halfway through the development of the plane. Instead of cutting their losses, they continued with the original plan despite complications and setbacks. This is an example of:
   a. a representativeness heuristic.
   b. the sunk-cost fallacy.
   c. functional fixedness.
   d. the conjunction fallacy.
7. Where was the first intelligence test developed?
   a. Japan
   b. France
   c. Australia
   d. America
8. When her mother had her tested, 5-year-old Emily scored the mental age of a 6-year-old. Her ratio IQ is approximately:
   a. 85.
   b. 95.
   c. 110.
   d. 120.
9. Ratio IQ scores produce a normal curve that is shaped like a(n):
   a. rectangle.
   b. inverted bell.
   c. bell.
   d. square.
10. When IQ scores are mapped on a bell curve, the average score is:
    a. 90.
    b. 100.
    c. 110.
    d. 120.
11. If you were in charge of hiring new employees, what kind of test would you choose as the most useful in predicting the job performance of those you interview?
    a. achievement test
    b. spatial memory test
    c. intelligence test
    d. vocabulary test
12. The statistical test that Charles Spearman used in developing his two-factor theory of intelligence was:
    a. the chi square.
    b. the test of mean differences.
    c. the analysis of determinants.
    d. factor analysis.

13. Which of the following is NOT one of psychologist Howard Gardner's eight distinct kinds of intelligence?
    a. humility
    b. linguistic
    c. spatial
    d. musical
14. Which of the following psychologists believed that intelligence was largely inherited?
    a. Francis Galton
    b. Alfred Binet
    c. Lewis Terman
    d. Charles Spearman
15. Which of the following would likely be used to quantify those differences in individual intelligence scores that are explained by differences in genetics?
    a. genetic coefficient
    b. heritability coefficient
    c. summative coefficient
    d. nature–nurture coefficient
16. Which of the following children is likely to be the most intelligent?
    a. Mari, who lives with her grandmother in a rural part of South Africa.
    b. Amanda, whose mother is a doctor in the United States.
    c. Chuy, who lives with his eight brothers and sisters in a poor part of Mexico City.
    d. Ravi, who lives with his single mother in inner-city Los Angeles

"HEY, GUESS WHAT I LEARNED IN PYCHOLOGY TODAY?" (AN ESSAY QUESTION)

We're guessing there's someone in your life who is interested in the quality of your educational experiences, is reasonably intelligent, but knows little about psychology. This might be your roommate, a previous teacher, your mom, or some other person you have access to and want to share your thoughts and feelings with.

1. What would you tell that person about language and thought? How would you describe the influence of language on thought? How would you explain the fact that most people are good at judging frequencies but not so good at judging probabilities?
2. What would you tell that person about intelligence? How would you describe the measurement of intelligence? What would you say about the cultural sensitivity of intelligence testing?

THINGS TO PONDER

You've learned a lot of information in this chapter about language, thought, and intelligence. When you put it all together, you may start to ponder how all of this relates to other issues in this textbook. For example, you may ask yourself:

- How has the brain evolved to process language and thought?

  Think about the studies from the chapter that show differential activation of specific brain areas for language production (Broca's area) versus language comprehension (Wernicke's area), or the additional density in the parietal lobe as a result of bilingualism.

  Consider fMRI data showing different areas of activation for naming animals versus tools, or that the dorsal parietal area shows activation as a result of belief-neutral reasoning, whereas the left temporal area shows enhanced activation during belief-laden reasoning.

- How is memory involved in language and language development?

  Note that by the time you are in college you have the meaning of roughly 200,000 words stored in your memory.

  Reflect on the idea that fast mapping, where a single exposure allows an individual to map a word onto an underlying concept, appears to be a special case of rapidly acquired and enduring memory.

- Does emotion have an impact on our ability to make good decisions?

  Consider the theories of categorization and concepts and how comparing things in an existing situation to a prototype or exemplars will often depend on your individual experience(s), whether they are good or bad, with the items compared.

  Weigh the consequences of biases, framing effects, and fallacies on the decision-making process. For example, the emotion attached to the investment in the sunk-cost fallacy results in more resources being squandered in hopes that things will get better, or to make you feel better about your faulty initial decision.

- Are errors in speech and decision making an indicator of a psychological or neurological disorder?

  We read about people who are detached from risky decisions as the result of prefrontal cortex damage. We will also learn that similar symptoms are seen in people with psychological disorders such as bipolar disorder and schizophrenia.

  Speech anomalies, such as pressured speech or "word salad," are often indicators of psychological problems, like bipolar disorder and schizophrenia, respectively.

- When it comes to intelligence, is a bigger brain better than a smaller one?

  Think about the McDaniel (2005) study that found a slightly positive correlation between brain size and higher intelligence, suggesting that bigger is better.

  Also consider the McGill University study that showed a correlation between cortical thickness, the delay in growth of that cortex, and the related levels of intelligence. Bigger may be slightly better, but it seems that slower and thicker may be even more important than overall size.

- Is there a pill out there that will make me smarter?

  There are definitely some marketers out there who would like you to believe that they have the "smart pill," but there isn't any good evidence of effective cognitive enhancers having much of an effect.

  Reflect on the idea that changing some genes, maybe like the one that codes for the NMDA receptor or hippocampal development that Joseph Tsien has manipulated, could make us smarter, and the use of techniques like PGD could make those kinds of choices available before a child is born.

- Do really smart people just have good memories or is it something else?

  Consider the fact that the most common intelligence test, the WAIS, does have some memory components, yet it also tests several other components of intelligence such as spatial ability, analytical ability, and mathematics.

  Working on your memory will almost certainly help in most occupations and assessments of general intelligence.

- Does being extremely intelligent doom you to a life of social awkwardness?

  There is no good evidence to suggest that highly intelligent people are any more socially awkward than people of average or below average intelligence, despite the stereotype of the goofy nerd.

  You will encounter, in reading and in life, some personality types and even some psychological abnormalities that include high intelligence as a feature; keep that in mind as you ponder this question.

WEB LINKS AND SUGGESTED READING

Strunk, William—Elements of Style—Bartleby.com: http://www.bartleby.com/141/

- An online version of the classic text that covers many of the basic rules of writing and grammar.

Brians, Paul—Common Errors in English Usage: http://www.wsu.edu/~brians/errors/errors.html

- An online version of the written text by the same name. This site/search engine lists words and phrases that are commonly misused, alphabetically. It also has a great list of links at the bottom for other language related issues.

Kreuz, Roger—The Psychology of Language Page of Links: http://www.psyc.memphis.edu:88/POL/POL.htm

- A list of dozens of researchers, labs and programs, organizations, meetings, books, journals, software, and related disciplines.

The Society for Judgment and Decision Making: http://www.sjdm.org/

- Lists the topics addressed by the APA Division and links to other related sites.

Chomsky, Noam (1996). *Powers and Prospects: Reflections on Human Nature and the Social Order.* Boston: South End Press.

- The first collection to examine the relations between Chomsky's philosophy and his politics. Essays on the Middle East, the scientific method, and linguistics.

Wrightsman, Lawrence (1999). *Judicial Decision Making: Is Psychology Relevant?* New York: Plenum Publishers.

- This book examines decision making by appellate judges from a psychological viewpoint.

Dean, W., Morgenthaler, J., and Fowkes, F. Smart Drugs 2—The next generation: http://nootropics.com/index.html

- An online reference for the book of the same title; it contains an extensive list of links to information on research and products related to cognitive enhancers.

Neuroscience for Kids—Smart Drugs: http://faculty.washington.edu/chudler/smartd.html

- A University of Washington site that has great starter questions and references on neuroscience topics.

Hawkins, J., and Blakeslee, S. (2004). *On Intelligence.* New York: Times Books.

- The creator of the Palm Pilot and a science writer take on neuroscience and computing as they relate to ideas of intelligence.

Thomas, D., and Inkson, K. (2004). *Cultural Intelligence: People Skills for Global Business.* San Francisco: Berret-Koehler.

- Advice on a kind of intelligence that isn't typically taught in the standard education system: how to relate to people in other cultures, particularly when conducting business.

ANSWERS

Chapter Overview

Language and Communication: Nothing's More Personal

Human language is characterized by a complex organization, from **phonemes**, the smallest units of sound recognizable as speech, to morphemes to phrases and finally **sentences**. Each level of human language is constructed and understood according to **grammatical** rules, none of which are taught explicitly. Children appear to be biologically predisposed to process **language** in ways that allow them to extract grammatical rules from the language that they hear. This language **acquisition device** emerges as a child matures. The biological predisposition is represented by **neurological** specialization. Our abilities to produce and comprehend language depend on distinct regions of the brain, with **Broca's** area critical for language production and **Wernicke's** area critical for comprehension. Recent studies on color processing and **time** judgments point to an influence of language on thought. However, it is also clear that language and **thought** are separate to some extent.

Concepts and Categories: How We Think

We store our knowledge in three main ways: our **experiences** in terms of individual memories, generalizations that take the form of **prototypes**, and factual information that is codified in terms of **rules**. The brain organizes concepts into distinct **categories**, such as living things and human-made things. We acquire concepts differently according to three theories: **family** resemblance theory, which states that items in the same category share certain features, if not all; prototype theory, which uses the most "**typical**" member of a category to assess new items; and **exemplar** theory, which states that we compare new items with stored memories of other members of the category. We use concepts and categories to solve problems, make **inferences**, and guide judgments.

Judging, Valuing, and Deciding: Sometimes We're Logical, Sometimes Not

Human decision making often departs from a completely **rational** process, and the mindbugs that accompany this departure tell us a lot about how the human **mind** works. The values we place on **outcomes** weigh so heavily in our judgments that they sometimes overshadow objective **evidence**. We excel at estimating **frequencies**, defining categories, and making similarity judgments, but we do not make **probability** judgments very well. Errors in decision making often take the form of **biases**. Because we feel that **avoiding** losses is more important than achieving gains, **framing** effects can affect our choices. **Prospect** theory was developed in part to account for these tendencies. **Emotional** information also strongly influences our decision making, even when we are not aware of it.

Intelligence

Early intelligence tests were designed to predict a child's **scholastic** performance but were eventually used to calculate an intelligence **quotient** either as a ratio of mental to physical age or as a deviation of a test score from the average score of those in the same age group. **Intelligence** is a hypothetical property that cannot be directly measured, so intelligence tests measure **responses** to questions and tasks that are known to be correlated with consequential **behaviors** that are thought to be made possible by intelligence. These consequential behaviors include **academic** performance, job performance, health, and **wealth**, all of which are enhanced by intelligence.

A person's score on one test of **mental** ability is likely to be highly correlated with his or her score on another. This pattern led Charles **Spearman** to suggest that performances require *g* (**general** intelligence) and *s* (**specific** abilities). Modern research reveals that *g* and *s* are **middle**-level abilities. The **bottom-up** approach suggests that there are eight of these, but the **top-down** approach suggests that there may be middle-level abilities that intelligence tests don't measure. **Cultures** may disagree about what constitutes intelligence, but Western scientists agree that it involves reasoning, solving problems, thinking **abstractly**, comprehending complex ideas, and learning quickly from **experience**.

The Origins of Intelligence: From SES to DNA

Genes exert a significant influence on intelligence. The **heritability** coefficient (h^2) tells us what percentage of the difference between the intelligence scores of different people is attributable to differences in their genes, and this **statistic** changes depending on the **socioeconomic** level and the age of the people being measured. Genes may directly influence intelligence, and they may also influence it indirectly by determining the **environments** to which people are drawn and by which they are shaped. Some groups of people have lower **average** intelligence test scores than others. Part of the **difference** between groups is clearly attributable to environmental factors, and it is not yet determined whether or not some of the difference is also **attributable** to genetic factors.

Education increases intelligence, but its impact is smaller, **narrower**, and more short-lived than we might wish. **Cognitive** enhancers can also increase intelligence, though it is not clear by how much. People who are extremely intelligent are not necessarily happier, and their gifts tend to be highly **specialized**.

Quick Quiz #1

1. **B.** Language allows individuals to exchange information about the world through the meaning of words organized grammatically.
2. **D.** Deep processing refers to the meaning of words and concepts, while surface structure refers to how the words in a sentence are arranged.
3. **A.** Chomsky and other nativists believe that language can be acquired through an innate language acquisition device.
4. **D.** The prototype theory of categorization compares new stimuli to the most typical member of a category, based on several observations of what is typical.
5. **B.** Although it often sounds more likely when things are more specific, the probability of two events co-occurring simultaneously is always less likely than the probability of either event occurring separately.
6. **B.** Binet and Simon are credited with creating the first intelligence test in the late 1800s, when they were asked by French authorities to design a test that could identify children in need of remedial educational programs. Watson and Skinner were behaviorists. Stern and Terman devised the idea of the intelligence quotient, but they did not create the first test. Spearman and Thurstone worked in the area of general and specific abilities.
7. **B.** IQ scores tend to fall along a bell curve, with a score of 100 as the mean. A score of 102 indicates that Ian's mental age and his physical age are roughly the same.
8. **C.** The ratio IQ score is used to describe the intelligence levels of children, not adults. The deviation IQ score was created to give a more accurate picture of adult intelligence. This score compares an adult's test score to the average test score of those in the same age group and is multiplied by 100. For both types of score, the mean is 100, that is, 100 is the score of the largest percentage of test takers.
9. **D.** The Stanford-Binet is based on Binet and Simon's original intelligence test but has been modified many times (specifically, by Lewis Terman, a researcher at Stanford University, hence the name of the modern test).
10. **D.** Until Spearman proposed his two-factor theory of intelligence, the prevailing idea had been that there was one general intelligence, and someone who scored high on this would undoubtedly perform well on just about everything. Spearman's research proved this was not true, and he believed that individuals have a general ability (*g*) and skills that are specific to each particular task (*s*).
11. **C.** Spearman devised the two-factor theory of intelligence. There is no such thing as an Adult/Adolescent Intelligence Scale. Thurstone, with his primary mental abilities, said there were a few stable and independent mental abilities (among them word fluency, verbal comprehension, and number).
12. **B.** A savant has low intelligence but an extraordinary ability typically in one general area.
13. **A.** If the twins are genetic copies of each other, then they must be identical, or monozygotic, twins. Identical twins develop from the splitting of a single egg that was fertilized by a single sperm. Fraternal

(dizygotic) twins develop from two different eggs that were fertilized by two different sperm. "Maternal twins" is a meaningless term.

14. **C.** Males typically score higher than females on tests that require visual or spatial transformation, as well as on tests of certain motor skills, spatiotemporal responding, and fluid reasoning in some mathematical and science domains. There may be other reasons for this than gender differences (e.g., testing situations, culturally biased tests), but the actual scoring differences are a fact. Therefore, Lucas would likely score higher because he is male.
15. **D.** Intelligence has been steadily increasing with time. It is true that fluid intelligence decreases over the life span of an individual, but it has tended to increase across generations. This is called the Flynn effect and may be due to a number of factors (e.g., better nutrition, better schooling).

Quick Quiz #2

1. **C.** Phonemes are the smallest unit of sound that is recognizable as speech.
2. **C.** Children between 1 and 4 average a vocabulary of roughly 10,000 words.
3. **C.** Difficulty in producing or comprehending language is called aphasia. Apraxia is difficulty in producing some speech and dystaxia is also a movement condition.
4. **C.** Family resemblance theory specifically states that every member of the category may not possess features used to group category members.
5. **B.** Studies have shown that people are quite good at estimating the frequency with which things occur, but we do not make probability judgments well.
6. **A.** The certainty effect states that when making decisions, people give greater weight to an outcome that is a sure thing, rather than calculating the probabilities of an outcome and deciding on the best potential payoff.
7. **D.** In the late 1800s French officials, wanting to provide a primary school education for all children of every social class, asked Alfred Binet and Theodore Simon to create a test that would identify young students who lagged behind their peers in order to identify those who would need remedial programs.
8. **A.** To calculate Jeannetta's ratio IQ, divide her mental age by her physical age and then multiply by 100: $11/10 \times 100 = 110$.
9. **C.** IQs for adults, called deviation IQs, are calculated with a slightly different formula from the ratio IQ used for children. To compute a deviation IQ, the adult's test score is divided by the average test score of people in the same age group, and then multiplied by 100. Since your aunt is most likely an adult, her IQ score would be calculated as a deviation IQ score.
10. **A.** By definition, a prodigy has normal intelligence and an extraordinary ability in some area. With an IQ of 101, Aaron's intelligence is considered average, and his command of the violin makes him a prodigy. (A savant has low intelligence and an extraordinary ability in some area.)
11. **B.** Because the twins are different sexes, they are fraternal, or dizygotic, twins; they developed from two different eggs. Identical twins, or monozygotic twins, would have to be the same sex since they come from the splitting of the same egg. "Supernal twins" is a meaningless term.
12. **C.** Wealthy children are assumed to have fairly similar environments that likely include ample nutrition, homes with books, and so on. This is likely the reason that the heritability factor is high. We can be fairly certain that poor children lack these advantages, and research has suggested a heritability factor of .10, substantially lower than that of wealthy children.
13. **D.** For example, a task force appointed by the American Psychological Association to study whether there were any genetic differences in intelligence between African Americans and Whites concluded that there was no empirical evidence that one ethnicity was genetically more intelligent than the other. We do know that intelligence is influenced by environment (e.g., nutrition, books, good parenting) and by heredity (intelligent parents tend to produce intelligent offspring).
14. **A.** Intelligence changes in some domains more than others. Although most people show marked decline over the life span on

tests that are timed or have abstract material, intelligence changes very little over the life span on tests that measure vocabulary or verbal reasoning. There is increasing evidence of a decline in general intelligence through the years that may be due to a slowing of the brain's processing speed.

15. **C.** Staying in school appears to increase IQ. Intelligence levels of children decline in the summer, particularly for those children that spend time on the least academically oriented activities. Students born in the last three months of the year, making them start school a full year later than children born during the first nine months, tend to have lower IQ scores. Similarly, when children take the summer off, their IQs fall.

Quick Quiz #3

1. **C.** Grammar is defined as a set of rules that specify how units of language can be combined to produce meaningful messages
2. **B.** Matching a word sound to an underlying concept after only a single exposure is defined as fast mapping.
3. **A.** Broca's area, which is important for speech production, is located in the left frontal cortex near other motor areas of the brain.
4. **B.** Although it may seem like Brett has amnesia, his condition is the result of a category-specific deficit.
5. **C.** Genetic dysphasia is the syndrome inhibiting learning of grammatical structure.
6. **B.** The sunk-cost fallacy is a framing effect that affects decision making based on previous investment in the situation.
7. **B.** Alfred Binet and Theodore Simon were asked by French officials to create a test that would identify children in need of remedial educational programs.
8. **D.** Using the formula for computing ratio IQ, mental age/physical age × 100: 6/5 × 100 = 120. Emily's ratio IQ is 120, well above the average IQ score of 100.
9. **C.** When IQ scores are plotted as a ratio, the shape that results is looks like a bell. Most of the scores fall in the middle, the top part of the bell. Fully 96% of IQ scores fall between 70 and 130.
10. **B.** The largest percentage of the population falls in the midrange of IQ scores; the mean or average score is 100.
11. **C.** Analysis of thousands of studies has revealed that intelligence test scores are the best predictors of how well prospective employees will perform. This is likely so because intelligence scores correlate highly with academic performance as well as performance in numerous other areas.
12. **D.** When Charles Spearman was trying to determine if one general intelligence really existed, he looked at a large number of correlations in terms of a small number of factors. In other words, he used a new statistical technique called factor analysis. Chi square, another statistical test, was not used in the study of intelligence. There is no "test of mean differences" or "analysis of determinants."
13. **A.** While Howard Gardner identified eight distinct kinds of intelligence, he did not include humility. Some have argued that Gardner's theory is strictly Western because other cultures may conceive of intelligence differently—for example, Asian cultures may conceive of intelligence as including cooperativeness.
14. **A.** Francis Galton focused on the role of genetics in intelligence. Binet, Terman, and Spearman all worked on intelligence tests themselves, not the role of genetics.
15. **B.** We know that identical twins have extremely similar intelligence scores whether or not they share experiences. The heritability coefficient describes the proportion of the difference between individuals' scores that can be explained by differences in their genetic makeup. The other three choices are meaningless terms.
16. **B.** The child raised in a wealthier environment is likely to have a higher intelligence. Amanda, whose mother is a doctor in the United States, in all likelihood is growing up in a home environment richer in many kinds of resources than are the other children named.

"Hey, Guess What I Learned In Psychology Today?" (An Essay Question)

1. What might you tell your Mom about language and thought?

- You might start by talking about how concepts that are relatively complex, like the way that we accumulate our knowledge about vocabulary, grammatical rules, concepts, categories, and judgments, are learned very rapidly and without much formal instruction. This would open the door to a description of the most basic components of language, phonemes and morphemes, through to the theories about how language develops throughout the life span and across generations. That would be a good segue into our neurological specialization that allows language to develop, that is, areas of the brain that have evolved to process language specifically. Then you could ask, "So Mom, do you think language is what separates us from the other animals?" She might say "yes" or come up with her own ideas about higher-order cognitive processes, like our abilities to judge, determine values, and make decisions, that make us different from the neighbor's cat. Then you have an opening to discuss the organization of thought, biases, heuristics, and the theories about how we solve problems.
- You could open with a provocative question, such as, "How would we express anything about our thoughts without language?" It is kind of an "if a tree falls in the forest but nobody hears it, does it make a sound?" question. This is a good time to mention that some theorists have stated exactly that point. In fact, the linguistic relativity hypothesis states that language shapes the nature of thought. Then your Mom will remind you about the discussion you had after the methods chapter in this book and ask you for some data on the issue. You can then point out that recent studies on color processing and time judgments point to an influence of language on thought, but that language and thought are separate to some extent. It might be tempting to whip out your recently acquired copy of Boroditsky's 2001 article from *Cognitive Psychology* on time and schedules, but I would recommend against it.
- Two words: biological preparedness. This is a great opportunity to talk about something that seems like a mindbug in terms of how we have evolved to be better at some things than others. You don't necessarily need to quote the frequency format hypothesis, but you could explain a scenario where it would make sense to notice the frequency of things over their probability. It is always fun to talk about evolutionary scenarios in terms of cave people. You explain that Lothar, the caveman, would notice that there were 15 berry bushes, 3 freshwater springs, and 7 protected caves on his walk back from a recent hunting journey because they would be helpful for the survival of his family and tribe. He would also notice that there were 4 saber-toothed tigers sitting on the ridge near those things and most likely make the decision that nobody should be packing their things for a move. Lothar wouldn't calculate the probability of being eaten by the big cats; he would just notice that there are several and that they are to be avoided. Probabilities and percentages are evolutionarily new, so we don't do a very good job of calculating losses versus gains or profit margins without a lot of training, but we know that when it comes to saber-toothed tigers, one is too many.

2. What might you tell your mom about intelligence?

- You might begin by talking about people who have extraordinary abilities in one area but who are considered below average intelligence otherwise—people like those with Williams syndrome, or autistic savants. These people possess abilities that most others would consider highly intelligent in a particular context but who would probably score quite low on a standardized intelligence test. This would be a good way to initiate a conversation about the complexities of intelligence and how difficult it has been in the past to define and measure this quality.
- You might point out that for the very reason definition and measurement have been so elusive, psychologists have worked backward in their study of intelligence. Early intelligence testing was developed without much knowledge about how to frame an operational definition of intelligence: Binet and Simon were testing children for intelligence before anyone had really addressed the question of what intelligence actually is. Meanwhile, people like Goddard were using the idea of intelligence as a social instrument to affect laws and public policies. Intelligence tests have been misused to legitimize prejudice and discrimination. Our definitions of intelligence are now much better, our tests of intelligence are more objective, and we have a better understanding of

how biology and the environment interact to influence each person's level of intelligence. Modern tests of intelligence assess skills and qualities that most people would agree accurately represent intelligence, if not completely, at least in large part. These tests have been replicated hundreds of thousands of times and tend to correlate with attributes that predict aptitude and achievement later in life.

- You could discuss with your mom traditions of your family's heritage—would you expect people of a different cultural, social, or economic background to be familiar with them? Not necessarily. Yet the questions that were originally on the WAIS pertained to particular experiences not shared by all test takers. The new tests are not completely objective; there are still questions that require a basic understanding of industrialized society, but the questions are less tilted than those on the original tests. You might also mention things we know about genetics versus the environment and the heritability of intelligence. Different groups of people have evolved to retain certain traits that could influence intelligence, either positively or negatively.

8

Consciousness

THE BIG PICTURE

Ian is sitting in his organic chemistry class trying not to think about the stunning young woman who gently flirted with him at the coffee shop this morning while they were waiting in line. He had seen her around campus and noted that she was attractive but probably out of his league. As Ian's attention drifts back to class he thinks, "Oh man, did the professor say that compound was chiral or achiral? I've got to stop thinking about her." The harder he tries to suppress thoughts about his encounter, the more his mind drifts back to it: "I wish I could have seen her name on the order ticket but that big oaf was in the way." Then Ian drifts into a full-blown daydream in which mystery girl literally bumps into him at the fountain, and then strikes up a conversation; a phone number and a date follow. On the date a shadowy figure, maybe a mugger, starts climbing the steps toward their outdoor table, but Ian can't move, and the figure says, "Would you like to draw this stereospecific reaction, Mr. Spencer?" Now Ian has realized that he has fallen asleep in class and the figure is really Professor Walden, standing in front of him. Ian quickly wipes his mouth with his sleeve, realizing that he can move again, gulps down the remainder of his cold triple espresso, hoping that the caffeine will kick in during the slow and lonely walk to the chalkboard at the front of the lecture hall. On the way down those stairs he quickly promises God that if he can get through this equation, he'll never go out on Thirsty Thursday again and he'll get more than two hours of sleep the night before organic chemistry.

For what percentage of this story was Ian conscious? Most psychologists would say that he was conscious throughout, but experiencing different, or altered, states of consciousness. Some, however, would argue that Ian was unconscious while he was asleep. These questions have been debated for a long time. How do we define consciousness? How do you give people tickets to your Cartesian theater? Why do people seek to alter their current state of consciousness? The story about Ian doesn't provide answers per se, but it does provide examples of several issues addressed in Chapter 8. In the story we saw the classic mindbug of thought suppression and the theory of ironic processes of mental control, as Ian tried to focus on class and not on the young woman whom he met earlier. We then saw how he probably passed through alpha EEG activity as he daydreamed and then passed all the way through the different stages of sleep into REM, or dreaming sleep. When the dream started to integrate Ian's real-world experiences, he experienced brief sleep paralysis before returning to wakefulness. Before class, in an attempt to ward off the effects of sleep deprivation and the lingering depressant effects of alcohol consumed the night before, Ian drank a beverage that contained concentrated amounts of caffeine, a mild stimulant. Finally, he may have tried to briefly achieve a religious experience on his walk to the board, but it was more of an attempt to avoid embarrassment than to achieve mystical rapture.

Consciousness is both fascinating and frustrating because it is subjective and private. Wouldn't it be fun to know how John Malkovich sees the world? Wait . . . that's been done. The point is that the things that make each of us different—the "black box" of how other people think and experience things (what it's like to be a movie star, for example) fascinates us. Of course, these issues of consciousness are central to other areas of psychology that have been covered in the text and those that are coming up. The brain (Chapter 3) dictates how each one of us experiences different sensations (Chapter 4) and how those experiences will be remembered (Chapters 5 and 6). Our personal experiences and perceptions are vital for decision making (Chapter 7). Our sleep patterns and use of psychoactive drugs can have a big impact on our emotional state and levels of motivation (Chapter 9). Because we recall our previous experiences and mature over the years (Chapter 10), our subjective experience of the world is constantly changing. We will find that abnormal sleep patterns and drug use can be stressful and detrimental to health (Chapter 14), and they can be symptoms of psychological disorders (Chapter 12). Some of those same psychoactive drugs can also be used to treat psychological disorders (Chapter 13).

Chapter 8 covers a lot of information and probably leaves you with more questions than answers. That's good—we need good scientists to address these complex issues about sleep, drugs, and other areas of consciousness. We all stop and ponder how our experiences are different from everyone else's once in a while. It is in our social nature to want to share our experiences, including our dreams and other altered states of consciousness, with our families and friends. But you might take a lesson from Ian and explore those dreamy ideas outside chemistry class!

CHAPTER OBJECTIVES

After studying this chapter, you should be able to:

1. Define *consciousness*, noting how the metaphor of the *Cartesian Theater* applies to our phenomenological experience of consciousness.
2. Explain the *problem of other minds*, noting the dilemma we are faced with when trying to perceive the consciousness of others.
3. Explain the *mind–body problem*, examining the various views of how the mind and brain are linked to one another.
4. Describe the *intentionality of consciousness*, explaining how consciousness is directed toward some object of attention.
5. Describe the *unity* of consciousness, noting how divided attention tasks reveal consciousness' resistance to division.
6. Describe the *selectivity* of consciousness, explaining how the *cocktail party phenomenon* illustrates this property.
7. Describe the *transience of consciousness*, commenting on the metaphor of a "stream of consciousness."
8. Contrast *minimal consciousness, full consciousness*, and *self-consciousness*, discussing the evidence for each state of awareness.
9. Explain how the notion of *current concerns* illustrates conscious contents.
10. Discuss the research evidence on *thought suppression*, with particular attention to the *rebound effect* and the *ironic processes of mental control*.
11. Contrast Freud's idea of the *dynamic unconscious* with the more modern idea of the *cognitive unconscious*. Discuss the work on *subliminal perception* in regard to the general concept of "consciousness below the surface."
12. Describe the stages of sleep over the course of a typical night. Discuss how sleep and wakefulness are part of a larger cycle, or *circadian rhythm*.
13. List some of the benefits of a good night's sleep, and some of the consequences of sleep deprivation.
14. Discuss the sleep disorders of *insomnia, sleep apnea, somnambulism, narcolepsy, sleep paralysis*, and *night terrors*.
15. Describe the five major characteristics of dream consciousness that distinguish it from the typical waking state.
16. Compare the psychoanalytic theory of dreams with the *activation–synthesis model*.

17. Explain how *drug tolerance*, physical dependence, and psychological dependence occur in the ingestion of psychoactive substances.
18. Compare the categories of psychoactive substances, noting how *depressants, stimulants, narcotics, hallucinogens*, and *marijuana* differ in their potential for overdose, physical dependence, and psychological dependence.
19. Discuss why *hypnosis* qualifies as an altered state of consciousness.
20. Describe research findings on the effects of hypnosis, with particular attention to lost memory and *hypnotic analgesia*.
21. Explain how practices such as *meditation* or ecstatic religious experiences can produce altered states of consciousness.

CHAPTER OVERVIEW

Use the terms below to fill in the following exercises. Terms may not be used more than once. The answers can be found at the end of this chapter.

addiction	hallucinogens	remembers
alcohol	heroin	sedative
altered	imagination	selectivity
amphetamines	inhalants	self
analgesia	intentionality	social
apnea	involuntarily	sound
behavior	ketamine	stimulants
body	LSD	stimulants
brain	marijuana	subliminal
codeine	meditation	suggestibility
cognitive	minds	susceptible
cycle	motor	symbolism
dangers	narcolepsy	synthesis
decrease	neurotransmitters	temporal
disorders	opium	tolerance
dreaming	perceptions	unconscious
ecstasy	physical	unwanted
EEG	psychoactive	waking
enthusiasts	religious	
epilepsy	REM	

Conscious and Unconscious: The Mind's Eye, Open and Closed

Consciousness is a mystery of psychology because other people's ______________ cannot be perceived directly and also because the relationship between mind and ______________ is perplexing. Nonetheless, people's reports of their consciousness can be studied, and these reports reveal basic properties such as ______________, unity, ______________, and transience. Consciousness can also be understood in terms of levels—minimal consciousness, full consciousness, and ______________-consciousness—and can be investigated for contents such as current concerns, and ______________ thoughts. ______________ processes are sometimes understood as expressions of the Freudian dynamic unconscious but are more commonly viewed as processes of the ______________ unconscious that create and influence our conscious thoughts and behaviors. The cognitive unconscious is at work when ______________ perception influences our thought or behavior without our awareness.

Sleep and Dreaming: Good Night, Mind

The sleep ______________ involves a regular pattern of sleep and ______________ that creates altered states of consciousness. ______________ measures have revealed that during a night's sleep, the ______________ passes through a five-stage sleep cycle, moving in and out of lighter sleep stages, from slow-wave sleep stages to the ______________ sleep stage, in which most dreaming occurs. Sleep needs ______________ over the life span, but deprivation from sleep and dreams has psychological and ______________ costs. Sleep can be disrupted through ______________, which include insomnia, sleep ______________, somnambulism, ______________, sleep paralysis, and night terrors. Dreaming is an ______________ state of consciousness in which the dreamer uncritically accepts changes in emotion, thought, and sensation, but poorly ______________ the dream on awakening. The contents of dreams are related to ______________ life and can be understood by examining the areas of the brain that are activated when we dream. Theories of dreaming include Freud's psychoanalytic theory, which focuses on ______________ and the unconscious, and more current views such as the activation–______________ model.

Drugs and Consciousness: Artificial Inspiration

______________ drugs influence consciousness by altering the brain's chemical messaging system and intensifying or dulling the effects of ______________. Drug ______________ can result in overdose, and physical and psychological dependence can lead to ______________. Specific effects on consciousness and ______________ occur with different classes of psychoactive drugs. These classes include depressants, ______________, narcotics, ______________, and marijuana. Depressants are substances that reduce the activity of the central nervous system, producing a ______________ or calming effect. Examples of depressants are ______________, barbiturates, benzodiazepines, and toxic ______________. ______________ are substances that excite the nervous system and include caffeine, ______________, nicotine, cocaine, and ______________ (MDMA). Narcotics are highly addictive drugs derived from ______________, such as ______________, morphine, methadone, and ______________. Hallucinogens produce altered sensations and ______________; examples include ______________, psilocybin, mescaline, PCP, and ______________. ______________, the leaves and buds of the hemp plant, produces heightened sensations but impairs memory and ______________ skills. Each of the major classes of psychoactive drugs was developed for medical, ______________, or religious reasons, and each has different effects and presents a different array of ______________.

Hypnosis: Open to Suggestion

Although many claims for hypnosis overstate its effects, this altered state of consciousness characterized by ________________ does have a range of real effects on individuals who are ________________, making them feel that their actions are occurring ________________ and leading them to follow the hypnotist's suggestions. Inductions of hypnosis can also influence memory reports, create ________________, and even change brain activation in a way that suggests that hypnotic experiences are more than ________________.

Meditation and Religious Experiences: Higher Consciousness

Meditation and ________________ ecstasy can be understood as altered states of consciousness. ________________ involves contemplation that may focus on a specific thought, ________________, or action, or may be an attempt to avoid any focus. The practice of meditation promotes relaxation in the short term, but the long-term benefits claimed by ____________ have not been established. Ecstatic religious experiences may have a basis in the same brain region—the right anterior ________________ lobe—as meditation; this region is also associated with some forms of ________________.

QUICK QUIZ #1

1. Phenomenology refers to:
   a. how things seem to the conscious person.
   b. how things seem to a person during a dream.
   c. the comparison of a single phenomenon to a transcendental state.
   d. the practice of determining traits by examining bumps on the skull.
2. Recent research on conscious will has revealed that before you can begin to text message your friend:
   a. you think about text messaging your friend.
   b. electrical activity begins in your brain.
   c. your brain processes the image of the friend.
   d. you react emotionally to the sight of your friend.
3. Which of the following is not affiliated with REM sleep?
   a. sleep spindles
   b. sawtooth waves
   c. atonia
   d. low-amplitude fast activity
4. Lindsey required more and more Vicodin over time to control her shoulder pain. This is called:
   a. biopsychosocial dependence.
   b. psychological dependence.
   c. drug ladder.
   d. drug tolerance.

5. After going to the bar with his friends on a weekly basis for most of the semester, Ruben was somewhat surprised to find that he had to increase the number of beers he drank in order to get a buzz. This is most likely due to:
   a. biopsychosocial dependence.
   b. psychological dependence.
   c. drug tolerance.
   d. drug ladder.
6. Monica had a few beers with her friends Saturday evening, and when she got home to an empty house she felt really despondent. How would you explain this phenomenon to Monica?
   a. Alcohol is a stimulant when you're with friends but a depressant when you are alone.
   b. Alcohol is a depressant.
   c. Alcohol, like any stimulant, can change the way you view the world.
   d. This reaction may indicate that you are an alcoholic.
7. Which of the following drugs is NOT classified as a depressant?
   a. alcohol
   b. sleeping pill
   c. Valium
   d. LSD

QUICK QUIZ #2

1. The ability to hear clearly what a friend is saying across a crowded cafeteria while filtering out the conversation of others nearby is a result of:
   a. the dichotic listening technique.
   b. dual attention.
   c. the cocktail party phenomenon.
   d. the unity of attention.
2. You have been sleeping—it's the middle of the night. Your 2-year-old daughter comes to you and asks if she can get in the bed with you. You are able to respond to her because you are in a state of:
   a. self-consciousness.
   b. transience of consciousness.
   c. minimal consciousness.
   d. REM consciousness.
3. In his famous "white bear" study, researcher Daniel Wegner demonstrated that thought suppression:
   a. is successful when participants are very focused.
   b. is a valuable tool to distract one's conscious mind.
   c. is successful only if the participant is not under stress.
   d. does not work.
4. Mitch told Helen that he had been asked to be best man at his friend's upcoming funeral. His misspeaking was the result of:
   a. word confusion.
   b. repression.
   c. thought suppression.
   d. a Freudian slip.

5. A high level of brain activity occurs during:
   a. stage 4 sleep.
   b. REM sleep.
   c. stage 3 sleep.
   d. stage 1 sleep.
6. Reggie rarely gets enough stage 3 and stage 4 sleep at night because the guys in the room next door party until quite late. It is likely that Reggie will:
   a. experience memory loss.
   b. be excessively aggressive.
   c. be very tired during the day.
   d. experience an increase in daydreaming.
7. Cole, a 3-year-old child, sometimes wakes around 9:00 p.m. crying and frightened, but he never remembers the episode the next day. It is likely that Cole is experiencing:
   a. night terrors.
   b. nightmares.
   c. somnambulism.
   d. narcolepsy.
8. A normal human circadian rhythm is approximately:
   a. 20 hours.
   b. 25 hours.
   c. 30 hours.
   d. 35 hours.
9. The body's naturally occurring endorphins are known to produce the same effects as:
   a. Valium.
   b. opiates.
   c. amphetamines.
   d. hallucinogens.
10. Cocaine is a(n):
    a. stimulant.
    b. hallucinogen.
    c. depressant.
    d. narcotic.

QUICK QUIZ #3

1. Your fraternity brother believes he can study with his iPod on. Research on the unity of consciousness suggests that:
   a. some people are able to do this if they have practiced it a lot.
   b. he may forget the information more quickly.
   c. he will be able to do this if the iPod is not turned up too loud.
   d. he is wrong in his belief.
2. When Jon yelled for help at the zoo, his parents were able to hear him even over the noise of other children and animals. This is called:
   a. dichotic listening.
   b. the cocktail party effect.
   c. routine parenting.
   d. the dual attention phenomenon.

3. The most effective way to study what is on people's minds is to:
   a. hypnotize them.
   b. ask them to think aloud.
   c. have them keep dream journals.
   d. have them focus on a white bear.
4. Sleeping medications such as Seconal and Ambien are classified as:
   a. amnesics.
   b. hallucinogenics.
   c. stimulants.
   d. depressants.
5. Which of the following drugs is NOT classified as a depressant?
   a. alcohol
   b. caffeine
   c. minor tranquilizers
   d. barbiturates
6. GABA is a neurotransmitter whose activity is increased when we ingest:
   a. narcotics.
   b. stimulants.
   c. marijuana.
   d. depressants.
7. Adolfo had a very frightening dream. It is likely that the __________ of his brain was very active while he was experiencing the dream.
   a. hypothalamus
   b. thalamus
   c. amygdala
   d. cerebral cortex
8. Alcohol is known to be a(n) __________ because it reduces the activity of the central nervous system.
   a. stimulant
   b. depressant
   c. inhibitor
   d. narcotic
9. Methedrine is a(n) __________ because it increases the levels of dopamine in the brain.
   a. amphetamine
   b. stimulant
   c. depressant
   d. hallucinogen

"HEY, GUESS WHAT I LEARNED IN PSYCHOLOGY TODAY?" (AN ESSAY QUESTION)

We're guessing there's someone in your life who is interested in the quality of your educational experiences, is reasonably intelligent, but knows little about psychology. This might be your roommate, a previous teacher, your mom, or some other person you have access to and want to share your thoughts and feelings with. What would you tell that person about consciousness? How would you describe what we know about sleep? What would you say about the nature of drug addiction?

THINGS TO PONDER

You've been provided a lot of information in this chapter about consciousness. When you put it all together, you may start to ponder how it all relates to other issues in this textbook. For example, you may ask yourself:

- What is the minimal amount of brain activity that is considered consciousness?

  Think about the studies cited in the chapter that showed differential activation of specific brain areas for different states of consciousness; then think about the many levels of consciousness. The answer is controversial.

  Consider special cases of consciousness, like the definition of a persistent vegetative state or how to specify when life begins. These are hotly debated social and political topics that have their roots in the nature of consciousness.

- Why do people want to alter their perceptions?

  We know that perception is different from sensation, and some people find the same interpretations of the same stimuli boring.

  Reflect on the idea that some people want to escape the troubles in their life and others are looking for a competitive advantage. We have identified several methods in this chapter for changing the ways that things are perceived; some of them are bizarre or dangerous.

- When are we aware of our own identity?

  Consider the studies examining this question in other species by marking the head of an animal when it is sleeping and allowing it to observe the mark in its own reflection when it wakes up. Very few species (e.g., chimpanzees and some dolphins) can dissociate self from others in this test, including young infants. We know a bit about when this dissociation happens for humans, but not a lot about how it happens.

  Investigate other cultures and the ways they identify self-awareness or the absence of it.

- Am I really unique or is something wrong with me?

  Review the information about the Cartesian Theater and the problems of studying and sharing subjective experiences. You are definitely unique!

  Differences in personality based on our different experiences are fascinating; however, some behaviors considered socially unacceptable or bizarre might be indicators of psychological disorders.

WEB LINKS AND SUGGESTED READINGS

WebMD: http://www.webmd.com/

- An online database that allows you to search for information about different drugs and medicines, and could help you identify problems with sleep.

US Department of Health and Human Services—Substance Abuse and Mental Health Services Administration—Office of Applied Studies: http://www.drugabusestatistics.samhsa.gov/

- The United States government's published data on the prevalence of drug use and abuse, emergency room episodes, and the efficacy of drug abuse treatment programs.

YouTube—Inside Edition—Skeeter the Narcoleptic Dog

- A brief video of a dog that suffers from narcolepsy, an often debilitating sleep disorder. *Please note that the content on YouTube is subject to change.*

Damasio, A. (1999). *The Feeling of What Happens: Body and Emotion in the Making of Consciousness.* Orlando, FL: Harcourt.

- Antonio Damasio, a prominent neurologist and scholar, follows his wildly successful book *Descartes' Error* (1994) by examining the role of feelings in what makes us all conscious.

Dennett, D. C. (1991). *Consciousness Explained.* Boston: Little, Brown.

- "Daniel C. Dennett, the director of the Center for Cognitive Studies at Tufts University, is one of a handful of philosophers who feel this quest is so important that they have become as conversant in psychology, neuroscience and computer science as they are in philosophy. *Consciousness Explained* is his attempt, as audacious as its title, to come up with a scientific explanation for that feeling, sometimes painful, sometimes exhilarating, of being alive and aware, the object of one's own deliberations." (From George Johnson's review in *The New York Times*, November 10, 1991.)

Leary, T., Matzner, R., and Alpert, R. (1995). *The psychedelic experience: A manual based on the Tibetan Book of the Dead.* New York: Citadel Press.

- As the subtitle states, this is a manual on how to have psychedelic experiences, from the political icon and activist Timothy Leary and his colleagues.

ANSWERS

Chapter Overview

Conscious and Unconscious: The Mind's Eye, Open and Closed

Consciousness is a mystery of psychology because other people's **minds** cannot be perceived directly and also because the relationship between mind and **body** is perplexing. Nonetheless, people's reports of their consciousness can be studied, and these reports reveal basic properties such as **intentionality**, unity, **selectivity**, and transience. Consciousness can also be understood in terms of levels—minimal consciousness, full consciousness, and **self**-consciousness—and can be investigated for contents such as current concerns, and **unwanted** thoughts. **Unconscious** processes are sometimes understood as expressions of the Freudian dynamic unconscious but are more commonly viewed as processes of the **cognitive** unconscious that create and influence our conscious thoughts and behaviors. The cognitive unconscious is at work when **subliminal** perception influences our thought or behavior without our awareness.

Sleep and Dreaming: Good Night, Mind

The sleep **cycle** involves a regular pattern of sleep and **dreaming** that creates altered states of consciousness. **EEG** measures have revealed that during a night's sleep, the **brain** passes through a five-stage sleep cycle, moving in and out of lighter sleep stages, from slow-wave sleep stages to the **REM** sleep stage, in which most dreaming occurs. Sleep needs **decrease** over the life span, but deprivation from sleep and dreams has psychological and **physical** costs. Sleep can be disrupted through **disorders**, which include insomnia, sleep **apnea**, somnambulism, **narcolepsy**, sleep paralysis, and night terrors. Dreaming is an **altered** state of consciousness in which the dreamer uncritically accepts changes in emotion, thought, and sensation, but poorly **remembers** the dream on awakening. The contents of dreams are related to **waking** life and can be understood by examining the areas of the brain that are activated when we dream. Theories of dreaming include Freud's psychoanalytic theory, which focuses on **symbolism** and the unconscious, and more current views such as the activation–**synthesis** model.

Drugs and Consciousness: Artificial Inspiration

Psychoactive drugs influence consciousness by altering the brain's chemical messaging system and intensifying or dulling the effects of **neurotransmitters**. Drug **tolerance** can result in overdose, and physical and psychological dependence can lead to **addiction**. Specific effects on consciousness and **behavior** occur with different classes of psychoactive drugs. These classes include depressants, **stimulants**, narcotics, **hallucinogens**, and marijuana. Depressants are substances that reduce the activity of the central nervous system, producing a **sedative** or calming effect. Examples of depressants are **alcohol**, barbiturates, benzodiazepines, and toxic **inhalants. Stimulants** are substances that excite the nervous system and include caffeine, **amphetamines**, nicotine, cocaine, and **ecstasy** (MDMA). Narcotics are highly addictive drugs derived from **opium**, such as **heroin**, morphine, methadone, and **codeine**. Hallucinogens produce altered sensations and **perceptions**; examples include **LSD**, psilocybin, mescaline, PCP, and **ketamine. Marijuana**, the leaves and buds of the hemp plant, produces heightened sensations but impairs memory and **motor** skills. Each of the major classes of psychoactive drugs was developed for medical, **social**, or religious reasons, and each has different effects and presents a different array of **dangers**.

Hypnosis: Open to Suggestion

Although many claims for hypnosis overstate its effects, this altered state of consciousness characterized by **suggestibility** does have a range of real effects on individuals who are **susceptible**, making them feel that their actions are occurring **involuntarily** and leading them to follow the hypnotist's suggestions. Inductions of hypnosis can also influence memory reports, create **analgesia**, and even change brain activation in a way that suggests that hypnotic experiences are more than **imagination**.

Meditation and Religious Experiences: Higher Consciousness

Meditation and **religious** ecstasy can be understood as altered states of consciousness. **Meditation** involves contemplation that may focus on a specific thought, **sound**, or action, or may be an attempt to avoid any focus. The practice of meditation promotes relaxation in the short term, but the long-term benefits claimed by **enthusiasts** have not been established. Ecstatic religious experiences may have a basis in the same brain region—the right anterior **temporal** lobe—as meditation; this region is also associated with some forms of **epilepsy**.

Quick Quiz #1

1. **A.** Phenomenology refers to how things seem to the conscious person. Dreams are not considered consciousness and examining skull bumps is phrenology.
2. **B.** Any thought, or any behavior, begins with electrical activity in the brain.
3. **A.** During REM sleep, the body becomes very aroused and yet the muscles are essentially paralyzed. A rise in blood pressure is a characteristic of arousal.
4. **D.** Most people tend to require stronger and stronger medication to handle a given level of pain because the body begins to build a resistance to the drug. Although one pill initially handled the pain, eventually two or more will be required to get the same effect.
5. **C.** As the body adjusts to the beer being consumed, it begins to build a resistance to the effects. Just as with other drugs, the individual will require more of the alcohol to get the same effect. The brain is equipped to help us adapt to our environment, and this includes what we ingest.
6. **B.** The exact way in which alcohol affects neural mechanisms is not known but we do know that alcohol reduces the activity of the central nervous system, and it is likely this leads to a feeling of despondency.
7. **D.** Alcohol and sleeping pills are depressants, while Valium is a muscle relaxant. LSD is a hallucinogenic.

Quick Quiz #2

1. **C.** The cocktail party effect is the reason you can pay attention to one voice out of many. The dichotic listening technique is an experimental technique in which participants receive a different message in each ear; "dual attention" refers to attention to two sources of information at the same time. "The unity of attention" is a made-up distractor.
2. **C.** You would have to be minimally conscious to be able to respond to your daughter's voice. There are no such psychological terms as transience of consciousness or REM consciousness. Self-consciousness refers to another level of consciousness in which the individual focuses on self.
3. **D.** Wegner's "white bear" study concluded that it is impossible NOT to think of a white bear if you are told not to think about one. In his study, even the most focused individuals still could not keep from thinking about a white bear.
4. **D.** Freud believed such slips were evidence of the unconscious mind; Mitch was indicating his true feeling about the upcoming wedding.
5. **B.** Brain activity is at its highest during REM sleep. REM sleep is often referred to as paradoxical sleep because the EEG patterns are more similar to being awake or aroused, which is quite different than the slower EEG patterns associated with the other stages of sleep.
6. **C.** Lack of stage 3 and 4 sleep can lead to extreme fatigue the following day. The only reliable symptom of a lack of these stages of sleep is fatigue. A person may be aggressive or have a difficult time remembering some things as a result of the fatigue, but these symptoms are much less common.
7. **A.** Night terrors, which tend to occur early in the evening, frighten parents but children rarely remember them. Nightmares are frightening dreams that are remembered; somnambulism is, literally, "sleepwalking"; narcolepsy is a disorder in which attacks of sudden sleep come in the middle of waking activities.
8. **B.** Even when people remain in settings where no time cues are available and allowed to sleep when they want to, they tend to have a rest/activity cycle of about 25.1 hours. Obviously, this is very close to the 24-hour cycle that we adhere to when we have clocks and the sun to guide us.
9. **B.** The brain naturally produces endogenous opiates, which are important in helping the body cope with pain. When individuals ingest

artificial opiates, flooding the brain's endorphin receptors, the brain begins to produce less endorphins.

10. **A.** Stimulants increase the activity of the body's nervous system, causing an individual to feel more stirred up and energetic.

Quick Quiz #3

1. **D.** Research has shown that any kind of distraction decreases the ability to concentrate fully on the subject at hand.
2. **B.** Jon's parents, like all parents, were able to hear their child's voice over any other noises at the zoo.
3. **B.** The most efficient way to study what is on people's minds is to simply ask them to think aloud.
4. **D.** Sleeping medications are barbiturates; barbiturates are classified as depressants.
5. **B.** Alcohol, minor tranquilizers, and barbiturates are all classified as depressants; caffeine is a stimulant.
6. **D.** Although the cause of changes in neural mechanisms is not completely understood, we do know that when the central nervous system is depressed by the ingestion of alcohol or barbiturates, activity of the neurotransmitter GABA is increased.
7. **C.** The area of the brain that is active during dreaming is the limbic system. The amygdala, in particular, is involved since it affects strong emotions. None of the other choices are part of the limbic system.
8. **B.** Any psychoactive drugs that act on the CNS are known as depressants. Alcohol, barbiturates/benzodiazepines, and toxic inhalants are all depressants.
9. **B.** Substances that excite the CNS are known as stimulants. Use of stimulants, such as Methedrine and Dexedrine (amphetamines) cause an increase in the levels of norepinephrine and dopamine in the brain.

"Hey, Guess What I Learned in Psychology Today?" (An Essay Question)

What might you tell your mom about consciousness?

- You might start by posing a Cartesian mind–body question, such as, "Do you think your feelings for me result from different patterns of neural firing?" If you are asking your mom this question, more than likely, she will tell you her love for you has to be something more than brain activity. (We don't recommend this line of questioning if you are talking to a new boyfriend or girlfriend.) Whatever her answer, you've opened the door to a discussion of what consciousness means and how we all experience the world around us differently. You could acknowledge her sentiment and still talk about what else there might be that makes you feel the way you do with your mom that is different from the way you feel with other people. This can lead to talking about different levels of consciousness and different theories that attempt to explain how we all experience things differently. You could use the last point as a segue into talking about altered states of consciousness, whether induced by sleep or drugs or religious experiences.
- The best way to start this conversation might be to say, "Did you know that scientists don't really understand sleep very well—that it's known we all need it, but we don't really know why?" Then back up and talk about the things that we do know about sleep: different patterns of brain activity relevant to different phases of sleep, the cycles of sleep that we progress through in the night, the changes in sleep throughout the life span, when dreams occur and what they might be for, and the host of things that can go wrong during sleep—its disruptions and disorders.
- You could ask your mom, "What do you think the new number one cause of death in young adults in West Virginia is in 2008?" She'll likely guess car accidents or gun violence. You can give her the fact: drug overdose. But your mom may be as knowledgeable as you and say, "Drug overdoses." Your follow-up question could be, "What kind of drug do you think is responsible?" Many people, including your mom, might immediately think of a heroin junkie in an alley, slumped over with a syringe dangling from an arm. "Actually," you reply, "it's prescription pain medication, by a long shot." Then you could discuss some of the other misconceptions about drugs, what counts as a psychoactive drug, and why many legal and illegal drugs can be dangerous because they alter consciousness. You could discuss how few people intend to become addicted, but there are physical and psychological processes related to drug use that are very powerful and can change the way we think and behave.

9

Emotion and Motivation

THE BIG PICTURE

Jason and Cleon are walking back to their cars, enjoying a raspberry sports drink after a long game of pick-up basketball. Cleon turns to Jason and says, "You played worse than usual today. Something bothering you?" Jason forces a crooked smile in an attempt to conceal his embarrassment and says, "Well, I guess I do have a lot of things on my mind. We're trying to buy that house, work is really busy right now, and Sophie needs braces, but I still think I played better than you." Cleon stops dead in his tracks. His expression serious and angry, he demands: "You want to go right here?" Jason's heart races and he flushes as he tries to assess whether or not his friend is really ready to fight. Cleon waits a second, then bursts out laughing and says, "I had you worried there for a minute, huh?" As they both chuckle about the near fisticuffs, they round the corner of the recreation center and bump into a short, dark-haired man wearing a white T-shirt with the number 24 and the DuPont emblem on the front. The red juice spills all over all three men. Jason realizes that they have just plowed into Jeff Gordon, his favorite NASCAR driver, and starts trying to think of how to apologize. Cleon says to Gordon, "You just got juice all over my new shoes!" Gordon says to Cleon, "Then maybe you should watch where you're going!" Jason jumps between the two and begins apologizing, stumbling over his words, a silly grin on his face. "We're so sorry. I'm a . . . uh, a big fan. Sorry! Sorry Mr., um, Gordon." He pulls Cleon aside as they walk away. "Don't you know who that is?" "Nope—he your boss or something?" Jason tells Cleon that he nearly got into a fight with a famous NASCAR driver, to which Cleon replies, "You should spend less time watching cars drive in a circle and more time working on that thing you call a jump shot."

What were the emotional and motivational principles at work in this story? We saw the range of valence and arousal in the two main characters in a short period of time. The two friends went from kidding around to nearly fighting to excitement in one case and considerable irritation in the other. Jason had to interpret his physiological arousal to the threat from Cleon—was it a fake or not? This leads to consideration of the classic theories of emotion—is one theory more likely to be correct than the others? As Jason's heart was racing and his face flushed, he knew that the reason for his response—the stimulus—was the angry man in front of him; did his brain figure this out before he experienced the emotion? We saw how body posture and facial expression (the asymmetry of the fake smile was a giveaway) are important for communicating our emotions as Cleon's fake anger and Jason's fake smile were both replaced by genuine laughter, laughter that in Cleon's case was then replaced by violent anger. Both men might have also been a little more on edge than usual because of their drives—to quench their thirst and possibly to sleep after their game. Finally, there was the matter of affective forecasting in the Jeff Gordon encounter: Jason was probably thinking about how great it was going to be to meet his favorite driver, when in fact the meeting ended awkwardly. Cleon, who had no idea who Jeff Gordon is, had a very different appraisal of what's likely to happen when you bump into some guy and spill your juice.

Chapter 9 introduces the topsy-turvy world of emotion and motivation, concepts that have been notoriously difficult to define and measure in the past. We have now made some progress in these areas and you can see how our new knowledge affects other areas of psychology. We've talked about some areas of the brain (Chapter 3) that quickly evaluate a situation and others that have evolved to be more comprehensive but are relatively slower than the more primitive areas. You saw how perception (Chapter 4) and appraisal are critical in determining how each of us experiences emotions in different situations. You understand the mechanisms that make emotional memories more salient and durable than nonemotional memories (Chapter 5). There are several lines of evidence that indicate that we can learn (Chapter 6) to modify our emotions and drives on the basis of our thoughts (Chapter 7) and appraisals. Reappraisal has been touted as an important tool for the treatment of certain kinds of psychological disorders (Chapters 12 and 13). Drives and motivation are clearly linked to our physical health (Chapter 14), and, specifically, our sexual motivations play an integral role in our social interactions (Chapter 15).

At some level we are all hedonists. We approach things that are pleasurable and avoid things that are uncomfortable or painful. That translates into a huge effect on most behavior, including whom we choose for a partner, what job will result in both money and personal satisfaction, and avoiding the ridicule of a friend regarding a less than stellar jump shot.

CHAPTER OBJECTIVES

After studying this chapter, you should be able to:

1. Explain how emotions can be mapped along the two dimensions of valence and arousal, and how this mapping helps us to define what an *emotion* is.
2. Compare the *James-Lange, Cannon-Bard,* and *two-factor theories* of emotion, noting their major similarities and differences.
3. Offer four reasons why Cannon and Bard thought their view of emotional experience was more appropriate than the James-Lange theory.
4. Describe the two factors in the two-factor theory of emotion and note how the theory has been both supported and refuted by subsequent research.
5. Explain how the amygdala is involved in the *appraisal* of emotion, noting the fast pathway and slow pathway that emotional information can take through the brain.
6. Define the process of *emotion regulation* and explain how *reappraisal* is one primary means of regulating our emotional states.
7. Define *emotional expression* and explain why facial expressions of emotion, compared to other channels of communication, are capable of communicating the greatest degree of specificity regarding underlying emotional experiences.
8. Describe two lines of evidence supporting the *universality hypothesis* for facial expressions of emotion and list emotions that have been shown to have a universal quality.
9. Discuss evidence for the *facial feedback hypothesis*, and describe how the pathway of emotional experience can be bidirectional.
10. Describe *display rules* and give examples of each of the four different types.
11. List four sets of features of facial expressions that allow a trained observer to detect whether an expression is sincere or not.
12. Define *motivation* and describe its linguistic and functional connections to emotion.
13. State the *hedonic principle* and note how it is an example of emotions serving to motivate behavior.
14. Discuss why instinct theory and *drive* theory enjoyed some initial success in explaining motivated behavior.
15. Explain how hunger arises, noting the functions of signals to eat and stop eating, ghrelin, the lateral hypothalamus, and the ventromedial hypothalamus.

16. Describe some of the forces that produce *anorexia* and *bulimia* and discuss some of the reasons why overeating and obesity can occur; define metabolism and explain how it is implicated.
17. Discuss the factors that contribute to sexual interest.
18. Describe the stages of the *human sexual response cycle.*
19. Compare *intrinsic* and *extrinsic motives*, and note some of the factors that can enhance or detract from these types of motivation.
20. Compare *conscious* and *unconscious motives.*
21. Compare *approach* and *avoidance motives*, noting how each type of motivation can direct our behavior.

CHAPTER OVERVIEW

Use the terms below to fill in the following exercises. Terms may not be used more than once. The answers can be found at the end of this chapter.

action	eating	polygraph
amygdala	effective	poor
arousal	error	punishments
avoidance	expressions	reappraisal
badness	extrinsic	regulate
body	face	research
Cannon-Bard	hedonic	rules
cause	hunger	sexes
classified	identify	sexual
comprehensive	indirectly	signify
correct	inhibits	sincere
cortex	James-Lange	specific
cortical	mating	testosterone
cultures	motivations	two-factor
Darwin	obesity	universally
directly	pain	utterances
display	physiological	valence
drive	pleasure	

Emotional Experience: The Feeling Machine

Emotional experiences are difficult to describe, but psychologists have identified their two underlying dimensions: arousal and ________________. Psychologists have spent more than a century trying to understand how emotional experience and ________________ activity are related. The ________________ theory suggests that a stimulus causes a physiological reaction that leads to an emotional response; the ________________ theory suggests that a stimulus causes both an emotional experience and a physiological reaction simultaneously; Schachter and Singer's ________________ theory suggests that a stimulus causes undifferentiated physiological arousal about which we draw inferences. None of these theories is entirely ____________, but each has elements that are supported by ____________.

Emotions are produced by the complex interaction of ____________ and subcortical structures in the brain. Information about a stimulus is simultaneously sent to the ____________ (which makes a quick appraisal of the "goodness" or "____________" of the stimulus) and the ____________ (which does a slower and more ____________ analysis of the stimulus). In some instances, the amygdala triggers an emotional experience that the cortex later ____________. We care about our emotional experiences and use many strategies to ____________ them. ____________ involves changing the way we think about an object or event, and it is one of the most ____________ strategies for emotion regulation.

Emotional Communication: Msgs w/o Wrds

The voice, the ____________, and the ____________ all communicate information about someone's emotional state. ____________ suggested that these emotional expressions are the same for all people and are ____________ understood, and research suggests that this is generally true. Emotional expressions are caused by the emotions they ____________, and they can also ____________ those emotions. Emotional mimicry allows us to experience and hence ____________ the emotions of others.

Not all emotional expressions are ____________ because we use display ____________ to help us decide which emotions to express. Different ____________ have different ____________ rules, but they are universally obeyed by use of the same set of techniques. There are reliable differences between sincere and insincere emotional ____________, just as there are reliable differences between truthful and untruthful ____________, but we are generally ____________ at determining when an expression or an utterance is sincere. Although machines such as the ____________ can make this determination with better than chance accuracy, their ____________ rates are dangerously high.

Motivation: Getting Moved

Emotions motivate us ____________ by providing information about the world, and they also motivate us ____________. The ____________ principle suggests that we approach ____________ and avoid ____________ and that this motivation underlies all others. All organisms are born with some ____________ and acquire others through experience.

When the body experiences a deficit, we experience a ____________ to remedy it. Biological drives such as ____________ and ____________ generally take precedence over others. ____________ is the result of a complex system of physiological processes, and disturbances in this system can lead to eating disorders and ____________, both of which are very difficult to overcome. With regard to ____________ drives, men and women tend to be more similar than different. Both ________________ experience the same sequence of physiological ________________, engage in sex for most of the same reasons, and have sex drives that are regulated by ________________.

We have many motivations, which can be ________________ in many ways. Intrinsic motivation can be undermined by ________________ rewards and ________________. We tend to be aware of our more general motivations unless difficulty in producing ________________ forces us to be aware of our more ________________ motivations. For most people—not all—________________ motivations are generally more powerful than approach motivations.

QUICK QUIZ #1

1. Psychologists used the technique of __________ and asked participants to approximate the distance between emotional concepts; their responses allowed the mapping of emotions on a two-dimensional scale.
   a. multidimensional mapping
   b. multidimensional scaling
   c. global scaling
   d. pinpoint mapping
2. The __________ theory of emotion asserts that you would not experience emotion without first experiencing a specific physiological state.
   a. two-factor
   b. Cannon-Bard
   c. Schachter-Singer
   d. James-Lange
3. One of the major weaknesses of the Schachter-Singer two-factor theory of emotion is that:
   a. there are specific physiological states that correspond to each emotion.
   b. there are actually four factors involved in the experience of emotion.
   c. later research identified physiological responses specific to certain emotions.
   d. later research showed that norepinephrine is not related to arousal.
4. In monkeys, temporal lobe syndrome results in all the following symptoms except:
   a. indiscriminate sexuality.
   b. sham rage.
   c. increased eating behavior.
   d. decreased fear in response to snakes.
5. Two pathways of information about a fear stimulus travels through the brain before a fear response is activated: the fast route goes directly from the __________ to the amygdala; the slow pathway makes an extra stop in the __________ before reaching the amygdala.
   a. thalamus; septum
   b. hippocampus; cortex
   c. cortex; hippocampus
   d. thalamus; cortex

6. Colonel Rogers is feeling pleased about his recent promotion from lieutenant colonel, but before he must speak to the family of a dead soldier he thinks of a time in battle when he lost a buddy. What strategy of emotion regulation is he employing?
   a. cheer down
   b. negative transference
   c. over-blunting
   d. reappraisal
7. The __________ muscle pulls up the corners of the lips during a smile.
   a. cheek extensor
   b. cheek retractor
   c. obicularis major
   d. zygomatic major
8. The universality hypothesis:
   a. states that emotional expressions have the same meaning in all cultures, except in preliterate ones.
   b. states that emotional expressions have the same meaning for everyone.
   c. has been largely disproved.
   d. states that feelings are universal across all cultures.
9. Researchers have found that __________ produces a higher heart rate than does __________.
   a. fear; anger
   b. anger; disgust
   c. sadness; fear
   d. disgust; anger

QUICK QUIZ #2

1. What are the two dimensions on which emotions are mapped?
   a. intensity and consciousness
   b. valence and intensity
   c. arousal and consciousness
   d. arousal and valence
2. Kelly is crossing a ravine on a rickety, swaying bridge. Her heart is racing and her hands are sweating. Safely across, she meets Terrence on the other side of the ravine; he gives her a wink and asks her to dinner. Kelly says yes and finds herself strangely attracted to Terrence, who isn't really her type. Which theory of emotion best describes Kelly's emotions?
   a. two-factor theory
   b. Cannon-Bard theory
   c. Willams-James theory
   d. James-Lange theory
3. A 1936 experiment rendered a monkey hypersexual and hyperphagic; this behavior has become known as the:
   a. James-Lange syndrome.
   b. Kluver-Bucy syndrome.
   c. Schachter-Wegner syndrome.
   d. Korsakoff's syndrome.

4. Changing one's emotional experience by changing the meaning of the emotion-eliciting stimulus is called:
   a. experience reacquisition
   b. reappraisal.
   c. cognitive transference.
   d. emotional transformation.

5. Two-day-old infants respond to sweet tastes with ____________ and to bitter tastes with an expression of ____________.
   a. a chuckle; disgust
   b. a smile; disgust
   c. a smile; fear
   d. a smile; happiness

6. People who are born blind can:
   a. make the same facial expressions associated with the basic emotions that sighted people make.
   b. not make the same facial expressions associated with the basic emotions that sighted people make.
   c. make nearly all of the same facial expressions associated with the basic emotions that sighted people make.
   d. make their facial expressions as recognizable as those made by sighted people.

7. The feeling of happiness causes:
   a. the temperature of the brain to rise dramatically.
   b. the temperature of the brain to fall dramatically.
   c. a slow change in affective state.
   d. the zygomatic major muscles to contract.

8. People who take drugs that impair neurotransmission in the amygdala do not have superior memory for:
   a. emotionally evocative words.
   b. events of their recent past.
   c. their childhood.
   d. abstract terms.

QUICK QUIZ #3

1. Which of the following terms describes a positive or negative experience that is associated with a particular pattern of physiological activity?
   a. motive
   b. drive
   c. emotion
   d. instinct

2. On the scale that maps the two dimensions of emotion, *miserable* and *distressed*, both dimensions have:
   a. negative valence.
   b. low arousal.
   c. high arousal.
   d. positive valence.

3. According to the Cannon-Bard theory of emotion, we experience:
   a. interpretation of an event followed by feelings of relief.
   b. general physiological arousal followed by emotion.
   c. emotion followed by specific physiological arousal.
   d. specific physiological arousal and emotion at the same time.

4. What part of the brain is primarily responsible for appraising the emotion-related aspects of a stimulus?
   a. amygdala
   b. nucleus accumbens
   c. insular cortex
   d. septum

5. The amygdala becomes active in response to an emotional photograph; the reappraisal of the photograph as a result of additional information activates the:
   a. hypothalamus.
   b. hippocampus.
   c. cortex.
   d. cerebellum.

6. An observable sign of an emotional state is called a(n):
   a. symbol.
   b. emotional expression.
   c. expressive signature.
   d. arousal.

7. Which one of the following needs is at the bottom of Abraham Maslow's hierarchy of needs?
   a. physiological
   b. safety and security
   c. belongingness
   d. esteem

8. Which of the following is NOT a sign that someone is a liar?
   a. A liar speaks more slowly than a truthful person does.
   b. A liar takes longer to respond to questions than a truthful person does.
   c. A liar responds in greater detail than a truthful person does.
   d. A liar is more uncertain than a truthful person is.

9. Which of the following statements is correct?
   a. The James-Lange theory suggests that a stimulus causes an emotional experience and a physiological reaction to occur simultaneously.
   b. The Cannon-Bard theory suggests that a physiological reaction to a stimulus leads to an emotional experience.
   c. The two-factor theory suggests that people have different psychological reactions to all emotional stimuli, which explains why they then go on to respond differently as well.
   d. Our emotions are produced by the complex interaction of limbic and cortical structures.

"HEY, GUESS WHAT I LEARNED IN PSYCHOLOGY TODAY?" (AN ESSAY QUESTION)

We're guessing there's someone in your life who is interested in the quality of your educational experiences, is reasonably intelligent, but knows little about psychology. This might be your roommate, a previous teacher, your mom, or some other person you have access to and want to share your thoughts and feelings with. What would you tell that person about emotion? About motivation? How would you describe the connection between emotion and motivation?

THINGS TO PONDER

You've been provided a lot of information in this chapter about emotion and motivation. When you put it all together, you may start to ponder how it all relates to other issues in this textbook. For example, you may ask yourself:

- Why do we have redundant neural systems for processing fear?

  Think about our evolution and how it must have been important for our ancestors' survival to be able to identify danger quickly and escape that danger.

  Consider that we don't face many of those dangers and we have evolved a way to discriminate threats in more detail than our ancestors did to avoid behaving too rashly.

- How do our bodies know when to become sexually motivated?

  There are biological processes that are modulated by hormones and puberty that dictate preparedness for sexual behavior.

  Reflect on the idea that in humans sexual behavior is not merely for procreation. We have developed social cues and rituals to mark sexual maturity, and these vary widely in different societies.

- Why is it so important for many of us to be right about things?

  Consider the power that comes along with accuracy in social or working relationships.

  Look at the information in the text that indicates how we are not very good at forecasting, appraising, or even remembering many things.

- Why is reappraisal important for mental and physical health?

  Therapists use reappraisal to help patients find new ways to think about the events that happen to them; these new ways of thinking can alleviate depression and the signs of physical stress.

  Consider the limitations of therapy if we were not able to change the way we think about things in our lives, and the fact that the inability to do so may be a contributor to some mental disorders.

WEB LINKS AND SUGGESTED READING

Encyclopedia of Psychology—Motivation—http://www.psychology.org/links/Environment_Behavior_Relationships/Motivation/

- An online reference for many of the theories and concepts related to motivation in different realms within and outside psychology.

American Psychological Association—Emotional Health—http://www.apa.org/topics/topicemotion.html

- Links to books, videos, journals, and press releases on emotional health.

Damasio, A. (2003). *Looking for Spinoza: Joy, Sorrow, and the Feeling Brain.* Orlando, FL: Harcourt.

- "Antonio Damasio pursues a unifying theory in *Looking for Spinoza.* Why Spinoza? The philosopher, whom Damasio calls a "protobiologist," firmly linked mind and body, paving the way for modern ideas of neurophysiology. Damasio examines this linkage, which ran counter to all scientific and religious thinking of Spinoza's day, and lays out the reasoning and evidence behind its truth. Damasio also defines his terms, which is crucial, as he means something very specific when he says *feeling* ("always hidden, like all mental images") instead of *emotion* ("actions or movements . . . visible to others as they occur in the face, in the voice, in specific behaviors"). Using an impressive array of biological and psychological research, Damasio makes a compelling case for his idea of the feeling brain as crucial for survival and sense of self." (From Amazon.com editorial review)

Weiner, B. (1992). *Human Motivation: Metaphors, Theories, and Research.* Newbury Park, CA: Sage Publications.

- Encompassing research and theory, the psychologist Bernard Weiner surveys classical and recent motivation theories and offers an exciting and challenging perspective.

ANSWERS

Chapter Overview

Emotional Experience: The Feeling Machine

Emotional experiences are difficult to describe, but psychologists have identified their two underlying dimensions: arousal and **valence**. Psychologists have spent more than a century trying to understand how emotional experience and **physiological** activity are related. The **James-Lange** theory suggests that a stimulus causes a physiological reaction that leads to an emotional response; the **Cannon-Bard** theory suggests that a stimulus causes both an emotional experience and a physiological reaction simultaneously; Schachter and Singer's **two-factor** theory suggests that a stimulus causes undifferentiated physiological arousal about which we draw inferences. None of these theories is entirely **correct**, but each has elements that are supported by **research**.

Emotions are produced by the complex interaction of **cortical** and subcortical structures in the brain. Information about a stimulus is simultaneously sent to the **amygdala** (which makes a quick appraisal of the "goodness" or **"badness"** of the stimulus) and the **cortex** (which does a slower and more **comprehensive** analysis of the stimulus). In some instances, the amygdala triggers an emotional experience that the cortex later **inhibits**. We care about our emotional experiences and use many strategies to **regulate** them. **Reappraisal** involves changing the way we think about an object or event, and it is one of the most **effective** strategies for emotion regulation.

Emotional Communication: Msgs w/o Wrds

The voice, the **body**, and the **face** all communicate information about someone's emotional state. **Darwin** suggested that these emotional expressions are the same for all people and are **universally** understood, and research suggests that this is generally true. Emotional expressions are caused by the emotions they **signify**, and they can also **cause** those emotions. Emotional mimicry allows us to experience and hence **identify** the emotions of others.

Not all emotional expressions are **sincere** because we use display **rules** to help us decide which emotions to express. Different **cultures** have different **display** rules, but they are universally obeyed by use of the same set of techniques. There are reliable differences between sincere and insincere emotional **expressions**, just as there are reliable differences between truthful and untruthful **utterances**, but we are generally **poor** at determining when an expression or an utterance is sincere. Although machines such as the **polygraph** can make this determination with better than chance accuracy, their **error** rates are dangerously high.

Motivation: Getting Moved

Emotions motivate us **indirectly** by providing information about the world, and they also motivate us **directly**. The **hedonic** principle suggests that we approach **pleasure** and avoid **pain** and that this motivation underlies all others. All organisms are born with some **motivations** and acquire others through experience.

When the body experiences a deficit, we experience a **drive** to remedy it. Biological drives such as **eating** and **mating** generally take precedence over others. **Hunger** is the result of a complex system of physiological processes, and disturbances in this system can lead to eating disorders and **obesity**, both of which are very difficult to overcome. With regard to **sexual** drives, men and women tend to be more similar than different. Both **sexes** experience the same sequence of physiological **arousal**, engage in sex for most of the same reasons, and have sex drives that are regulated by **testosterone**.

We have many motivations, which can be **classified** in many ways. Intrinsic motivation can be undermined by **extrinsic** rewards and **punishments**. We tend to be aware of our more general motivations unless difficulty in producing **action** forces us to be aware of our more **specific** motivations. For most people—not all—**avoidance** motivations are generally more powerful than approach motivations.

Quick Quiz #1

1. **B.** Psychologists used multidimensional scaling to map different emotions according to valence and arousal; the values for the "data points" were determined by the responses of many participants asked to estimate distances between various emotions.
2. **D.** The James-Lange theory stated that you would not experience emotion without first experiencing physiological activity; the Cannon-Bard theory assumed simultaneous activation; and the two-factor (Schachter-Singer) theory suggested a more general state of arousal, opposed to specific arousal, before experiencing fear.
3. **C.** The two-factor theory holds that emotion is determined after general, undifferentiated physical arousal; this position is weakened by research linking specific physical responses to specific emotions.
4. **B.** Sham rage is the inappropriate expression of fear or the showing of fear for no particular reason. The monkeys with temporal lobe syndrome showed an eerie lack of fear to things that they are normally afraid of, such as snakes and experimenters.
5. **D.** A fear stimulus travels quickly from the thalamus to the amygdala for a "quick-and-dirty" appraisal and speedy response; the slower route travels from the thalamus to the cortex and then to the amygdala before a fear experience or response is generated.
6. **A.** The colonel is attempting to "cheer down" so that his demeanor with the family will be suitable to the occasion. Cheering down is one of many cognitive strategies used to regulate emotions.
7. **D.** The zygomatic major pulls up the lips to smile; the obicularis oculi crinkles the edges of the eyes. "Cheek extensor" and "cheek retractor" are made-up distracters.
8. **B.** The universality hypotheses (suggested by Darwin), stating that emotional expressions have the same meaning in all cultures, is today considered largely correct.
9. **B.** Anger, fear, and sadness each produce a higher heart rate than disgust.

Quick Quiz #2

1. **D.** The two dimensions on which emotions are mapped are arousal and valence. Consciousness is linked with motivation; intensity is similar to arousal but lacks the specificity, particularly a negative component, necessary to map emotions.
2. **A.** The two-factor theory best describes Kelly's emotions because she is interpreting her general physiological arousal as attraction, instead of experiencing a specific physiological state that leads to attraction.
3. **B.** The excessive sexual and eating behavior was the result of a medial temporal lobectomy performed by Heinrich Kluver and Paul Bucy. The monkey had a difficult time distinguishing between "good" and "bad" food or mates and had an extremely reduced sense of fear.
4. **B.** Reappraisal is the ability to change one's emotional experience by changing the meaning of the emotion-eliciting stimulus. The three other choices are not related to the process of emotion regulation.
5. **B.** Studies (by Jacob Steiner) showed that two-day-old infants respond to sweet tastes with a smile and to bitter tastes with an expression of disgust. The studies support the universality of expression because these responses are not learned.
6. **A.** Congenitally blind people can make the same facial expressions as those who can see; however, some of their expressions are slightly more difficult to recognize than those made by sighted people.
7. **D.** The zygomatic major muscles control the turning up of the corners of the lips.
8. **A.** Damage to the amygdala or impairment of neurotransmission within the amygdala results in blunted affect; there is no boost to memory for words that are generally emotionally evocative.

Quick Quiz #3

1. **C.** "Emotion" is the term that best answers the question. Drives and instincts are components of motives.
2. **A.** Both "miserable" and "distressed" have negative valence; "miserable" is classified as lower arousal and "distressed" is classified as higher arousal.
3. **D.** The Cannon-Bard theory predicts that we experience a specific physiological arousal and the emotion simultaneously. The other

choices refer to a general physiological state, which is affiliated with the two-factor theory, different organization of the experience, or a state of relief that is not predicted by any of the theories.

4. **A.** The part of the brain that is primarily responsible for appraising the emotion-related aspects of a stimulus is the amygdala. The nucleus accumbens, septum, and insular cortex are also considered part of the limbic system, but they play different roles in the emotional process.
5. **C.** Whereas the amygdala is initially activated by an emotional image, the cortex is activated to reappraise the scene and effectively turns down the activity of the amygdala.
6. **B.** An emotional expression is an observable sign of an emotional state. Arousal is more a state than a behavior or expression; symbols are arbitrary designations of the things they represent; "expressive signature" is a made-up term.
7. **A.** Physiological needs must be met first, according to Maslow, before any of the other needs can be addressed.
8. **C.** Research by DePaulo et al. (2003) has shown that when people lie, many of their verbal and nonverbal behaviors are altered. Besides including less detail, the story the liar tells is just a little too good to be true.
9. **D.** Information about a stimulus is sent simultaneously to the amygdala (which quickly appraises the stimulus's goodness or badness) and the cortex (which analyzes the stimulus more slowly and comprehensively).

"Hey, Guess What I Learned in Psychology Today?" (An Essay Question)

What might you tell your mom about emotion and motivation?

- You could sneak up behind your mom and clap your hands loudly behind her head. If she startles you can ask her if she experienced the emotion of surprise first or if her body reacted first and then she tried to figure out what—or who—was trying to scare her. This question is a great lead into consideration of the evidence for each of the theories that attempts to predict how we come to experience emotions. You might talk about the two pathways in her brain that processed information about the event as it was happening, and how they connect to other areas of the brain that are important for making sense out of the event and responding appropriately.
- Another good opener is, "How do you know not to pick up a rattlesnake and kiss it?" The answer will probably be something like, "Because they're dangerous and scary and creepy." Dangerous, yes—but your mom didn't always know that. And most people haven't had the personal experience of being bitten by a rattlesnake, or seeing someone bitten. This fear is an instinct, passed down through your DNA, not absorbed through any formal learning process. Similarly, you don't have to learn what it means to be hungry; hunger is a drive, an internal state generated by a departure from physiological optimality. Something has changed in your body, probably because you haven't eaten in five hours, and you are not running at 100%. That state initiates a signal that tells your body, "Hey, go get me a sandwich!" There are similar drives for sex and thirst and other biological processes. You could then talk about how instincts and drives lead to motivation that can be intrinsic or extrinsic, conscious or unconscious, and result in approach or avoidance.
- Here's a question of connections you could talk about. Emotions often lead to motivations; motivations can affect emotions. If you see a rabid, snarling wolf running at you from the edge of the dark woods you will most likely experience an emotion (fear), which will result in some motivation (avoidance), which will lead to some behavior (running away). Psychologists are interested in the origins of behavior, and determining the motivation for a behavior tells us a lot about how that behavior is generated and controlled. Even though these relatively abstract ideas of emotions and motivation are hard to pin down, when we do begin to understand them, the benefits reaped can be great.

10

Development

THE BIG PICTURE

The Giving Tree by Shel Silverstein (1964), a classic children's book, is also a wonderful and relatively thorough review of developmental psychology. The story is a short moral tale about a young boy and a tree. The tree loves the boy like a mother. She always provides the boy with what he wants and needs in life throughout the different stages of development. When the boy is a small child the tree provides branches for him to swing from, shade to sit under, apples to snack on; the tree is a playmate in the boy's fantastic and creative games. We can almost see the boy progressing through Erik Erikson's stages of development as the story unfolds and he explores his independence through his imagination. We would categorize the boy as securely attached, given his ability to venture away from the caregiver tree without stress or ambivalence, and the boy clearly loves the tree. As he enters Erikson's fifth stage, identity vs. role confusion, his focus shifts from the tree to peer relationships, and when he enters young adulthood, he brings a young lady to sit by the tree and carves their initials in the trunk of the tree. As the boy enters middle adulthood (the stage of generativity vs. stagnation) he asks more and more of the tree (her apples to sell, her branches to build a house, and her trunk for a boat to sail the world). Again, these are the crises and key events that Erikson identifies for the seventh stage of human development. Another interesting aspect of the story is the perspective of the tree, who is always happy to see the boy and takes great joy in providing for him in any way that she can. This attitude is relevant in the work of Harlow, Bowlby, and Ainsworth, which suggests that development, particularly early in life, is a complex interaction between the temperament of the child and the parenting style of the caregiver. At the end of the story the boy, now an old man, returns to the tree after being away for many years and the tree says, "I have nothing left to give you." The boy replies that all he needs is a quiet place to sit and rest as he awaits death (ego integrity vs. despair). The tree straightens her trunk and happily obliges the boy. In the story, this final scene is somber and may be the least representative of actual development; people tend to focus on the positive in the waning years of life.

Chapter 10 introduces many concepts about how we develop over the life span. Since the chapter describes the entire journey of life, it relates to all the other topics discussed in this textbook. The brain develops rapidly after conception, continues to develop throughout the early years of life, and will slowly decline as we journey through adulthood (Chapter 3). The way that we see and hear also, initially primitive and cloudy, sharpens to a peak in young adult life, and then slowly declines with age (Chapter 4). Much of Chapter 10 is dedicated to the early processes of how we learn about the world (Chapter 6), with very different rules and schemas early in life compared to the way we deal with the complexities of adulthood. The unique processes and behaviors of human beings (language, thought, consciousness, and intelligence; Chapters 7–8) begin to develop in early childhood and continue to develop, for most of us, throughout our entire lives. There are several theories about the changing motivations (Chapter 9) and stressors (Chapter 14) that each of us encounters as we grow from child to adult. There is also a considerable discussion of forecasting of adult personalities (Chapter 11) and successes that are based on the social relationships (Chapter 15) established early in life.

Life is a wonderful journey. The central tenet of the ancient eastern philosophy Taoism is the "way," or the "path"— the way we perceive the world around us and interact with life. Consider your own way: the manner in which you perceive reality influences your way of being in the world, your path of action. The life of the boy in the story changes as his motivations and choices change. At first it was enough to swing from the tree's branches and play make-believe games. Then he wanted new relationships, money, a family of his own, to travel the world. That was the story of his development. Your motivations, your choices, your actions are the story of yours. There are a lot of things to see and do before the final offer from the generous caregiver, "Come, boy, sit down. Sit down and rest," will sound appealing to you.

CHAPTER OBJECTIVES

After studying this chapter, you should be able to:

1. Offer a definition of *developmental psychology* that encompasses the notions of continuity and change.
2. Outline the stages of development that take place prenatally, including the *zygote, germinal stage, embryonic stage,* and *fetal stage.*
3. Discuss how *teratogens* and conditions such as *fetal alcohol syndrome* can affect a developing fetus.
4. Describe the major achievements of *motor development* that take place during the *infancy* stage (from 0 to 24 months).
5. Describe the *cephalocaudal rule* and the *proximodistal rule,* and note how they apply to motor development during infancy.
6. Outline Jean Piaget's four stages of *cognitive development,* noting the major milestones that characterize each stage.
7. Compare the processes of *assimilation* and *accommodation,* and describe how they relate to *object permanence.*
8. Explain the principle of *conservation,* and provide two examples of how a child in the *concrete operational stage* might misapply that principle.
9. Describe how children make the cognitive journey from *egocentrism* to developing a *theory of mind.* How is the process the same or different for children with autism or deafness?
10. Compare the ways in which children discover other minds with the ways in which they discover their cultures.
11. Describe the different *attachment* styles that can develop between an infant and a primary caregiver.
12. Contrast Jean Piaget's view of moral development with Lawrence Kohlberg's view of moral development.
13. Explain how children act as moral intuitionists, and the general ways in which children distinguish between similar but nuanced moral judgments.
14. Discuss the *primary* and *secondary sex characteristics* that girls and boys evidence during *adolescence.*
15. Consider some of the myths and realities associated with protracted adolescence, such as the onset of *puberty,* moodiness, and raging hormones.
16. Describe some of the issues surrounding sexuality among adolescents, particularly noting the role that sex education can play in informing adolescents about the causes and consequences of sexual activity.
17. Discuss some of the explanations for the development of sexual orientation.
18. Comment on the relative influence of parents and peers on adolescent development.

19. List the abilities that change during *adulthood*, noting both gains and losses that take place.
20. Explain why changes in orientation to information take place during adulthood.
21. Consider whether events that most people think will make them happy as adults, such as marriage or having children, actually contribute to psychological well-being.

CHAPTER OVERVIEW

Use the terms below to fill in the following exercises. Terms may not be used more than once. The answers can be found at the end of this chapter.

adolescence	exist	puberty
attracted	expertise	retrieval
biology	fetus	risky
caregivers	four	see
center	growth	sexual
change	harm	social
child	identities	suffering
children	intentions	temperament
chromosomes	intuitions	teratogens
cliques	later	theories
compensate	married	tobacco
continuity	minds	tools
cultures	moral	vision
down	outcomes	voice
earlier	peer	women
embryo	Piaget	zygote
emotionally	prenatal	
enduring	psychological	

Prenatality: A Womb with a View

Developmental psychology studies ________________ and ________________ across the life span. The ________________ stage of development begins when a sperm fertilizes an egg, producing a ________________. The zygote, which contains ________________ from both the egg and sperm, develops into a/an ________________ at two weeks and then a ________________ at eight weeks. The fetal environment has important physical and ________________ influences on the fetus. In addition to the food a pregnant woman eats, ________________, agents that impair fetal development, can affect the fetus. Some of the most common teratogens are ________________ and alcohol. Although the fetus cannot ________________ much in the womb, it can hear sounds and become familiar with those it hears often, such as its mother's ________________.

Infancy and Childhood: Becoming a Person

Infants have a limited range of ______________, but they can see and remember objects that appear in their visual field. They learn to control their bodies from the top ______________ and the ______________ out. Infants slowly develop ______________ about how the world works. ______________ believed that these theories developed through ______________ stages, in which children learn basic facts about the world, such as the fact that objects continue to ______________ even when they are out of sight, and the fact that objects have ______________ properties that are not changed by superficial transformations. Children also learn that their ______________ produce representations of objects, so the objects themselves may not be as they appear, and other people may not see them the way the ______________ does. Cognitive development also comes about through social interactions in which children are given ______________ for understanding that have been developed over millennia by members of their ______________.

At a very early age, humans develop strong emotional ties to their primary ______________. The quality of these ties is determined both by the caregiver's behavior and the child's ______________. People get along with each other by learning and obeying ______________ principles. Children's reasoning about right and wrong is initially based on an action's ______________, but as they mature, children begin to consider the actor's ______________ as well as the extent to which the action obeys abstract moral principles. Moral ______________ may also be derived from one's emotional reactions to events, such as the ______________ of others.

Adolescence: Minding the Gap

______________ begins with a ______________ spurt and with ______________, the onset of sexual maturity of the human body. Puberty is occurring ______________ than ever before, and the entrance of young people into adult society is occurring ______________. During this in-between stage, adolescents are somewhat more prone to do things that are ______________ or illegal, but they rarely inflict serious or enduring ______________ on themselves or others. During adolescence, ______________ interest intensifies, and in some cultures, sexual activity begins. Although most people are ______________ to members of the opposite sex, some are not, and research suggests that ______________ plays a key role in determining a person's sexual orientation. As adolescents seek to develop their adult ______________, they seek increasing autonomy from their parents and become more ______________-oriented, forming single-sex cliques, followed by mixed-sex ______________; finally, they pair off as couples.

Adulthood: The Short Happy Future

Older adults show declines in working memory, episodic memory, and ______________ tasks, but they often develop strategies to ______________. Gradual physical decline begins early in adulthood and has clear psychological consequences, some of which are offset by increases in skill and ________________. Older people are more oriented toward ________________ satisfying information, which influences their basic cognitive performance, the size and structure of their ________________ networks, and their general happiness. For most people, adulthood means leaving home, getting ________________, and having ________________. People who marry are typically happier, but children and the responsibilities that parenthood entails pre-sent a significant challenge, especially for ________________.

QUICK QUIZ #1

1. The single cell that contains the chromosomes from both a sperm and an egg is called a:
   a. blastocyst.
   b. fetus.
   c. embryo.
   d. zygote.

2. A newborn chimp's brain is nearly ____________% of its adult weight; a newborn human human's brain is nearly ____________% of its adult weight.
   a. 50; 80
   b. 60; 25
   c. 60; 75
   d. 25; 50

3. Which of the following statements is evidence that a fetus can hear its mother's voice during gestation?
   a. Two-hour-old infants suck a nipple more vigorously when they hear the sound of their mother's voice than when they hear a female stranger.
   b. Newborns whose mothers had repeatedly read aloud a specific passage during pregnancy react to the passage the same way as newborns whose mothers read unfamiliar passages.
   c. A fetus kicks more at sound of the voice of a sibling than at the voice of its mother.
   d. A fetus responds to low-frequency sounds more than to high-frequency sounds.

4. Which of the following was not a stimulus involved in the Johnson et al. (1991) study testing the ability of newborns to respond to social stimuli?
   a. a blank disk
   b. a disk with scrambled facial features
   c. a disk with a regular face
   d. a disk with a monkey face

5. Which of the following is not a factor in determining the emergence of motor skills in children?
   a. a baby's incentive for reaching
   b. body weight
   c. the child's general level of activity
   d. disciplined instruction according to timetables

6. ___________ is occurring when infants apply their schemas in novel situations; ___________ is occurring when infants revise their schemas in light of new information.
   a. Accommodation; assimilation
   b. Assimilation; accommodation
   c. Assimilation; commendation
   d. Commendation; accommodation
7. According to Erik Erikson's stages of human development, what crisis do adolescents face?
   a. industry vs. inferiority
   b. intimacy vs. isolation
   c. identity vs. role confusion
   d. ego integrity vs. guilt
8. According to ___________ theory, younger adults are generally oriented toward the acquisition of information that will be useful to them later, and older people seek information that is emotionally satisfying.
   a. attachment
   b. psychoanalytic
   c. socioemotional selectivity
   d. socioeconomic transition
9. ___________ women live longer than ___________ men; both groups live longer than men and women who were ___________.
   a. Married; widowed; never married or divorced
   b. Widowed; married; divorced
   c. Married; married, never married or divorced
   d. Widowed; widowed; married

QUICK QUIZ #2

1. ___________ is the study of continuity and change across the life span.
   a. Sociology
   b. Anthropology
   c. Developmental psychology
   d. Sociobiology
2. Alcohol is a ___________, an agent that damages the process of development.
   a. carcinogen
   b. teratogen
   c. antigen
   d. pathogen
3. Infancy is the developmental stage that begins ___________ and lasts between ___________.
   a. at birth; 18 and 24 months
   b. at birth; 6 and 12 months
   c. at 12 months; 18 and 24 months
   d. at 2 years; 1 and 2 years

4. The tendency for infants to move their mouths toward any object that touches their cheek is called the:
   a. sucking reflex.
   b. Babinsky reflex.
   c. rooting reflex.
   d. tracking reflex.

5. Who of the following is considered the father of modern developmental psychology?
   a. Lev Vygotsky
   b. Jean Decety
   c. Lawrence Kohlberg
   d. Jean Piaget

6. Object permanence is the idea that:
   a. objects that move are not real.
   b. objects continue to exist even when they are not visible.
   c. words written in permanent marker describe physical objects.
   d. objects disappear when they are hidden.

7. Paul, who is 3 years old, is standing in a courtyard around the corner from Mike, who is standing on the sidewalk next to the street. When Jean asks Paul what he thinks Mike sees, he describes the courtyard instead of the street or sidewalk. What developmental concept describes this lack of understanding of another's mind?
   a. centration
   b. mental representations
   c. egocentrism
   d. narcissism

8. Across a variety of tasks, older adult brains show ____________ and young adult brains show ____________.
   a. bilateral activation; unilateral activation
   b. bilateral activation; bilateral inhibition
   c. unilateral inhibition; bilateral activation
   d. unilateral activation; unilateral inhibition

9. In general, research suggests that children ____________ their parents' happiness.
   a. increase
   b. decrease
   c. have no affect on
   d. eliminate

QUICK QUIZ #3

1. What is the order of the prenatal stages of development?
   a. germinal, embryonic, fetal
   b. germinal, fetal, embryonic
   c. fetal, embryonic, germinal
   d. zygotal, embryonic, fetal

2. Short eye openings, a flat midface, an indistinct or flat ridge under the nose, and a thin upper lip are all indicators of:
   a. trisomy 21.
   b. autism.
   c. fetal alcohol syndrome.
   d. Williams syndrome.
3. The level of detail that a newborn can see at a distance of ____________ is roughly equivalent to the level of detail that an adult can see at ____________.
   a. 6 feet; 60 feet
   b. 20 feet; 600 feet
   c. 20 feet; 60 feet
   d. 2 feet; 20 feet
4. The tendency for motor skills to emerge in sequence from the head to the feet is called the:
   a. proximodistal rule.
   b. cephalocaudal rule.
   c. anterioposterior rule.
   d. head-shoulders-knees-and-toes rule.
5. What is the order of Jean Piaget's four stages of cognitive development?
   a. preoperational, concrete operational, sensorimotor, formal operational
   b. preoperational, sensorimotor, concrete operational, formal operational
   c. sensorimotor, preoperational, concrete operational, formal operational
   d. sensorimotor, preoperational, formal operational, concrete operational
6. Childhood, the period that follows infancy, begins at about ____________ and lasts until ____________.
   a. 18 to 24 months; death
   b. 3 years; adolescence
   c. 18 to 24 months; 5 years
   d. 18 to 24 months; between 11 and 14 years
7. What two groups of children lag behind their peers in acquiring a theory of mind?
   a. autistic and deaf
   b. autistic and blind
   c. deaf and rural
   d. autistic and urban
8. The four attachment styles described by John Bowlby, Mary Ainsworth, and others occur in American infants in the following order of prevalence:
   a. secure > disorganized > ambivalent > avoidant.
   b. secure > ambivalent > avoidant > disorganized.
   c. secure > avoidant > ambivalent > disorganized.
   d. ambivalent > avoidant > secure > disorganized.
10. Research suggests that negative affect ____________ and positive affect ____________ with age.
   a. increases; increases
   b. decreases; increases
   c. increases; decreases
   d. decreases; decreases

"HEY, GUESS WHAT I LEARNED IN PSYCHOLOGY TODAY?" (AN ESSAY QUESTION)

We're guessing there's someone in your life who is interested in the quality of your educational experiences, is reasonably intelligent, but knows little about psychology. This might be your roommate, a previous teacher, your mom, or some other person you have access to and want to share your thoughts and feelings with. What would you tell that person about development? What would you tell that person about the different styles of attachment between a caregiver and an infant? In light of what you learned in this chapter, what tips might be useful to a new parent?

THINGS TO PONDER

You've been provided a lot of information in this chapter about development. When you put it all together, you may start to ponder how it all relates to other issues in this textbook. For example, you may ask yourself:

- When are drugs and alcohol most dangerous for the developing nervous system of a fetus?

  While there is no safe time to ingest drugs during pregnancy, think about the progression of the development of the nervous system, which begins around the third or fourth week and is relatively complete by six months of gestation.

  Also consider the severe pathologies that are associated with fetal alcohol syndrome, including the severely malformed brains of children whose mothers drank heavily during pregnancy.

- How does something like gaze duration tell us about cognitive development in infants?

  Remember the concept of habituation and responses to novelty that were discussed in the chapters on sensation and perception and on learning.

  Reflect on the idea that humans, as well as many other animals, have evolved to respond to new and interesting things in our environments in order to track important stimuli and stay alive.

- Why do social constructions have such an impact on moral development in adolescence?

  Consider the impact of social mores and relationships in developing personality in general.

  Look at the evidence that secondary sexual characteristics develop at different rates in different cultures and the underlying interaction of biology and social constructions.

- Why has the dogma about the determination of sexual orientation changed from being almost totally dependent on upbringing to a focus on genetics and shared environments?

  Think about the history of psychology and the fact that psychoanalytical theories dominated psychology for some time. The emphasis on parenting and parenting styles has given way to evidence that genetics and non-shared environmental influences are better predictors of sexual orientation than parenting.

  Consider the evidence for the hormonal milieu's contribution to sexual orientation as well as genetics and environmental factors.

WEB LINKS AND SUGGESTED READINGS

Alzheimer's Association: http://www.alz.org/index.asp

- An online resource on Alzheimer's disease, including news feeds, information for caregivers, conferences and scholarly publications, and fundraising.

Spock, Benjamin. (1945). *The Common Sense Book of Baby and Child Care*. New York: Simon & Shuster.

- The standard of child-care books in the 1950s. By 1998 it had sold over 50 million copies, second only to the Bible. Although many of the suggestions are out of date or irrelevant today, these suggestions provided important questions for developmental psychologists to study in the years since the book was published.

Weissbluth, Marc (1999). *Healthy Sleep Habits, Happy Child*. New York: Ballantine.

- The author, a pediatrician and father of four, addresses the often difficult task of getting a child to bed, during the day and at night. He emphasizes nap schedules and gives advice on how to deal with children of all different temperaments.

Silverstein, Shel (1964). *The Giving Tree*. New York: HarperCollins.

- The story of a boy who grows up with a tree as a friend and caregiver. The boy asks for many things from the tree and the tree happily provides for him throughout his lifetime development.

ANSWERS

Completed Chapter Overview

Prenatality: A Womb with a View

Developmental psychology studies **continuity** and **change** across the life span. The **prenatal** stage of development begins when a sperm fertilizes an egg, producing a **zygote**. The zygote, which contains **chromosomes** from both the egg and sperm, develops into an **embryo** at two weeks and then a **fetus** at eight weeks. The fetal environment has important physical and **psychological** influences on the fetus. In addition to the food a pregnant woman eats, **teratogens**, agents that impair fetal development, can affect the fetus. Some of the most common teratogens are **tobacco** and alcohol. Although the fetus cannot **see** much in the womb, it can hear sounds and become familiar with those it hears often, such as its mother's **voice**.

Infancy and Childhood: Becoming a Person

Infants have a limited range of **vision**, but they can see and remember objects that appear in their visual field. They learn to control their bodies from the top **down** and the **center** out. Infants slowly develop **theories** about how the world works. **Piaget** believed that these theories developed through **four** stages, in which children learn basic facts about the world, such as the fact that objects continue to **exist** even when they are out of sight, and the fact that objects have **enduring** properties that are not changed by superficial transformations. Children also learn that their **minds** produce representations of objects, so the objects themselves may not be as they appear, and other people may not see them the way the **child** does. Cognitive development also comes about through social interactions in which children are given **tools** for understanding that have been developed over millennia by members of their **cultures**.

At a very early age, humans develop strong emotional ties to their primary **caregivers**. The quality of these ties is determined both by the caregiver's behavior and the child's **temperament**. People get along with each other by learning and obeying **moral** principles. Children's reasoning about right and wrong is initially based on an action's **outcomes**, but as they mature, children begin to consider the actor's **intentions** as well as the extent to which the action obeys abstract moral principles. Moral **intuitions** may also be derived from one's emotional reactions to events, such as the **suffering** of others.

Adolescence: Minding the Gap

Adolescence begins with a **growth** spurt and with **puberty**, the onset of sexual maturity of the human body. Puberty is occurring **earlier** than ever before, and the entrance of young people into adult society is occurring **later**. During this in-between stage, adolescents are somewhat more prone to do things that are **risky** or illegal, but they rarely inflict serious or enduring **harm** on themselves or others. During adolescence, **sexual** interest intensifies, and in some cultures, sexual activity begins. Although most people are **attracted** to members of the opposite sex, some are not, and research suggests that **biology** plays a key role in determining a person's sexual orientation. As adolescents seek to develop their adult **identities**, they seek increasing autonomy from their parents and become more **peer**-oriented, forming single-sex cliques, followed by mixed-sex **cliques**; finally, they pair off as couples.

Adulthood: The Short Happy Future

Older adults show declines in working memory, episodic memory, and **retrieval** tasks, but they often develop strategies to **compensate**. Gradual physical decline begins early in adulthood and has clear psychological consequences, some of which are offset by increases in skill and **expertise**. Older people are more oriented toward **emotionally** satisfying information, which influences their basic cognitive performance, the size and structure of their **social** networks, and their general happiness. For most people, adulthood means leaving home, getting **married**, and having **children**. People who marry are typically happier, but children and the responsibilities that parenthood entails present a significant challenge, especially for **women**.

Quick Quiz #1

1. **D.** The single cell that contains the chromosomes from both a sperm and an egg is the zygote. The zygote begins to divide, and by about day 5 it forms a blastocyst, a collection of cells that is the stage between zygote and embryo. An embryo is the stage between weeks 2 and 8 of development, and the fetus is the stage from week 9 to birth.
2. **B.** A newborn chimp's brain is nearly 60% of its adult weight, but a newborn human human's brain is nearly 25% of its adult weight. As the size of the adult human brain increased over the course of evolution, it became necessary to have much of the brain's development occur after birth.
3. **A.** Sucking the nipple in response to the mother's voice is the only evidence presented in the text that matches the responses. The fetus does hear low-frequency sounds, but that isn't specific to a mother's voice. The other choices are altered or fabricated findings.
4. **D.** All the stimuli listed except the disk with the monkey face were used in the study examining newborns and social cues. The infants tracked the regular face longer than they did the other disks, indicating that they recognized upright faces.
5. **D.** Other factors include muscular development, and mobiles have been shown to increase the incentive to reach.
6. **B.** The processes of assimilation and accommodation were described and named by Jean Piaget, who believed that it is through these processes that infants build an understanding of the world.
7. **C.** According to Erikson, we develop a sense of self in relationship to others and to their own internal thoughts and desires in adolescence. The other choices are the crises in the latency stage (choice a) and the young adulthood stage (choice b); choice d mixes the crisis elements of two different stages.
8. **C.** Socioemotional selectivity theory holds that younger adults are generally oriented toward the acquisition of information that will be useful to them later, and older people seek information that is emotionally satisfying. Attachment has to do with the social relationships of infants. Psychoanalytic theory doesn't really address the issues of the elderly.
9. **A.** In sum, statistically speaking, the loss of a wife is always bad, but the loss of a husband is bad only if he's still alive.

Quick Quiz #2

1. **C.** Sociology and anthropology both study groups of people; developmental psychology is the study of individual behavior across the life span. Sociobiology is the study of biological changes throughout life in reference to social interaction, but doesn't necessarily include other aspects of development.
2. **B.** Carcinogens are cancer-causing agents. Alcohol is a risk factor for cancer, but not specifically a carcinogen, and its connection to cancer is not specifically related to developmental processes. Similarly, antigens and pathogens disrupt normal biological processes, but they are not specific to development.
3. **A.** Infancy begins at birth and lasts for 18 to 24 months. A great deal of motor development occurs during this stage of development.
4. **C.** The tendency for infants to move their mouths toward any object that touches their cheek is called the rooting reflex. The sucking and the Babinsky reflexes are not orienting reflexes.
5. **D.** Jean Piaget (1896–1980) is generally considered to be the father of modern developmental psychology. Lev Vygotsky was a Soviet developmental psychologist whose theories emphasized the role that social life plays in cognitive development. Jean Decety is a neurobiologist now at the University of Chicago; his interests include social cognition and empathy. Lawrence Kohlberg picked up where Piaget left off and offered a more detailed theory of the development of moral reasoning.
6. **B.** Object permanence is the idea that objects continue to exist even when they are not visible—the the opposite of the notion in choice d. Choices a and c simply play on words about movement and permanence.
7. **C.** Egocentrism is the failure to understand that the world appears differently to different observers. Paul cannot relate to Mike because he is too young to have

developed an understanding of the viewpoints of others and so falls prey to egocentrism.

8. **A.** That older adult brains show bilateral activation and young adult brains show unilateral activation may be a way for older brains to compensate for declining abilities.
9. **B.** Most studies show that parental dissatisfaction peaks around their children's teenage years then recovers somewhat when the children leave home.

Quick Quiz #3

1. **A.** The germinal stage is the 0–2 weeks from conception, followed by the embryonic stage, from 2 to 8 weeks, and then the fetal stage from 9 weeks to birth. It all begins with the zygote, but there is no "zygotal stage" as such.
2. **C.** These are all the hallmarks of the physical features associated with fetal alcohol syndrome. While some of these features are seen in people with trisomy 21 or Williams syndrome, the complete set is indicative of FAS.
3. **B.** The level of detail that a newborn can see at a distance of 20 feet is roughly equivalent to the level of detail that an adult can see at 600 feet. Despite the lack of detail, infants track moving stimuli very well.
4. **B.** The tendency for motor skills to emerge in sequence from the head to the feet is called the cephalocaudal (that is, the "head to tail") rule. The proximodistal rule is the tendency for motor skills to develop inside to outside. An anterioposterior rule (which in fact does not exist) would refer more to front-to-back development. Choice d is not a motor skills rule.
5. **C.** The child goes from using the senses primarily to interact with the world to understanding the physical properties of objects and hypothetical situations.
6. **D.** Childhood starts at the end of infancy, at 18 to 24 months, and lasts until adolescence, roughly between 11 and 14 years.
7. **A.** Blind children may also lag somewhat, but there is less evidence of a severe lag. Whether children live in a rural or urban environment is not a significant predictor of when they will acquire a theory of mind.
8. **C.** Sixty percent of American infants are securely attached. An avoidant attachment style (20%) is slightly higher than an ambivalent one (15%), and disorganized attachment (5%) is the least common.
9. **D.** Research suggests that negative affect decreases and positive affect decreases with age; negative affect decreases more than positive affect, resulting in a net increase in overall happiness.

"Hey, Guess What I Learned in Psychology Today?" (An Essay Question)

What might you tell your mom about development?

- You might start by making sure that your Mom understands that development doesn't end when childhood ends (we bet she knows this). Then you could talk about some critical point in your development that would illustrate an early stage of development—you could ask her, "Do you remember how old I was when playing peek-a-boo stopped being completely fascinating to me?" Her reminiscence would lead to discussion of other similar behaviors—a good lead into Piaget's four stages of cognitive development. You could talk about the processes that allowed you to proceed through those stages, compare Piaget's ideas to Vygotsky's ideas, and then venture into Erikson's eight stages of human development. Erikson's theories provide great places to jump off and talk about the issues facing teenagers, young adults, and older adults.
- What is not to love, pardon the pun, about Harry Harlow's work? Ask your mom if she thinks providing food or affection would be more important to a baby monkey. Of course, the monkey wouldn't survive without food, but posing the question is a good way to introduce Harlow's finding that his monkeys, when given a choice, spent much more time with the cuddly cloth surrogate than with the cold, wire, feeding surrogate. This result, in conjunction with Konrad Lorenz's studies of imprinting with geese and ducks, led John Bowlby and Mary Ainsworth to study the types of attachments that develop between infants and their primary caregivers. Then you can describe Ainsworth's strange situation and how that led to the categorization of infants into those with secure,

avoidant, ambivalent, or disorganized attachment to their caregiver. You can talk about the dynamics of attachment and the likelihood that this early social relationship will affect the personality of the infant in adulthood, including social relationships with others.

- Pick a few of the key findings that you think would be useful for new parents to know and turn them into tips. For example, research has shown that a fetus recognizes the mother's voice and that deep sounds penetrate to the womb. You could advise a mother-to-be to read her favorite story aloud, and if she is going to play music for the baby, bass solos will be a lot easier for him or her to hear than the jazz flute. Studies have shown that the best predictor of language development is the number of words that a young child hears every day. You could advise new parents to point at objects and name them, even if the baby doesn't seem to be paying attention. But watch your language! If you don't want the little tyke's first word to be profane, start using terms like "oh, marshmallows" when you get cut off by that careless motorist.

11

Personality

THE BIG PICTURE

Most dreaded intro to a conversation: "I had the weirdest dream last night." Dreaded because nothing on earth will stop the dreamer from telling you about it. (Interesting, though, how many of us do this, while—unless professionally involved—we're bored out of our wits by other people's dreams.)

At any rate, Ramon speaks the dread remark to his friend Alan. Alan is a nice guy and Ramon's good friend, so he obliges: "Really? What was it about?" And Ramon tells him: "I was late to my speech class where I was supposed to give the final speech of the semester, which counted as fifty percent of my grade, when I realized that I was running across the middle of campus naked. I couldn't go back to get my clothes, so I went to give the speech naked and everyone laughed at me as soon as I walked to the front of the room." Alan says that this all sounds like a typical fear or anxiety dream, which makes sense because Ramon does have a big presentation due soon and he is something of an introvert. "This is where it gets weird, though," Ramon continues. "I nail the speech anyway. Then, as the professor walks back to the front of the room, her face morphs into my mom. She's really mad and whacks me on the knuckles with a ruler." Alan's a little more interested now—he sees how the dream might connect with things they've discussed in their psychology class. He tells his friend, "Ramon, your speech performance is a symbol wish fulfillment or one resolution of the person–situation controversy, depending on the theory you subscribe to, and the presence of your judging mother could be a whole host of issues that you haven't resolved from childhood. Freud might say that you're fixated and Rogers would say that you might have lacked unconditional positive regard as a child. Your mom and your professor and a nun that whacked you on the knuckles in third grade all represent authorities in your life." Ramon blinks, but he can see that Alan has been paying close attention to the coursework on personality and nods in agreement. Then he says, "In the end, I turn into a pink Tyrannosaurus rex and eat my mom-professor." Alan stares at him blankly for a second and replies, "Um . . . I've got nothing."

Chapter 11 defines personality, explains how researchers have attempted to measure it, and discusses the theories that have tried to account for how it develops in each one of us. Because personality is essentially what we all carry around with us at all times, it is easy to see how it affects other aspects of psychology. Just as your brain is responsible for your behavior (Chapter 3), it is responsible for a great deal of your personality. You have seen that your personal experiences (Chapters 5 and 6) and biases can change the way you perceive some of the stimuli that you sense (Chapter 4). Your personal thoughts and the way that you express them (Chapter 7) make up your self-perception and the way that others perceive your personality. Freud and his contemporaries believed that much of what determines your adult personality is based on things outside of your conscious mind (Chapter 8) and on the resolution of conflicts in early childhood (Chapter 10). You will see that personality extremes and pathologies contribute to psychological disorders (Chapters 12 and 13), and that much of what determines whether someone has a personality disorder is the way that person interacts, or fails to interact, with other people (Chapter 15).

Every person on the planet is unique, even if you share 100% of your DNA with your identical twin and the two of you were reared in essentially the same environment. From the day you were born, arguably from the day you were conceived, you began to have different experiences from anyone else in the world. The way that you react to each situation, the way your parents talk to you, the relationships that you forge, the schools you attend, even the food that you eat, combine to make up the individual personality that is you. (Even if you do turn out to be a pink dinosaur!)

CHAPTER OBJECTIVES

After studying this chapter, you should be able to:

1. Define *personality*, noting how it involves thought, feeling, and behavior.
2. Explain the difference between what people are like and why people are the way they are.
3. Compare *self-report* measures of personality and *projective* measures of personality, note some strengths and weaknesses of both approaches, and provide examples of each type of personality measure.
4. Describe the *trait* approach to studying personality, and discuss some of the questions that arose during the search for core traits.
5. List the *Big Five* personality dimensions, and provide examples of each.
6. Discuss the evidence regarding the heritability of personality traits, noting the contributions of both genes and environment to the development of personality traits.
7. Describe the psychodynamic structure of the mind, explaining the functions and properties of the *id, ego,* and *superego.*
8. Compare the *pleasure principle* and the *reality principle,* and note how each helps guide behavior according to the psychodynamic approach.
9. Describe seven *defense mechanisms,* provide an example of each, and explain how each helps reduce anxiety for an individual.
10. Describe the five stages of psychosexual development, provide an example of the conflicts that occur during each stage, and discuss how fixation is a possibility at each stage.
11. Explain the *Oedipus conflict,* and note how it played a central role in the psychodynamic view of personality.
12. Explain the basic approach to personality adopted by the humanist and existential psychologists.
13. Explain the basic tenets of the *social-cognitive approach* to personality and discuss how the notions of *person–situation controversy,* personal constructs, and locus of control illustrate aspects of this general approach.
14. Describe how the *self-concept* is organized.
15. List some sources of *self-esteem,* and note why self-esteem is not synonymous with self-concept.
16. Define the *self-serving bias,* and draw parallels between it and *narcissism.*

CHAPTER OVERVIEW

Use the terms below to fill in the following exercises. Terms may not be used more than once. The answers can be found at the end of this chapter.

acceptance	environmental	personality
angst	episodic	philosophical
anxiety	esteem	potentials
arousability	evaluation	projective
behaving	extraversion	psychosexual
beliefs	feedback	reality
better	feeling	Rorschach
biological	fixated	self-actualization
concept	Freud	self-report
conscientiousness	genetics	sexual
consistency	goals	situations
consistent	inventories	standards
construct	measure	status
core	mind	superego
defense	mortality	thinking
describe	narcissism	trait
dimensions	neuroticism	want

Personality: What It Is and How It Is Measured

Personality is a person's characteristic style of ______________, ______________, and ______________. Personality psychologists seek ways to ______________, explain and ______________ these different characteristic styles. Personality ______________, such as the MMPI and other ______________ questionnaires, can be used to assess people's views of themselves and their own personality characteristics. ______________ techniques, such as the ______________ Test and the Thematic Apperception Test, can be used to assess aspects of people's personalities of which they may be unaware.

The Trait Approach: Identifying Patterns of Behavior

The trait approach tries to identify personality ______________ that can be used to characterize individual behavior. Researchers have attempted to refine the gigantic array of things that we do, think, and feel into some ______________ personality dimensions. Many personality psychologists currently focus on the Big Five personality factors: ______________, agreeableness, ______________, openness to experience, and ______________. The emphasis in these theories is on broad personality dispositions that are relatively ______________ across situations. Trait psychologists often look to ______________ factors to explain the existence of traits. Behavioral ______________ research generally supports the biological underpinning of traits. Some propose that traits arise from neuropsychological factors, such as the ________________ of the cortex.

The Psychodynamic Approach: Forces That Lie Beneath Awareness

________________ believed that personality results from a complex interplay of biology and ________________ experience. The psychodynamic approach sees the ________________ as consisting of the interacting systems of id, ego, and ________________, which are aimed at satisfying our drives while dealing with ________________ and our internalized standards of conduct. Freud explained personality in terms of the ________________ and aggressive forces that drive us, our characteristic ways of using ________________ mechanisms to deal with ________________, and the degree to which we are able to move through a series of developmental ________________ stages relatively unhindered. Some people can become ________________ at a specific developmental stage, which then shapes their adult ________________.

The Humanistic–Existential Approach: Personality as Choice

The humanistic–existential approach to personality grew out of ________________ traditions that are very much at odds with most of the assumptions of the ________________ and psychoanalytic approaches. Humanists see personality as directed by an inherent striving toward ________________ and the development of our unique human ________________. Existentialists focus on ________________ and dread, and the defensive response people often have to these experiences.

The Social-Cognitive Approach: Personalities in Situations

Behavior is determined not only by personality but also by how we respond to the ________________ we encounter. The social-cognitive approach describes the ________________ of behavior observed in particular situations. Kelly's personal ________________ theory suggests that situations and persons mean different things to different people. Core elements of personality involve ________________ and expectancies about the likelihood of goal attainment. If you are trying to negotiate the world, the social-cognitive approach emphasizes how you see things and what you ________________ in each situation.

The Self: Personality in the Mirror

The human capacity for self-reflection allows us to form a self-________________ and develop a characteristic level of self-________________. The content of the self-concept ranges from ________________ memories of behavior and self-narratives to specific ________________ about personality traits. Our self esteem is influenced by ________________ about the self that is filtered by processes of self-________________. Sources of self-esteem also include secure ________________ from others as well as evaluations from comparing against ________________. Theories have attempted to explain the positive feelings associated with positive self-evaluations, including locating these feelings in perceptions of ________________, or belonging, or of being protected against ________________. Most people see themselves as ________________ than average. ________________ is the trait of excessive high self-esteem.

QUICK QUIZ #1

1. ____________ is an individual's characteristic style of behaving, thinking, and feeling.
   a. A trait
   b. Personality
   c. Humanism
   d. Dynamism
2. "MMPI" stands for:
   a. Missouri Multiphasic Personality Inventory.
   b. Minnesota Managerial Personality Inventory.
   c. Massachusetts Multiphasic Personality Identifier.
   d. Minnesota Multiphasic Personality Inventory.
3. The main weakness of projective tests is that:
   a. they are difficult to administer:
   b. the results are subjective and interpretations vary wildly.
   c. they produce nearly the same results every time they are administered.
   d. nobody really wants to project themselves into the future.
4. Which one of the following is NOT one of the traits in the Big Five factor model of personality?
   a. conscientiousness
   b. extraversion
   c. gender identity
   d. neuroticism
5. Studies of identical twins reared apart suggest that ____________ factors are more predictive of differences in personalities than ____________ factors.
   a. nonshared environmental; shared environmental
   b. shared interuterine; shared environmental
   c. shared educational; shared relational
   d. shared environmental; nonshared environmental
6. Which structure of the mind would have the motto, "I gotta have it, and I gotta have it now!"
   a. superego
   b. ego
   c. id
   d. alter ego
7. Sigmund Freud believed that the default defense mechanism is:
   a. regression.
   b. sublimation.
   c. reaction formation.
   d. repression.

8. Julie was told in her job evaluation that she is timid in meetings and passive with clients. However, she knows herself to be aggressive, and her friends and colleagues would agree. Now she goes out of her way to interrupt at meetings and hound clients. Julie is exhibiting what psychological tendency?
   a. narcissism
   b. high self-esteem
   c. sadism
   d. self-verification
9. Which of the following is NOT an example of the name-letter effect?
   a. Florence lives in Key West, Florida.
   b. Dennis has a practice in child dentistry.
   c. Laura Lane bought a house at 1522 Lazy Lane.
   d. Robert picked "B" as his favorite letter of the alphabet.

QUICK QUIZ #2

1. Explanations of personality differences are concerned with ___________ and ___________.
   a. prior events; anticipated events
   b. current events; anticipated events
   c. prior events; current events
   d. motivations; emotions
2. ___________ consist of a standard series of ambiguous stimuli designed to elicit unique responses that reveal inner aspects of an individual's personality.
   a. Self-reports
   b. Theatre techniques
   c. Projective techniques
   d. Existential exercises
3. Jenny is following a strict diet that doesn't allow processed sugar, but she can't resist taking a doughnut from a tray as she passes it. Now she feels guilty about cheating. Her feeling of guilt is a result of what structure of the mind?
   a. superego
   b. id
   c. ego
   d. alter ego
4. The stage in which the Oedipus conflict occurs is the:
   a. oral stage.
   b. anal stage.
   c. phallic stage.
   d. genital stage.
5. Our explicit knowledge of our own behaviors, traits, and other personal characteristics is called our:
   a. self-esteem.
   b. self-verification.
   c. self-loathing.
   d. self-concept.

6. ____________ is a grandiose view of the self, combined with a tendency to seek admiration from and exploit others.
   a. Narcissistic personality disorder
   b. Narcissism
   c. Self-serving bias
   d. Implicit egotism

QUICK QUIZ #3

1. The MMPI is classified as what type of personality test?
   a. projective
   b. apperception
   c. self-report
   d. inkblot
2. Allport and Odbert (1936) catalogued more than ____________ words in an English-language dictionary that could be used to describe personality traits.
   a. 1,000
   b. 8,000
   c. 18,000
   d. 38,000
3. What are the two sets of anchors for the trait dimensions in Hans Eysenck's model of personality traits?
   a. emotional and stable; introverted and extraverted
   b. emotional and stable; agreeable and uncooperative
   c. conscientious and careless; introverted and extraverted
   d. neurotic and secure; introverted and extraverted
4. Which of the following pairs is the most likely to have the highest degree of similarity between their personalities?
   a. nontwin brothers
   b. a father and his son
   c. fraternal twin sisters
   d. monozygotic twin sisters
5. Hans Eysenck proposed that the ____________ of the brain of extraverts is not easily stimulated.
   a. amygdala
   b. hippocampus
   c. hypothalamus
   d. reticular formation
6. The ____________ and ____________ do not operate according to the reality principle.
   a. id; ego
   b. id; superego
   c. ego; superego
   d. ego; preconscious

7. Jaime made a marketing pitch and won a big contract; then he dented a new Mercedes as he pulled out of the garage. Jaime tells his girlfriend: "I was amazing, but some jerk parked over the line in the garage and now I have to deal with a dent in his ridiculous oversize car." This is an example of what psychological concept?
   a. idiocy
   b. self-serving bias
   c. arrogance
   d. external refocusing

"HEY, GUESS WHAT I LEARNED IN PSYCHOLOGY TODAY?" (AN ESSAY QUESTION)

We're guessing there's someone in your life who is interested in the quality of your educational experiences, is reasonably intelligent, but knows little about psychology. This might be your roommate, a previous teacher, your mom, or some other person you have access to and want to share your thoughts and feelings with. What would you tell that person about personality? What would you tell that person about the different approaches to studying and defining personality?

THINGS TO PONDER

You've been provided a lot of information in this chapter about personality. When you put it all together, you may start to ponder how it all relates to other issues in this textbook. For example, you may ask yourself:

- What part of each person's personality is determined by genes?

  Recall that the only way of measuring heritability is by determining the likelihood of the appearance of a trait through population averages or twin studies.

  Also consider the findings indicating that the environmental component that contributes to personality comes from nonshared factors.

- Why can't you choose to change your traits?

  Remember that a trait is stable and enduring over a lifetime. If you can change some aspect of your personality, it's unlikely that that aspect is in fact a trait.

  Reflect on the ideas presented in the chapter on the social-cognitive approach to personality, and how adaptation to situations interacts with decision making (Chapter 7).

- Why has the dogma about what determines sexual orientation changed from being almost purely dependent on upbringing to a focus on genetics and shared environments?

Think about the history of psychology and the fact that psychoanalytical theories dominated psychology for some time. The emphasis on parenting and parenting styles has given way to evidence that genetics and nonshared environmental influences are better predictors of sexual orientation than parenting.

Consider the evidence for the hormonal milieu's contribution to sexual orientation as well as genetics and other environmental factors.

WEB LINKS AND SUGGESTED READINGS

Humanmetrics: Jung Typology Test—http://www.humanmetrics.com/cgi-win/JTypes2.asp

- Essentially an abbreviated version of the Myers-Briggs Type Indicator, which produces four-letter combinations that indicate personality traits on four different dimensions.

Robert J. Harvey, Job Analysis and Personality Research—http://harvey.psyc.vt.edu/Personality/resources.html

- Information about the Big Five, including PDFs of several personality inventories.

Theorists and Topics in Personality Psychology—http://personalitypedagogy.arcadia.edu/pmwiki/pmwiki.php?n=Topics.Index

- A wiki-style index of many of the major personality theorists and links to information about them.

Bandura, A. (1997). *Self-Efficacy: The Exercise of Control*. New York: W. H. Freeman.

- A presentation of Alfred Bandura's theory that those with high self-efficacy expectancies, or the belief that one can achieve what one sets out to do, are healthier, more effective, and generally more successful than those with low self-efficacy expectancies.

Freud, S. (1899). *The Interpretation of Dreams (Die Traumdeutung)*. Leipzig and Vienna: Franz Deuticke.

- Freud's infamous publication—now available in English in many editions, hardcover and paperback—that launched the theory of dream analysis that he famously described as "the royal road to the understanding of unconscious mental processes."

ANSWERS

Chapter Overview

Personality: What It Is and How It Is Measured

Personality is a person's characteristic style of **behaving**, **thinking**, and **feeling**. Personality psychologists seek ways to **describe**, explain and **measure** these different characteristic styles. Personality **inventories**, such as the MMPI and other **self-report** questionnaires, can be used to assess people's views of themselves and their own personality characteristics. **Projective** techniques, such as the **Rorschach** Test and the Thematic Apperception Test, can be used to assess aspects of people's personalities of which they may be unaware.

The Trait Approach: Identifying Patterns of Behavior

The trait approach tries to identify personality **dimensions** that can be used to characterize individual behavior. Researchers have attempted to refine the gigantic array of things that we do, think, and feel into some **core** personality dimensions. Many personality psychologists currently focus on the Big Five personality factors: **conscientiousness**, agreeableness, **neuroticism**, openness to experience, and **extraversion**. The emphasis in these theories is on broad personality dispositions that are relatively **consistent** across situations. Trait psychologists often look to **biological** factors to explain the existence of traits. Behavioral **genetics** research generally supports the biological underpinning of traits. Some propose that traits arise from neuropsychological factors, such as the **arousability** of the cortex.

The Psychodynamic Approach: Forces That Lie Beneath Awareness

Freud believed that personality results from a complex interplay of biology and **environmental** experience. The psychodynamic approach sees the **mind** as consisting of the interacting systems of id, ego, and **superego**, which are aimed at satisfying our drives while dealing with **reality** and our internalized standards of conduct. Freud explained personality in terms of the **sexual** and aggressive forces that drive us, our characteristic ways of using **defense** mechanisms to deal with **anxiety**, and the degree to which we are able to move through a series of developmental **psychosexual** stages relatively unhindered. Some people can become **fixated** at a specific developmental stage, which then shapes their adult **personality**.

The Humanistic–Existential Approach: Personality as Choice

The humanistic–existential approach to personality grew out of **philosophical** traditions that are very much at odds with most of the assumptions of the **trait** and psychoanalytic approaches. Humanists see personality as directed by an inherent striving toward **self-actualization** and the development of our unique human **potentials**. Existentialists focus on **angst** and dread, and the defensive response people often have to these experiences.

The Social-Cognitive Approach: Personalities in Situations

Behavior is determined not only by personality but also by how we respond to the **situations** we encounter. The social-cognitive approach describes the **consistency** of behavior observed in particular situations. Kelly's personal **construct** theory suggests that situations and persons mean different things to different people. Core elements of personality involve **goals** and expectancies about the likelihood of goal attainment. If you are trying to negotiate the world, the social-cognitive approach emphasizes how you see things and what you **want** in each situation.

The Self: Personality in the Mirror

The human capacity for self-reflection allows us to form a self-**concept** and develop a characteristic level of self-**esteem**. The content of the self-concept ranges from **episodic** memories of behavior and self-narratives to specific **beliefs** about personality traits. Our self-esteem is influenced by **feedback** about the self that is filtered by processes of self-**evaluation**. Sources of self-esteem also include secure **acceptance** from others as well as evaluations from comparing against **standards**. Theories have attempted to explain the positive feelings associated with positive self-evaluations, including locating these feelings in perceptions of **status**, or belonging, or of being protected against **mortality**. Most people see themselves as **better** than average. **Narcissism** is the trait of excessive high self-esteem.

Quick Quiz #1

1. **B.** Traits are part of personality, but they do not account for the entirety of the definition. Humanism, in psychology, is a theory of personality. The term "dynamism" has no particular psychological significance.
2. **D.** The Minnesota Multiphasic Personality Inventory is a questionnaire on which the test taker answers "true," "false," or "cannot say" to some 500 self-descriptive statements. The test yields amazingly consistent results and detects those who try to cheat or manipulate the test.
3. **B.** Although projective test results are subjective and their interpretations vary wildly, they are not particularly difficult to administer, however, the results can be confusing and the results with a single participant can vary from session to session.
4. **C.** Although gender identity is not one of the Big Five, many psychologists argue that sexuality and other components of personality should be added as additional factors.
5. **A.** Intrauterine and shared experiences after birth don't seem to contribute to personality differences as much as do nonshared experiences.
6. **C.** The id requires immediate gratification; that is, it operates on the pleasure principle.
7. **D.** Freud believed that motivated forgetting, or repression, pushes issues we don't want to deal with into the unconscious mind.
8. **D.** Julie is responding to the judgment of passivity by overcompensating to confirm her self-concept of being aggressive. Her actions could fit with sadism, narcissism, or high self-esteem, but her behavior in the given situation is best described by the concept of self-verification.
9. **D.** The first three choices are clear examples of the name-letter effect, that is, choices to live or work in places or professions that begin with the same letter as one's name. Choice d is not an example of the effect—unless Robert goes by "Bob."

Quick Quiz #2

1. **A.** Anticipated events are examined to determine motivations; the past, including the influence of genetics, is important in the shaping of personality.
2. **C.** Projective techniques are preferable to self-report tests when the aim is to access parts of the personality that the participant may not want to reveal.
3. **A.** Jenny feels guilty because her superego wants to impose the strict rule of her diet. Her id battles for the doughnut and wins, but her guilt results from her breaking the rules of the superego.
4. **C.** In the phallic stage, at 3 to 5 years of age, when the Oedipus conflict occurs, a boy focuses his desire toward his mother and sees his father as competition. He must then repress this desire and identify with his father to avoid fixation in this stage.
5. **D.** Self-esteem refers to feelings, as opposed to knowledge, about the self. Self-loathing and self-verifications are processes, not knowledge bases.
6. **B.** A personality disorder is not a trait, but a disruption of daily living. Although narcissists exhibit self-serving bias and implicit egotism, these are not traits but rather the effects of traits.

Quick Quiz #3

1. **C.** The MMPI is a self-report test of personality; it requires participants to respond to some 500 self-descriptive questions, labeling them "true," "false," or "cannot say." The other choices are all types of projective tests.
2. **C.** The trick, of course, was to figure out which words were the most important.
3. **A.** The other choices are different components of the Big Five factor model.
4. **D.** Monozygotic twins have all their genes in common. A parent and child, siblings, and fraternal twins have only 50% of their same genetic material in common.

5. **D.** The reticular formation is the part of the brain that is responsible for regulating alertness and arousal. Eysenck assumed that the reticular formation of extraverts is not easily stimulated, and also the reverse—that the reticular formation *is* easily stimulated in introverts.
6. **B.** The reality principle governs the ego, which tries to regulate desire for gratification by imposing real-world rules.
7. **B.** Jaime's bias toward emphasizing his success and downplaying his failure is self-serving. He may in fact also be arrogant or even a little dim, but those are not the best explanations for the effect in this situation.

"Hey, Guess What I Learned In Psychology Today?" (An Essay Question)

What might you tell your mom about personality?

- You might start by posing the following question: "Do you think that the way you raised me was crucial to the kind of person that I turned out to be?" Most parents assume that they had quite an impact on the adult personality of their child. Some parents might bring up the question of genetics versus environment, saying that they influenced you in two ways: by giving you half your genes and by trying to guide your behavior and instill a sense of right and wrong. From this point, you could discuss how different theories regard the importance of childhood experiences in influencing an individual's personality.
- Different approaches arose from different questions about personality and the various dogmas of different periods in the history of psychology. You could group the different theories on the basis of common features, or emphasize what distinguishes them. Which theories assume that your personality is fixed, or determined (psychoanalytic and trait approached), versus those that are flexible, or based on choices (humanistic and social-cognitive approaches)? You could establish which theories have a more positive outlook on life (for example, the humanistic) versus those that have a negative outlook (the psychoanalytic and existential). This provides an introduction to talking about the many theories that exist and the possibilities for more that may be better at explaining all facets of personality.

12

Psychological Disorders

THE BIG PICTURE

Gary is a manager at a top-ten marketing firm. Intelligent and hardworking, he can't understand why he has been passed over for promotion twice in the last 5 years. Gary has handled big accounts and most of his campaigns have been successful. The few that have not gone well appear to be the result of Gary's failure to get along with his team. Gary works hard himself and he often asks for tremendous—some feel outrageous—amounts of work from his designers and writers. If they don't meet his expectations, he chastises and belittles them. When management asks what has gone wrong with a project, Gary blames his team and says he doesn't understand why they can't follow his effective plan. He also has conflicts with his superiors; he has told his divisional manager more than once that he could do the job better than she does, and he doesn't understand why his marketing genius isn't being recognized. Gary's subordinates must endure his haughty tone and his often expressed fantasies of becoming the firm's CEO. If others don't agree with his goals he quickly abandons the conversation or yells at them for being jealous. This is the third marketing firm Gary has worked for, and in fact his job at this one is about to come to an end (he doesn't know it yet).

Gary has been dating Susan, a telemarketer and part-time model, for about 2 weeks. She constantly tells Gary how smart he is and how unfair it is that he is being treated so poorly. Gary is her eighth boyfriend this year. She can't understand why her relationships don't last more than a month or two (it is always the man who leaves). She spends all her time with each new man and follows his advice in many areas. She is devastated by each breakup and often misses work for several days afterward. She returns to work more for the social support it offers than for the salary. Although she is quite competent, she finds it difficult to hold a job. The fact that Gary and Susan both require excessive praise and reassurance will most likely doom their relationship.

Is there something seriously wrong with these two people or are they just difficult personalities? Is there a disorder described in the *DSM-IV-TR* that might fit each of them? Gary definitely has an inflated sense of self-importance, is absorbed by his fantasies of success, and exaggerates his accomplishments at the expense of others. Given that these behaviors are disrupting his work and his relationships, he might have narcissistic personality disorder. Susan is submissive and requires excessive approval, reassurance, and advice. Her clinging style in relationships, lack of self-confidence, and inability to be alone, combined with her sensitivity to breakups, suggest someone with dependent personality disorder. Again, her behaviors of dependence are interfering with her ability to work and have relationships. What is the difference between someone who has narcissistic traits and someone with narcissistic personality disorder? What is the difference between someone who is needy and someone with dependent personality disorder? Although the answers are not simple, when these personality features disrupt daily living, they can be classified as disorders. The text discusses these controversial personality disorders and notes that critics of these classifications question their existence as disorders altogether, or think that they may be better understood as extreme values of trait dimensions. Chapter 12 defines what many psychologists consider to be abnormal behavior, describes the classification of the different kinds of psychological disorders, and discusses the ways that clinicians identify and diagnose them.

The issues considered in this chapter are often the applications of concepts that are addressed in other parts of the text. To some degree, many of the psychological disorders described have a genetic or biological component (Chapter 3), such as a decreased level of serotonin that contributes to major depression. People with schizophrenia or schizotypal personality disorder may experience hallucinations or other distortions in perception (Chapter 4) and language (Chapter 7), such as disorganized speech. Those with dissociative amnesia and dissociative fugue definitely have impaired memory (Chapter 5). Many of the disorders can affect one's motivation (Chapter 9), one's perception of one's level of intelligence (Chapter 7), and one's ability to engage in suitable social relationships (Chapter 15). Many of the disorders have a developmental component (Chapter 10), in that some disorders are more common early in life and others are more prevalent later in adulthood. Psychological disorders often contribute to a decline in physical health (Chapter 14), whether as a direct result of the disorder or of its accompanying stressors.

It is the goal of psychologists everywhere to apply scientific findings to identify the mechanisms that contribute to normal behavior and abnormal behavior in hope of finding ways to help those who suffer from psychological disorders. Although the mind is an amazing thing, it occasionally has bugs. Psychological disorders are often the result of some of the most extreme versions of those mindbugs.

CHAPTER OBJECTIVES

After studying this chapter, you should be able to:

1. Describe some of the problems associated with defining abnormality, and discuss why a *medical model* of psychological abnormalities was eventually adopted.
2. Describe how the *Diagnostic and Statistical Manual* (*DSM-IV-TR*) is used to diagnose and classify mental disorders.
3. Explain how the *diathesis–stress model* contributes to our overall understanding of the classification and causes of psychological disorders.
4. Describe the central features of *anxiety disorders*, and describe the main differences between *generalized anxiety disorder*, *phobic disorders*, *panic disorder*, and *obsessive-compulsive disorder*.
5. Contrast *specific phobias* with *social phobia*, and comment on how *preparedness theory* might apply to phobic disorders.
6. Describe the central features of *dissociative disorders*, and note the main differences between *dissociative identity disorder*, *dissociative amnesia*, and *dissociative fugue*.
7. Describe the central features of *mood disorders*, and note the main differences between depression and bipolar disorder.
8. Compare some varieties of depression, such as *major depressive disorder*, *dysthymia*, *double depression*, *seasonal affective disorder*, and postpartum depression.
9. Summarize the research evidence that implicates biological factors in depression and *bipolar disorder*.
10. Summarize the research evidence that implicates psychological factors in depression and bipolar disorder.
11. Explain the central features of *schizophrenia*, and describe the main differences between the subtypes of schizophrenia.
12. Describe five symptoms of schizophrenia, and provide an example of each.
13. Discuss research evidence for the role of biological factors in schizophrenia, describing evidence from genetics, prenatal factors, biochemical factors, and neuroanatomy.

14. Describe the central features of *personality disorders,* and describe the main differences between the three clusters of personality disorders.
15. Describe the features of *antisocial personality disorder.*

CHAPTER OVERVIEW

Use the terms below to fill in the following exercises. Terms may not be used more than once. The answers can be found at the end of this chapter.

abnormal	environmental	moderate
agoraphobic	extreme	moral
amnesia	family	motivational
antisocial	fragmented	negative
attitudes	fugue	neurotransmitter
biological	global	nomination
brain	gray	obsessions
cause	hallucinations	overdiagnosed
chronic	high	panic
classification	home	paranoid
communication	hospitalizations	phobic
comorbidity	humiliation	predominant
compulsions	identity	prepared
dangerous	inflexible	rejection
detachment	inhibited	relating
diathesis–stress	insight	stable
disorders	internal	stigma
disorganized	irrational	stressful
dopamine	irritable	suicidal
DSM-IV-TR	label	swings
dysfunction	lithium	twice
dysthymia	mania	unipolar
eccentric	medical	weeks
emotion	memory	withdrawal

Identifying Psychological Disorders: What Is Abnormal?

The investigation of ________________ behavior not only enhances our understanding of the causes and treatments of mental ________________ but also offers insight about normal psychological functioning. Studies of psychological problems depend on the reliable identification and ________________ of mental disorders. Abnormal psychology follows a ________________ model in which symptoms are understood to indicate an underlying disorder. Psychologists and psychiatrists use the ________________ to diagnose disorders. The classification system includes a ________________ assessment of functioning and several categories of disorders. A mental disorder is defined as occurring when someone experiences disturbances of thought, ________________, or behavior that produce distress or impairment and that arise from ________________ sources. Mental disorders are best understood from a perspective that considers a combination of influences, including ________________, psychological, and ________________ factors. ________________ of disorders is common, that is, people with more than one diagnosable disorder frequently also have another. The ________________ model proposes that it is possible to possess a predisposition for a mental disorder that remains unexpressed until it is triggered by stress. It is an oversimplification to assume that the intervention that cures a disorder defines the ________________ of the disorder. When a mental disorder is diagnosed, the ________________ can be difficult to overcome because of the social ________________ that often accompanies that diagnosis.

Anxiety Disorders: When Fears Take Over

Anxiety disorders involve ________________ fears and worries that undermine well-being and result in ________________. The anxiety may be ________________, as in generalized anxiety disorder (GAD), or it may be tied to a specific object or situation, as in the ________________ disorders. Phobias typically involve stimuli that humans are evolutionarily ________________ to find threatening. People who experience ________________ disorder experience a sudden and intense attack of anxiety that is terrifying. Those who experience frequent panic attacks can gradually become ________________ and stay home for long periods of time for fear of public ________________. People with obsessive-compulsive disorder (OCD) experience recurring, anxiety-provoking thoughts, or ________________, that compel them to engage in ritualistic, irrational behaviors, or ________________. Overall, the anxiety disorders show a ________________ level of heritability.

Dissociative Disorders: Going to Pieces

The dissociative disorders involve severely ________________ cognitive processes that produce significant disruptions in ________________, awareness, or personality. People with dissociative ________________ disorder shift between two or more identities that are distinct from each other in their personal memories, behavioral characteristics, and ________________. Some therapists believe that DID is ________________ because of widespread media attention. Psychodynamic theorists speculate that DID arises when psychological ________________ is used as a means of coping with trauma, and a fractioning of integrated psychological functions results. Dissociative ________________ and dissociative ________________ involve significant memory loss that is not the result of normal forgetting and cannot be attributed to ________________ injury, drugs, or another mental disorder. This memory loss is often associated with ________________ life circumstances. People with dissociative fugue leave ________________ abruptly and assume a new identity.

Mood Disorders: At the Mercy of Emotions

The mood disorders are mental disorders in which the ________________ feature is a disturbance in mood. Major depression, or ________________ depression, is characterized by a severely depressed mood lasting at least 2 ________________, with symptoms that include excessive self-criticism, guilt, difficulty concentrating, ________________ thoughts, disturbances of sleep and appetite, and lethargy. Women are ________________ as likely to be diagnosed with depression than men. ________________ is a less severe form of depression that persists for at least 2 years. Depression shows a moderate level of heritability and is likely to involve ________________ imbalances. Patterns of ________________ thinking may also contribute to depression, such as the tendency to explain personal failures by attributing them to internal, ________________, and global causes. Depression-prone people may behave in ways that lead to social ________________ that serves to confirm a sense of low self-worth.

Bipolar disorder is an unstable emotional condition involving extreme mood ________________ of depression and ________________. The manic phase is characterized by periods of abnormally elevated or ________________ mood, lasting at least 1 week. Bipolar disorder has a ________________ rate of heritability. Stress and ________________ problems may also contribute to the onset and maintenance of the disorder. Some believe that norepinephrine and serotonin imbalances contribute to the disorder, but that does not explain why ________________ is effective as a drug treatment.

Schizophrenia: Losing the Grasp on Reality

Schizophrenia is a profound disorder involving ________________, delusions, disorganized thoughts, behavior, and speech, and emotional and social ________________. The ________________ and social deficits are schizophrenia's negative symptoms. Five subtypes of schizophrenia have been identified: ________________, catatonic, ________________, undifferentiated, and residual. Although schizophrenia affects approximately 1% of the U.S. population, it accounts for a disproportionate number of psychiatric ________________. Drugs that reduce the availability of ________________ sometimes reduce the positive symptoms of schizophrenia. Neuroimaging studies have shown that progressive loss of ________________ matter is a common feature of the progression of the disease. There is an increased risk of developing schizophrenia or experiencing a relapse in someone whose family has poor ________________ patterns and relationships.

Personality Disorders: Going to Extremes

Personality disorders are deeply ingrained, ________________ patterns of thinking, feeling, and ________________ to others, or controlling impulses that cause distress or impaired functioning. There are three clusters of personality disorders: odd/________________, dramatic/erratic, and anxious/________________. The classification, and even existence, of these disorders is controversial because they may just be ________________ versions of normal personality and they are often comorbid with other disorders. People with personality disorders often lack ________________ into their own disorders, making self-report difficult or useless, but peer ________________ procedures are relatively successful. Antisocial personality disorder (APD) is associated with a lack of ________________ emotions. Those with APD are usually manipulative, ________________, and reckless, often hurting others and sometimes hurting themselves. A disproportionate number of prison inmates have ________________ personality disorder.

QUICK QUIZ #1

1. Approximately __________ of the U.S. population will develop some type of mental disorder during the course of their lives.
   a. 2%
   b. 15%
   c. 40%
   d. 65%
2. Which of the following is NOT a key element that must be present for a cluster of symptoms to be considered a mental disorder?
   a. The disorder is manifested in symptoms that involve disturbances in behavior, thoughts, or emotions.
   b. The symptoms may be triggered by drug exposure and/or degeneration of the nervous system.
   c. The symptoms are associated with significant personal distress or impairment.
   d. The symptoms stem from an internal dysfunction.
3. The co-occurrence of two or more disorders in a single person is called:
   a. morbidity.
   b. mortality.
   c. comorbidity.
   d. duality.
4. Drugs that are effective in treating generalized anxiety disorder work by affecting the __________ system in the brain.
   a. glutamate
   b. GABA
   c. serotonin
   d. dopamine
5. Which of the following is NOT recognized as one of the five categories of specific phobias?
   a. clowns and dolls
   b. animals
   c. natural environments
   d. blood, injections, and injury
6. In those with dissociative identity disorder, if __________ is dominant it is typically unaware of __________, although they are aware of each other.
   a. the original personality; the host personality
   b. the host personality; alters
   c. the host personality; fractures
   d. the original personality; multipliers

7. Someone who has a moderately depressed mood that persists for at least 2 years and that is punctuated by periods of major depression has:
   a. dysthymia.
   b. major depression.
   c. double depression.
   d. All of these answers are correct.

8. What are the two phases that appear in bipolar disorder?
   a. manic and depressive
   b. neurotic and psychotic
   c. delirious and depressive
   d. manic and psychotic

9. Gina wears a pink-feathered boa to class with a low-cut half shirt and a miniskirt. She feigns a fainting spell for the fourth time this semester in hopes that her male peers will rush to her side. What personality disorder best describes Gina's behavior?
   a. paranoid
   b. borderline
   c. dependent
   d. histrionic

QUICK QUIZ #2

1. What is the theory that suggested that mental disorders could be diagnosed from facial features?
   a. physiognomy
   b. facial dystonia
   c. faciophrenology
   d. mirrorism

2. The global assessment of functioning scale:
   a. rates the number of disorders a person has from 0 to 10.
   b. assesses the severity of an individual's disorder.
   c. ranks severe disorders with higher numbers.
   d. classifies a person's disorder into specific axes and groups.

3. According to a 2001 study, those with major depression are more likely to have a secondary diagnosis of ____________ than another of the anxiety disorders.
   a. panic disorder
   b. social phobia
   c. obsessive-compulsive disorder
   d. generalized anxiety disorder

4. Belonging to which of the following groups increases one's likelihood of having generalized anxiety disorder?
   a. women
   b. the rich
   c. a rural population
   d. married people

5. Which of the following is NOT involved in the most common obsessions of those who suffer from obsessive-compulsive disorder?
   a. contamination
   b. reincarnation
   c. aggression
   d. disfigurement

6. Someone with dissociative __________ has a sudden loss of memory for significant personal information, whereas someone with dissociative __________ has a sudden loss of memory for his or her personal history, accompanied by an abrupt departure from home and the assumption of a new identity.
   a. fugue; amnesia
   b. fugue; identity disorder
   c. amnesia; identity disorder
   d. amnesia; fugue

7. Depression that occurs in a seasonal pattern is referred to as:
   a. the winter blues.
   b. melancholic seasonal disorder.
   c. seasonal affective disorder.
   d. solstice-trophic disorder.

8. The concordance rate in __________ twins for bipolar disorder is __________%.
   a. fraternal; 30
   b. identical; 16
   c. identical; 80
   d. fraternal; 40

9. What are the different types of schizophrenia?
   a. paranoid, catatonic, and disorganized
   b. paranoid, catatonic, disorganized, undifferentiated, and residual
   c. paranoid, catatonic, negative, undifferentiated, and residual
   d. disorganized, undifferentiated, and residual

QUICK QUIZ #3

1. The __________ is the conceptualization of psychological abnormalities as diseases that have symptoms and causes and possible cures.
   a. *DSM-IV-TR*
   b. diathesis–stress model
   c. medical model
   d. neuroses model

2. Jenny, who lost a close friend to a roadside bomb in the Iraq war, is now in a deep depression. She is 45 years old and until now has been spared the legacy of her family history of depression. What model best explains this?
   a. heritability model
   b. biopsychosocial model
   c. *ataque de nervios* model
   d. diathesis–stress model

3. A(n) __________ is a disorder involving an irrational fear of a particular object or situation that markedly interferes with one's ability to function.
   a. social phobia
   b. specific phobia
   c. generalized anxiety disorder
   d. obtuse phobia

4. Many who suffer from __________ also develop __________ as a result of the symptoms of the primary diagnosis.
   a. social phobia; specific phobia
   b. generalized anxiety disorder; schizophrenia
   c. panic disorder; agoraphobia
   d. agoraphobia; bipolar disorder

5. Some research suggests that increased activity in the __________ of the basal ganglia contributes to obsessive-compulsive disorder.
   a. amygdala
   b. caudate nucleus
   c. putamen
   d. cingulate gyrus

6. __________ do not include the grief that accompanies the death of a loved one; they are dysfunctional, chronic, and fall outside of the range of socially or culturally expected responses.
   a. Dissociative disorders
   b. Anxiety disorders
   c. Personality disorders
   d. Depressive mood disorders

7. The helplessness theory of depression suggests that those who are prone to depression attribute negative experiences to causes that are __________, __________, and __________.
   a. internal; stable; specific
   b. external; stable; global
   c. internal; stable; global
   d. internal; unstable; specific

8. Which of the following is NOT a negative symptom associated with schizophrenia?
   a. disorganized speech
   b. social withdrawal
   c. apathy
   d. poverty of speech

9. Which cluster of the personality disorders does antisocial personality disorder belong to?
   a. odd/eccentric
   b. dramatic/erratic
   c. anxious/inhibited
   d. odd/inhibited

"HEY, GUESS WHAT I LEARNED IN PSYCHOLOGY TODAY?" (AN ESSAY QUESTION)

We're guessing there's someone in your life who is interested in the quality of your educational experiences, is reasonably intelligent, but knows little about psychology. This might be your roommate, a previous teacher, your mom, or some other person you have access to and want to share your thoughts and feelings with. What would you tell that person about psychological disorders? How would you describe the difference between personal oddities and psychological disorders? How would you explain that schizophrenia is not a split personality?

THINGS TO PONDER

You've been provided a lot of information in this chapter about psychological disorders. When you put it all together, you may start to ponder how it all relates to other issues in this textbook. For example, you may ask yourself:

- How does an imbalance of a neurotransmitter lead to a complex psychological disorder like depression or generalized anxiety disorder (GAD)?

  Recall that the only way neurons can communicate is via neurotransmitters and that those signals are responsible for determining all behavior.

  Also consider the delicate balance of firing patterns of neurons and the release of several kinds of neurotransmitters for sensation or locomotion. Now add the complexity of heredity and predisposition for disorders, cognitions, trauma, and environmental factors, and consider how easy it would be to throw that balance off.

- What does learning have to do with the development of phobic overreactions?

  Recall that John Watson trained Little Albert to be afraid of a white rat in just a few short fear conditioning trials.

  Reflect on the fact that Little Albert's conditioned fear was not specific to the rat but generalized to other animals and to other white, furry things. Phobias may become other types of anxiety disorders (e.g., GAD or agoraphobia) by a similar mechanism.

- When does an extreme personality trait become a personality disorder?

  Understand that disorders are determined by a disruption of an ongoing lifestyle, among other factors.

  Annoying narcissistic traits do not define the narcissistic personality disorder; the disorder arises when self-love, jealousy, and need for praise significantly disrupt the ability to lead a relatively adjusted life.

- Why has the dogma about what determines sexual orientation changed from being almost totally dependent on upbringing to a focus on genetics and shared environments?

  Think about the history of psychology and the fact that psychoanalytical theories dominated psychology for some time. The emphasis on parenting and parenting styles has given way to evidence that genetics and nonshared environmetal influences are better predictors of sexual orientation than is the nature of parenting.

Consider the evidence for the contribution of the hormonal milieu to sexual orientation, as well as the influence of genetics and environmental factors.

WEB LINKS AND SUGGESTED READINGS

BehaveNet Clinical Capsule: APA Diagnostic Classification: *DSM-IV-TR*—http://www.behavenet.com/capsules/disorders/dsm4TRclassification.htm

- Essentially an abbreviated version of the *DSM-IV-TR* that lists the axes of mental disorders and their general classifications and symptoms; with links to more in-depth classification and diagnostic criteria.

National Institutes of Mental Health—http://www.nimh.nih.gov/

- The National Institutes of Mental Health is the largest scientific organization in the world dedicated to research focused on the understanding, treatment, and prevention of mental disorders and the promotion of mental health.

Brown, N. (2002). *Working with the Self-absorbed: How to Handle Narcissistic Personalities on the Job.* Oakland, CA: New Harbinger Publications.

- This text provides a no-nonsense approach to coping with, and overcoming, the stresses that accompany working with a narcissist without losing one's integrity or self-control. Nina Brown offers realistic strategies for changing expectations, listening and responding constructively, learning not to take things personally, and deciding when it's best to simply ignore outrageous behaviors.

Burke, R., Gates, R. and Hammond, R. (1996). *When the music's over: My journey into schizophrenia.* New York: Plume.

- The tragedy of schizophrenia cannot really be understood by anyone who has never been afflicted, but Ross David Burke takes the reader very close to his experience. Burke was in and out of mental hospitals and jails and plagued by paranoid schizophrenia. He wrote his memoir in prison. When it was finished, he took an overdose of drugs and ended his life. The reader shares the details of Burke's moments of reality and his delusions. In one of his suicide notes, he wrote, "I'm a paranoid schizophrenic and for us, life is hell; I'm sorry God."

ANSWERS

Chapter Overview

Identifying Psychological Disorders: What Is Abnormal?

The investigation of **abnormal** behavior not only enhances our understanding of the causes and treatments of mental **disorders** but also offers insight about normal psychological functioning. Studies of psychological problems depend on the reliable identification and **classification** of mental disorders. Abnormal psychology follows a **medical** model in which symptoms are understood to indicate an underlying disorder. Psychologists and psychiatrists use the ***DSM-IV-TR*** to diagnose disorders. The classification system includes a **global** assessment of functioning and several categories of disorders. A mental disorder is defined as occurring when someone experiences disturbances of thought, **emotion**, or behavior that produce distress or impairment and that arise from **internal** sources. Mental disorders are best understood from a perspective that considers a combination of influences, including **environmental**, psychological, and **biological** factors. **Comorbidity** of disorders is common, that is, people with more than one diagnosable disorder frequently also have another. The **diasthesis-stress** model proposes that it is possible to possess a predisposition for a mental disorder that remains unexpressed until it is triggered by stress. It is an oversimplification to assume that the intervention that cures a disorder defines the **cause** of the disorder. When a mental disorder is diagnosed, the **label** can be difficult to overcome because of the social **stigma** that often accompanies that diagnosis.

Anxiety Disorders: When Fears Take Over

Anxiety disorders involve **irrational** fears and worries that undermine well-being and result in **dysfunction**. The anxiety may be **chronic**, as in generalized anxiety disorder (GAD), or it may be tied to a specific object or situation, as in the **phobic** disorders. Phobias typically involve stimuli that humans are evolutionarily **prepared** to find threatening. People who experience **panic** disorder experience a sudden and intense attack of anxiety that is terrifying. Those who experience frequent panic attacks can gradually become **agoraphobic** and stay home for long periods of time for fear of public **humiliation**. People with obsessive-compulsive disorder (OCD) experience recurring, anxiety-provoking thoughts, or **obsessions**, that compel them to engage in ritualistic, irrational behaviors, or **compulsions**. Overall, the anxiety disorders show a **moderate** level of heritability.

Dissociative Disorders: Going to Pieces

The dissociative disorders involve severely **fragmented** cognitive processes that produce significant disruptions in **memory**, awareness, or personality. People with dissociative **identity** disorder shift between two or more identities that are distinct from each other in their personal memories, behavioral characteristics, and **attitudes**. Some therapists believe that DID is **overdiagnosed** because of widespread media attention. Psychodynamic theorists speculate that DID arises when psychological **detachment** is used as a means of coping with trauma, and a fractioning of integrated psychological functions results. Dissociative **amnesia** and dissociative **fugue** involve significant memory loss that is not the result of normal forgetting and cannot be attributed to **brain** injury, drugs, or another mental disorder. This memory loss is often associated with **stressful** life circumstances. People with dissociative fugue leave **home** abruptly and assume a new identity.

Mood Disorders: At the Mercy of Emotions

The mood disorders are mental disorders in which the **predominant** feature is a disturbance in mood. Major depression, or **unipolar** depression, is characterized by a severely depressed mood lasting at least 2 **weeks**, with symptoms that include excessive self-criticism, guilt, difficulty concentrating, **suicidal** thoughts, disturbances of sleep and appetite, and lethargy. Women are **twice** as likely to be diagnosed with depression than men. **Dysthymia** is a less severe form of depression that persists for at least 2 years. Depression shows a moderate level of heritability and is likely to involve **neurotransmitter** imbalances. Patterns of **negative** thinking may also contribute to depression, such as the tendency to explain personal failures by attributing them to internal, **stable**, and global causes. Depression-prone people may behave in ways that lead to social **rejection** that serves to confirm a sense of low self-worth.

Bipolar disorder is an unstable emotional condition involving extreme mood **swings** of depression and **mania**. The manic phase is characterized by periods of abnormally elevated or **irritable** mood, lasting at least 1 week. Bipolar disorder has a **high** rate of heritability. Stress and **family** problems may also contribute to the onset and maintenance of the disorder. Some believe that norepinephrine and serotonin imbalances contribute to the disorder, but that does not explain why **lithium** is effective as a drug treatment.

Schizophrenia: Losing the Grasp on Reality

Schizophrenia is a profound disorder involving **hallucinations**, delusions, disorganized thoughts, behavior, and speech, and emotional and social **withdrawal**. The **motivational** and social deficits are schizophrenia's negative symptoms. Five subtypes of schizophrenia have been identified: **paranoid**, catatonic, **disorganized**, undifferentiated, and residual. Although schizophrenia affects approximately 1% of the U.S. population, it accounts for a disproportionate number of psychiatric **hospitalizations**. Drugs that reduce the availability of **dopamine** sometimes reduce the positive symptoms of schizophrenia. Neuroimaging studies have shown that progressive loss of **gray** matter is a common feature of the progression of the disease. There is an increased risk of developing schizophrenia or experiencing a relapse in someone whose family has poor **communication** patterns and relationships.

Personality Disorders: Going to Extremes

Personality disorders are deeply ingrained, **inflexible** patterns of thinking, feeling, and **relating** to others, or controlling impulses that cause distress or impaired functioning. There are three clusters of personality disorders: odd/**eccentric**, dramatic/erratic, and anxious/**inhibited**. The classification, and even existence, of these disorders is controversial because they may just be **extreme** versions of normal personality and they are often comorbid with other disorders. People with personality disorders often lack **insight** into their own disorders, making self-report difficult or useless, but peer **nomination** procedures are relatively successful. Antisocial personality disorder (APD) is associated with a lack of **moral** emotions. Those with APD are usually manipulative, **dangerous**, and reckless, often hurting others and sometimes hurting themselves. A disproportionate number of prison inmates have **antisocial** personality disorder.

Quick Quiz #1

1. **C.** This figure represents substantial aggregate losses in productivity and emotional fulfillment.
2. **B.** The diagnoses of mental disorders explicitly exempts drug use and degenerative diseases as contributing factors to a mental disorder; otherwise, anyone who gets drunk would be classified as having a mental disorder. The other three choices are key features of disorders.
3. **C.** Comorbidity is the co-occurrence of two or more disorders in one person. The mortality of a disease is the number of deaths in a given time or place. The morbidity of a disease is its relative appearance in a given population. Dualism, in psychology, refers to the mind–body problem.
4. **B.** A stimulated GABA system increases inhibition and decreases anxiety.
5. **A.** Clowns and dolls are not recognized as one of the five categories of specific phobias. The other choices are among the categories of specific phobias, as is situations (for example, being in a constrained space like a bridge or a tunnel) and other phobias such as excessive fear of illness or death.
6. **B.** In people with dissociative identity disorder if the host personality is dominant, it is typically unaware of the *alters* or *alternate personality*, although they are aware of each other and the host.
7. **D.** Someone with double depression experiences ongoing dysthymia, a less severe depression, with periods of severe major depression. This is a special case of comorbidity.
8. **A.** The manic phase can result in psychoses, but that is not the defining feature of the disorder—the defining feature is the cycling between high and low moods.
9. **D.** Histrionic personality disorder is congruent with the extreme attention seeking and flamboyant style of dress that Gina is exhibiting. Her attention-seeking includes faking or exaggerating illness. While borderline and dependent personality disorders also have attention-seeking as a major characteristic, they are typically less dramatic about their attempts, particularly someone with dependent personality disorder.

Quick Quiz #2

1. **A.** Physiognomy, along with other nonempirical theories, has been discredited in favor of the medical model. Facial dystonia is a movement disorder of the face characterized by spasms and/or rigidity. "Faciophrenology" and "mirrorism" are made-up terms.
2. **B.** The global assessment of functioning scale indicates the severity of an individual's disorder by ranking function from 0 to 100, with lower scores indicating a greater degree of severity. Disorders are categorized in the *DSM* system.
3. **D.** Those with major depression are more likely also to have generalized anxiety disorder (~70%) than another of the other anxiety disorders, with social phobia (~40%) next, then panic disorder (~20%), and OCD (<10%) last.
4. **A.** Women are more likely than men to experience GAD. Residents of large cities, the poor, and those in enduring unpredictable or abusive relationships, are also more likely than the general population to have GAD.
5. **B.** Common obsessions are death, sex, disease, and orderliness. (Obsessions are intrusive thoughts; compulsions are the resulting ritualistic behaviors.)
6. **D.** Dissociative amnesia is the loss of personal information; dissociative fugue is the loss of personal history accompanied by vanishing to assume a new identity. Dissociative identity disorder is the fracturing of personality to cope with excessive trauma.
7. **C.** Actually, "winter blues" is a good description, but in the *DSM-IV-TR* the disorder is called "seasonal affective disorder" (SAD).
8. **C.** This is the highest rate of heritability among the mental disorders, indicating a strong genetic component that may be polygenic.
9. **B.** These five types of schizophrenia are based on the dominating features of the symptoms; however, the residual subtype is more characteristic of a schizophrenia that is in remission than one of the other, more severe, subtypes.

Quick Quiz #3

1. **C.** The medical model allows psychologists to think about mental disorders in a similar way as biological diseases, although not all mental disorders have an underlying biological component that has been identified. The *DSM* is a tool for diagnosing disorders; the diathesis–stress model refers to latent mental disorders triggered by stress.
2. **D.** The diathesis–stress model best explains Jenny's predisposition to depression and the fact that its appearance was triggered by a major stressor. Heritability distinguishes the likelihood that this would occur overall in a population, but not in a given person.
3. **B.** As its name implies, a specific phobia is a fear of a specific object or situation. Social phobia and GAD are more general disorders. There is no "obtuse phobia."
4. **C.** Sufferers of panic disorder may also develop agoraphobia because they fear having a panic attack in a public place, and that fear can keep them confined to home for considerable periods of time.
5. **B.** The caudate nucleus is important for initiation of intentional actions. Drugs that increase serotonin have been shown to decrease this activity and relieve some symptoms of OCD.
6. **D.** It is important to distinguish depressive mood disorders from the likely adaptive responses to grief and loss that we all experience.
7. **C.** The helplessness theory of depression suggests that those who are prone to depression blame themselves (internal cause), believe that their condition is unlikely to change (stable cause), and feel that their negative experience is a widespread phenomenon (global cause).
8. **A.** The negative symptoms of schizophrenia are the absence or insufficiency of normal behavior, motivation, and emotion. Disorganized speech, on the other hand, is one of the positive symptoms of the disorder.
9. **B.** Other personality disorders in the dramatic/erratic cluster are the borderline, histrionic, and narcissistic personality disorders.

"Hey, Guess What I Learned in Psychology Today?" (An Essay Question)

What might you tell your mom about psychological disorders?

- You might start talking about just what abnormal means—the difference between ordinary anxiety before an exam, or grief at the death of someone you love—and the persistent, uncontrollable, and harmful thoughts, feelings, and emotions that define psychological disorders. You could follow with the adaptation of a medical model of mental disorders in order to classify them, diagnose them, and justify treatment. Explain how these classifications have changed over time by pointing out how things such as being homosexual and being African American were considered disorders in early versions of the *DSM*. From this point, introduce the general categories and the axes of the *DSM-IV-TR*.
- Many people, at one time or another in their lives, have a psychological disorder, and the disorder can make life difficult or seemingly unmanageable. The personality disorders tend to be the extremes of normal personality traits. Traits such as extraversion or overconscientiousness taken to the extreme can result in disorders when they interfere with successful daily living. Similarly, people with what many would consider more severe disorders, such as schizophrenia or bipolar disorder, are not necessarily wandering the streets in tattered clothes talking to themselves, especially if they are receiving proper medication and therapy. You could also note that approximately 40% of the U.S. population will experience a mental disorder during their lifetime. That is, nearly half of the people that you know will suffer from a psychological disorder. Some will overcome the disorder and some will not. This may help to demonstrate that personal oddities are closer to abnormal thoughts, feelings, and emotions than most of us may think.
- You might talk about just what "schizophrenia" means, and how its nature is often misunderstood. The schism that is implied in the term is a split from reality, not a split personality or identity. The heritability component of schizophrenia is high; it is a severely disruptive disorder of thought that is not typically thought of as being brought on by environmental stimuli. Schizophrenia should not be confused—though it often is—with dissociative identity disorder (DID), more commonly known as multiple personality disorder, which is usually the result of exposure to trauma during childhood (e.g., ritualistic physical abuse). In DID the mind compartmentalizes the trauma by fracturing into separate identities, each with its own distinct characteristics.

13

Treatment of Psychological Disorders

THE BIG PICTURE

Charron and Emma meet at a mutual friend's party. "How do you know Jennifer?" Charron asks. Emma replies, "We used to be roommates during freshman year. How about you?" "We met in our abnormal psychology class this semester," Charron tells her. "So," says Emma, "are you a psych major too? I'm always afraid you people are trying to analyze me or I have to lie down on a couch to have a conversation." Charron begins an explanation that she has had to make several times before: "That's a common misconception, all right. But not all psychologists are therapists. In fact, a lot of psychologists don't deal directly with people at all, and only about thirty percent of therapists practice strictly psychodynamic therapy, the kind where you might lie on a couch and talk about your childhood to uncover things about your problems or a psychological disorder." "Really?" Emma seems interested. "What other kinds of therapy do psychologists use, then?" "Well," says Charron, "there are cognitive and behavioral therapies, which grew out of learning theory and the cognitive movement, there's humanistic therapy, which is much more free-flowing than the other, more prescribed psychotherapies, there's existential therapy, and then there are different eclectic combinations of several kinds of therapies. But psychotherapy isn't the only way to treat psychological disorders. There are lots of medications being developed to treat different mental illnesses and there are other kinds of treatments like transcranial magnetic stimulation and specific psychosurgeries." Emma is impressed: "It sounds like you know what you're talking about!" Charron says, "I hope so. After graduation this spring I'm going to work at Eli Lilly in their R & D department to work on a new class of antidepressant. I thought I wanted to be a therapist, like Jennifer, when I started off as a psychology major, but I learned that there are so many different ways to contribute to helping people with psychological disorders, and I'm pretty good at chemistry, so this seems like a good fit for me." Emma says, "I'm glad there are people like you to do that kind of thing. A couple of my relatives really depend on those medications, and therapy, but I've never thought about it much. Maybe I'll end up in the business office over at Lilly when I finish my finance degree!"

Chapter 13 discusses the reasons some people need treatment for psychological disorders, the major types of treatments that are available, and how effective those treatments are. The issues considered in this chapter are directly related to those in Chapter 12 and several that are covered in Chapter 14, which discusses stress and health. Freud's psychoanalytic therapy grew out of his theory of personality (Chapter 11) that relied heavily on early developmental conflicts (Chapter 10) and the ways that children deal, or don't deal, with those conflicts. Cognitive behavior therapy grew directly out of concepts of learning theory (Chapter 6) and complex thoughts (Chapter 7). The medical treatments reviewed in this chapter touch on the workings of the brain (Chapter 3) and the effects that drugs have on consciousness (Chapter 8). For many who seek treatment, the motivation (Chapter 9) is the desire for fulfilling relationships (Chapter 15) with friends and family.

Charron's description of the types of treatments that are available for psychological disorders was accurate, but brief (though long-winded enough for party chat). As you saw in this chapter, there are many different kinds of treatment options available to those with psychological disorders, and a great number of combinations of treatment approaches. Part of the difficulty in providing treatment is that many in need don't know how to find the appropriate treatment or fear the stigma attached to being labeled with a disorder or illness. There is also the question of compliance with treatment, and the effectiveness of treatment. For most of us who have chosen psychology as a major or a career, these are exciting challenges—and the rewards, both for clients and practitioners, can be great.

CHAPTER OBJECTIVES

After studying this chapter, you should be able to:

1. Summarize the benefits of receiving treatment for psychological disorders, and the reasons why some people cannot or will not seek treatment.
2. Compare the psychological and biological approaches to treatment.
3. Explain the differences between psychologists, psychiatrists, social workers, and counselors, and note the role of each.
4. Describe the approach of *eclectic psychotherapy.*
5. Explain the basic principles of psychoanalysis, drawing on its origins in the psychodynamic perspective on personality.
6. Discuss why the development of insight is a central goal of psychoanalysis, and explain how free association, dream analysis, interpretation, and analysis of *resistance* each contribute to that overall goal. Discuss transference.
7. Summarize the main departures from traditional psychoanalysis that were developed by Carl Jung, Alfred Adler, Melanie Klein, and Karen Horney.
8. Describe the central tenets of *interpersonal psychotherapy.*
9. Compare the techniques of *token economy, exposure therapy,* and *systematic desensitization,* noting their similarities and differences as types of behavior therapies.
10. Explain the similarities and differences between cognitive therapies and behavior therapies.
11. Describe the techniques of *cognitive restructuring* and *mindfulness meditation.*
12. Summarize the basic methods of *cognitive behavioral therapy.*
13. Explain how humanistic and existential therapies differ from psychodynamic and behavioral therapies.
14. Describe the basic features of couples and family therapy, *group therapy,* and self-help groups.
15. Describe how *antipsychotic drugs, antianxiety medications,* and *antidepressants* work at a biological level.
16. Discuss research evidence on the question of whether medication, *psychotherapy,* or a combination of the two approaches is effective in treating psychological disorders.
17. Describe biological treatments that do not involve medication, such as *electroconvulsive therapy, transcranial magnetic stimulation,* and *psychosurgery.*
18. Explain why treatment illusions can cloud the ability to determine the effectiveness of treatment for psychological disorders.
19. Compare outcome studies and process studies of treatment effectiveness, and summarize what has been learned from each approach.

20. Name some empirically supported psychological treatments and the disorders to which they apply.
21. Name some of the dangers associated with the treatment of psychological disorders.

CHAPTER OVERVIEW

Use the terms below to fill in the following exercises. Terms may not be used more than once. The answers can be found at the end of this chapter.

behavior	exhausted	mindfulness
biomedical	exposure	nonspecific
brain	family	person
chair	financial	placebo
cognitive	free association	problem
combined	Freudian	processes
congruence	Gestalt	psychodynamic
dangers	herbal	psychotherapy
depression	hundreds	psychotic
disorders	iatrogenic	regard
double-blind	illnesses	regulate
dream	improvement	resistance
efficacious	insight	side
electroconvulsive	irrational	token
embarrassed	learning	transcranial
emotive	lobotomies	untreated
established	medical	

Treatment: Getting Help to Those Who Need It

Psychological disorders and mental illness are often misunderstood, and consequently often go __________________. These disorders carry enormous social, __________________, and personal costs. Some people are unaware of their problems, while others are too __________________ to seek help. Psychological and __________________ treatments can lessen the overall costs of psychological disorders and provide a greater quality of life to those who have them. Clinical help typically comes in the form of __________________, or talking therapy, __________________ and biological therapy, or a combination of both.

Psychological Therapies: Healing the Mind Through Interaction

There are __________________ of different types of psychological therapies. The most common are the __________________, behavioral, __________________, and humanistic–existential. Psychodynamic therapy is based on __________________ psychoanalysis and focuses on helping a client develop __________________ into his or her psychological problems. Some of the techniques used in psychodynamic therapy include __________________, __________________ analysis, interpretation of a client's statements and behaviors, and the analysis of __________________ during treatment. ________________ therapy helps clients change maladaptive behaviors to more adaptive ones. Some techniques used in behavior therapy include establishing a ________________ economy, ________________ therapy, and systematic desensitization, which are all based on the principles of ________________ theory. Cognitive therapy teaches clients to challenge ________________ thoughts and beliefs. Some techniques used in cognitive therapy are rational________________ behavior therapy, cognitive restructuring, and ________________ meditation. Cognitive behavior therapy (CBT) combines the strategies of both cognitive therapy and behavior therapy. CBT is ________________ focused, action oriented, and transparent. Humanistic therapies, like ________________-centered therapy, and existential therapies, such as ________________ therapy, focus on helping clients develop a sense of personal worth and nurture growth. Humanistic therapies, emphasize ________________, empathy, and unconditional positive ________________ in the therapist's treatment of a client. Gestalt therapy uses methods such as focusing and the empty ________________ technique. Approaches to therapy can also involve more than one person working with a therapist; some of these are couples, ________________, and group therapy.

Medical and Biological Treatments: Healing the Mind through the Brain

Biomedical treatments have transformed therapy for a wide array of mental ________________. These treatments include medications, ________________ products, and techniques that intervene directly in the ________________. Many medications have been developed specifically to treat ________________ symptoms, anxiety disorders, bipolar disorder, and ________________. Unfortunately, the ________________ effects of many of these medications are unpleasant and annoying. Medications are often more useful when ________________ with psychotherapy. Herbal products may be useful in relieving some psychological symptoms, but little is done to ________________ these products. Those with depression who don't respond well to medications often turn to other biomedical treatments, such as ________________ therapy or ________________ magnetic stimulation. Today, psychosurgery is more focused and better defined than the broad and controversial ________________ of the past. This type of surgery is reserved for patients who have ________________ other treatment options.

Treatment Effectiveness: For Better or for Worse

________________ during treatment does not necessarily indicate the efficacy of the treatment. Scientific evaluation of treatment is necessary to determine whether or not other factors, such as natural improvement, ________________ treatment effects, the ________________ effect, or reconstructive memory processes (i.e., the exaggeration of pretreatment problems), contributed to an observed change in behavior. Studies of treatment efficacy focus on both outcomes and ________________. The preferred technique for studying treatment outcomes is the ________________ technique, in which neither client nor experimenter is aware of treatment conditions. Certain treatments have been found to be more beneficial for certain ________________ than others. Some psychological organizations are developing lists of treatments that are well ________________ or probably ________________ for certain disorders. There are significant ________________ of treatment, which include the side effects of drugs and the potential for the therapy itself to create ________________ psychological disorders that were not present when therapy began.

QUICK QUIZ #1

1. It is estimated that almost 1 in __________ Americans suffers from some type of mental illness.
   a. 2
   b. 5
   c. 10
   d. 50
2. What percentage of Americans, approximately, is diagnosed with depression or anxiety disorders that receive proper treatment?
   a. 30%
   b. 47%
   c. 83%
   d. 94%
3. The majority of therapists responding to a survey by the American Psychological Association Division of Psychotherapy said that they used __________ therapy in their practice.
   a. psychodynamic
   b. cognitive
   c. humanistic
   d. eclectic
4. Which of the following techniques did Sigmund Freud abandon because he found it to be highly unreliable?
   a. free association
   b. dream analysis
   c. hypnosis
   d. interpretation
5. Which of the following disagreed in particular with Sigmund Freud's treatment of the inherent differences between men and women, suggesting that the differences are cultural instead of biological?
   a. Melanie Klein
   b. Karen Horney
   c. Harry Stack Sullivan
   d. Carl Jung
6. Cognitive and behavioral therapies focus on dysfunctional __________ and maladaptive __________, instead of early developmental processes, as the source of psychological dysfunction.
   a. thoughts; behaviors
   b. thoughts; beliefs
   c. behaviors; beliefs
   d. karma; behaviors

7. Eliminating unwanted behaviors, a goal of behavior therapy, relies on evidence from operant conditioning that shows that behavior can be predicted by its __________ and its __________.
   a. punishers; reinforcers
   b. reinforcers; consequences
   c. antecedents; consequences
   d. antecedents; punishers
8. Cognitive behavioral therapy (CBT) is most frequently employed by therapists who treat __________ and __________.
   a. schizophrenia; bipolar disorder
   b. anxiety; depression
   c. anxiety; schizophrenia
   d. bipolar disorder; social phobia
9. Members of the self-help group __________ are encouraged to view their problem as a chronic disease over which they have little control.
   a. Jonestown
   b. Heavens Gate
   c. Alcoholics Anonymous
   d. Libertarians for Justice
10. The second generation of antidepressant drugs that were developed in the 1950s, including Tofranil and Elavil, are called __________ antidepressants.
   a. monoamine inhibitor
   b. tricyclic
   c. selective serotonin reuptake inhibitor
   d. monoamine oxidase inhibitor

QUICK QUIZ #2

1. The relatively new technique of virtual reality therapy is best classified as a __________ therapy.
   a. cognitive
   b. behavior
   c. exposure
   d. All of these answers are correct.
2. Which of the following is NOT considered a significant barrier to obtaining treatment in the United States for a psychological disorder?
   a. failing to recognize that a disorder exists
   b. government limits on the number of people who may receive treatment every year for mental illnesses
   c. the embarrassment of being labeled with a disorder
   d. gaining access to a treatment facility or therapist
3. __________ therapies explore childhood events and encourage individuals to use this understanding to develop insight into their psychological problems.
   a. Humanistic
   b. Cognitive behavioral
   c. Psychodynamic
   d. Existential

4. Gertrude, Hamlet's mother, says in Shakespeare's play, "The lady doth protest too much, methinks." Taken as a reference to someone's underlying beliefs, it best relates to the psychodynamic technique known as:
   a. interpretation
   b. transference
   c. free association
   d. analysis of resistance

5. The shift of psychodynamic therapy to a focus on helping clients improve current relationships resulted in the development of __________.
   a. interpersonal psychotherapy
   b. peer-to-peer therapy
   c. cognitive behavior therapy
   d. existential therapy

6. Who first coined the term *behavior therapy* in a description of changing schizophrenic symptoms based on the principles of learning?
   a. John B. Watson
   b. Edward L. Thorndike
   c. Ivan Pavlov
   d. B. F. Skinner

7. __________ founded rational emotive behavior therapy, a form of cognitive therapy.
   a. Alfred Adler
   b. Aaron Beck
   c. Albert Ellis
   d. Carl Jung

8. __________ therapy assumes that each individual is qualified to determine his or her own goals for therapy, for example, feeling more confident or making a career decision.
   a. Person-centered
   b. Cognitive behavioral
   c. Psychodynamic
   d. Behavioral

9. The drug __________ was the first in a series of __________ drugs produced to treat schizophrenia and other related psychotic disorders.
   a. diazepam (Valium); antipsychotic
   b. Prozac; neuroleptic
   c. lithium; antineurotic
   d. Thorazine; antipsychotic

10. Despite the side effects of nausea and weight gain associated with the drug, __________ is currently the most prescribed drug for the treatment of bipolar disorder.
   a. valproate
   b. lithium
   c. clozapine
   d. amitriptyline

QUICK QUIZ #3

1. One estimate of the annual cost to the affected individual and to society of anxiety disorders in the United States is:
   a. $10.1 million.
   b. $3.4 billion.
   c. $42.3 billion.
   d. $156.7 billion.
2. ___________ is an interaction between a therapist and client with the goal of providing support or relief from the client's psychological problem.
   a. Electroconvulsive therapy
   b. Psychotherapy
   c. Psychosurgery
   d. Pseudopsychological therapy
3. Although psychodynamic therapy has changed in many ways since Sigmund Freud developed the technique, modern psychodynamic therapies are still based on the belief that the path to overcoming psychological problems lies in developing insight into ___________ memories, impulses, wishes, and conflicts.
   a. unconscious
   b. preconscious
   c. conscious
   d. postconscious
4. At the end of his fifth therapeutic session, Tony tries to kiss his therapist as he is leaving her office. When she rebuffs him, Tony proclaims his newfound love for her. This is an example of:
   a. interpretation
   b. exposure therapy
   c. analysis of resistance
   d. transference
5. The concept developed by Carl Jung that describes culturally determined symbols and myths that are shared among all people is called:
   a. shared culturalism
   b. collective unconscious
   c. archetypal kibbutz
   d. communal mythology
6. Which of the following activities would have the highest fear ranking on an exposure hierarchy for social phobia?
   a. asking for directions at the gas station
   b. going for a job interview
   c. attending a holiday party without drinking
   d. eating lunch with co-workers
7. ___________ is a therapeutic approach that teaches clients to question beliefs, assumptions, and predictions that often lead to negative emotions and to replace negative thinking with more realistic and positive beliefs.
   a. Cognitive restructuring
   b. Mindfulness meditation
   c. Emotive behavior shifting
   d. Pessimistic elimination

8. Which of the following is NOT a basic quality that person-centered therapists are encouraged to demonstrate?
   a. congruence
   b. empathy
   c. unconditional positive regard
   d. determinism
9. ____________ medications, such as the benzodiazapine Xanax, enhance the ____________ neurotransmitter system in order to be effective.
   a. Antidepressant; serotonin
   b. Antipsychotic; glutamate
   c. Antianxiety; dopamine
   d. Antianxiety; GABA
10. ____________ is a disorder or symptom that occurs as a result of a medical or psychotherapeutic treatment.
   a. Neurosis
   b. Iatrogenic illness
   c. Psychosis
   d. Synesthesia

"HEY, GUESS WHAT I LEARNED IN PSYCHOLOGY TODAY?" (AN ESSAY QUESTION)

We're guessing there's someone in your life who is interested in the quality of your educational experiences, is reasonably intelligent, but knows little about psychology. This might be your roommate, a previous teacher, your mom, or some other person you have access to and want to share your thoughts and feelings with. What would you tell that person about the treatment of psychological disorders? How would you describe the differences between the major types of psychotherapies? What would you say if your mom told you that a friend of hers has severe depression that has not responded to medication or psychotherapy?

THINGS TO PONDER

You've been provided a lot of information in this chapter about the treatment of psychological disorders. When you put it all together, you may start to ponder how it all relates to other issues in this textbook. For example, you may ask yourself:

- How does a simple salt, such as lithium, work to reduce the symptoms of a disorder as severe and complex as bipolar disorder?

  Consider that we don't yet understand some of the basic mechanisms of the brain and there are many things that we don't understand about bipolar disorder. The puzzle of lithium remains, but lithium has been successful, and many treatment providers don't fight success.

- How did behavior therapy grow out of learning theory?

  Remember that extinction is an effective way to reduce many kinds of behaviors. Conversations between learning theorists and therapists led to techniques that extinguish many of the unwanted behaviors associated with a disorder.

  Reflect on the fact that exposure can lead to habituation and that habituation to a fearful stimulus can be a good thing.

- Is there any way to test for highly heritable disorders and head them off at the pass?

  Understand that heritability applies to groups and is impossible to test in one person, even when the heritability for a disorder is high.

  Think about the ailments for which there are genetic tests (e.g., Huntington's disease) and consider whether or not, if you were asymptomatic, you would want to know that you harbored a debilitating—and inevitable—illness.

- Why bother with treatments that aren't much better than no treatment or a placebo?

  Think about the life disruption that so many of those who live with psychological disorders confront daily. Would you take a little bit of relief from something that is extremely uncomfortable or intrusive if it was offered to you?

  Consider the evidence that combinations of therapies can work better than either medicine or psychotherapy alone.

WEB LINKS AND SUGGESTED READINGS

NIMH Outreach Partnership Program—http://www.nimh.nih.gov/health/outreach/partnership-program/index.shtml

- The Outreach Partnership Program is a vital element in the effort of the National Institute of Mental Health to inform the public, health professionals, constituency groups, and other interested parties. The 55 partners of the program also seek to help people find treatment and reduce the stigma surrounding mental illness.

Wigram, T.,and De Backer, J. (1999). *Clinical Applications of Music Therapy in Psychiatry*. London and Philadelphia: Jessica Kingsley.

- The authors describe the planning and evaluation of music therapy intervention, and how music therapy can be used for assessing complex organic and emotional disabilities.

O'Hanlon, B. (2006). *Change 101: A Practical Guide to Creating Change in Life or Therapy*. New York: W. W. Norton Professional Books.

- Bill O'Hanlon, a psychotherapist, has written several books about how to change, such as *Do One Thing Differently* and *Solution Focused Therapy*. The author believes this is his best book about change because it presents what he has learned through his work. In this book he backs away from the solution focus, finding that approach to be invalid.

ANSWERS

Chapter Overview

Treatment: Getting Help to Those Who Need It

Psychological disorders and mental illness are often misunderstood and consequently often go **untreated**. These disorders carry enormous social, **financial**, and personal costs. Some people are unaware of their problems, while others are too **embarrassed** to seek help. Psychological and **biomedical** treatments can help lessen the overall costs of psychological disorders and provide a greater quality of life to those who have them. Clinical help typically comes in the form of **psychotherapy**, or talking therapy, **medical** and biological therapy, or a combination of both.

Psychological Therapies: Healing the Mind Through Interaction

There are **hundreds** of different types of psychological therapies. The most common are the **psychodynamic**, behavioral, **cognitive**, and humanistic–existential. Psychodynamic therapy is based on **Freudian** psychoanalysis and focuses on helping a client develop **insight** into his or her psychological problems. Some of the techniques used in psychodynamic therapy include **free association**, **dream** analysis, interpretation of a client's statements and behaviors, and the analysis of **resistance** during treatment. **Behavior** therapy helps clients change maladaptive behaviors to more adaptive ones. Some techniques used in behavior therapy include establishing a **token** economy, **exposure** therapy, and systematic desensitization, which are all based on the principles of **learning** theory. Cognitive therapy teaches clients to challenge **irrational** thoughts and beliefs. Some techniques used in cognitive therapy are rational **emotive** behavior therapy, cognitive restructuring, and **mindfulness** meditation. Cognitive behavior therapy (CBT) combines the strategies of both cognitive therapy and behavior therapy. CBT is **problem** focused, action oriented, and transparent. Humanistic therapies, like **person**-centered therapy, and existential therapies, such as **Gestalt** therapy, focus on helping clients develop a sense of personal worth and nurture growth. Humanistic therapies emphasize **congruence**, empathy, and unconditional positive **regard** in the therapist's treatment of a client. Gestalt therapy uses methods such as focusing and the empty **chair** technique. Approaches to therapy can also involve more than one person working with a therapist; some of these are couples, **family**, and group therapy.

Medical and Biological Treatments: Healing the Mind through the Brain

Biomedical treatments have transformed therapy for a wide array of mental **illnesses**. These treatments include medications, **herbal** products, and techniques that intervene directly in the **brain**. Many medications have been developed specifically to treat **psychotic** symptoms, anxiety disorders, bipolar disorder, and **depression**. Unfortunately, the **side** effects of many of these medications are unpleasant and annoying. Medications are often more useful when **combined** with psychotherapy. Herbal products may be useful in relieving some psychological symptoms, but little is done to **regulate** these products. Those with depression who don't respond well to medications often turn to other biomedical treatments, such as **electroconvulsive** therapy or **transcranial** magnetic stimulation. Today, psychosurgery is more focused and better defined than the broad and controversial **lobotomies** of the past. This type of surgery is reserved for patients who have **exhausted** other treatment options.

Treatment Effectiveness: For Better or for Worse

Improvement during treatment does not necessarily indicate the efficacy of the treatment. Scientific evaluation of a treatment is necessary to determine whether or not other factors, such as natural improvement, **nonspecific** treatment effects, the **placebo** effect, or reconstructive memory processes (i.e., the exaggeration of pretreatment problems), contributed to an observed change in behavior. Studies of treatment efficacy focus on both outcomes and **processes**. The preferred technique for studying treatment outcomes is the **double-blind** technique, in which neither client nor experimenter is aware of treatment conditions. Certain treatments have been found to be more beneficial for certain **disorders** than others. Some psychological organizations are developing lists of treatments that are well **established** or probably **efficacious** for certain disorders. There are significant **dangers** of treatment, which include the side effects of drugs and the potential for the therapy itself to create **iatrogenic** psychological disorders that were not present when therapy began.

Quick Quiz #1

1. **B.** According to the 2002 study by Narrow and colleagues, approximately one in five people suffers from a mental disorder.
2. **A.** This finding was a result of a 2001 study, which also found that 83% of those surveyed had seen a health care provider in the previous year.
3. **D.** Thirty-six percent of the 1,000 therapists surveyed responded that they used eclectic therapy. The next most popular approach was psychodynamic therapy, used by 29% of the respondents.
4. **C.** Free association, dream analysis, and interpretation are all techniques that Freud developed and continued to use to explore the unconscious mind.
5. **B.** All these therapists disagreed with various aspect of Freud's original approach; Karen Horney focused on the cultural, rather than inherent, differences between men and women.
6. **A.** Cognitive and behavioral therapies do not focus on karma; they do try to restructure some beliefs.
7. **C.** Adjusting antecedents and consequences may help eliminate unwanted behaviors. Punishers and reinforcers are consequences, but without antecedents they do not predict behavior.
8. **B.** Schizophrenia and bipolar disorder are not as amenable to CBT as anxiety and depression because the thought disorganization is often more severe.
9. **C.** It is difficult to evaluate the effectiveness of AA's methods because members have not supported researchers' requests to evaluate the program.
10. **B.** MAOI drugs were the first generation of antidepressants; SSRIs are the third generation of antidepressants.

Quick Quiz #2

1. **D.** The virtual reality technique can be described as behavioral and cognitive because the client is acting on the fear in an attempt to change irrational thoughts. Exposure therapy is a type of behavioral therapy that exposes the client to the feared stimulus in a safe environment.
2. **B.** Although it may seem like it, the U.S. government does not have a quota for the number of people who can be treated for mental illness every year. Identification of the problem, embarrassment from the stigma, and access are all serious barriers to treatment.
3. **C.** CBT is more focused on changing behaviors and thoughts than insights; humanistic and existential therapies explore personal growth rather than the personal past.
4. **D.** Freud found the phenomenon of resistance particularly useful in therapy. The therapist suggests an interpretation that is unpalatable to the client and analyzes the amount of resistance to the interpretation in order to gain insight into the problem.
5. **A.** Interpersonal psychotherapy (IPT) grew out of Freud's original psychoanalytic therapy but shifted the focus from the past to helping clients improve current relationships. IPT was originally developed as a brief (12–16 week) treatment for depression.
6. **D.** The other choices name influential learning theorists who predated the development of behavior therapy.
7. **C.** Alfred Adler and Carl Jung were both influential psychodynamic therapists; Aaron Beck developed a gentler kind of cognitive therapy that helps a client discover errors in thinking.
8. **A.** Person-centered therapy is a humanistic therapy, developed by Carl Rogers, that is nondirective and assumes that the client has the best understanding of his or her own therapeutic needs.
9. **D.** Thorazine blocks dopamine and reduces the positive symptoms of schizophrenia. "Neuroleptic" is a synonym for "antipsychotic," but the drugs named are used in the treatment of other disorders.
10. **A.** Valproate is the most prescribed treatment for bipolar disorder, although lithium is still

used and was the drug of choice for many years. There are no known drugs that effectively treat the mania and depression of bipolar disorder without distressing side effects.

is unlikely to be brought on by treatment alone. Most psychologists no longer use the term *neurosis*. Synesthesia, the confusion of sensations, is not iatrogenic.

Quick Quiz #3

1. **C.** A 1999 study estimated the cost at $42.3 billion, or $1,542 per sufferer; the figures take into account the cost of treatment, diminished productivity, and absenteeism.
2. **B.** Psychotherapy is the general term used for the interaction between a therapist and someone suffering from a psychological problem, with the goal of providing support or relief from the problem. ECT and surgery are biological therapies.
3. **A.** Psychodynamic therapies are based on the concept that unwanted thoughts and conflicts are pushed into the unconscious. Therapists believe that successful treatment involves gaining insight into what is hidden in the unconscious mind.
4. **D.** Transference occurs when the analyst begins to assume a major significance in the client's life and the client reacts to the analyst on the basis of unconscious childhood fantasies.
5. **B.** Jung believed that the collective unconscious played the role Freud assigned to motives of sex and aggression.
6. **C.** Attending a holiday party for an hour without having a drink is slightly higher on the social phobia exposure hierarchy than going for a job interview. The other two choices rank relatively low.
7. **A.** Mindfulness meditation encourages the client to be fully present in each moment with a heightened sense of awareness; the other two choices are nonsense terms.
8. **D.** Rogers encouraged congruence (openness and honesty), empathy (trying to understand the client's point of view), and unconditional positive regard (providing a nonjudgmental and accepting environment).
9. **D.** Serotonin is typically more involved with depression; dopamine is associated with psychosis and substance abuse.
10. **B.** An iatrogenic illness (*iatros* is the Greek word for "doctor") is a disorder or symptom that occurs as a result of a medical or psychotherapeutic treatment itself. Psychosis

"Hey, Guess What I Learned In Psychology Today?" (An Essay Question)

What might you tell your mom about the treatment of psychological disorders?

- You might start by talking about the common misconception that psychodynamic therapy is the only kind of treatment available for psychological disorders—a good way to open a discussion about the history of psychodynamic therapy and how it dominated the field for some time. You could point out that the changes in treatment styles have outpaced the public perception of the field. You could note that while many therapists do use psychodynamic techniques, more and more are using a blend of those techniques in combination with other kinds of therapies, such as cognitive behavioral therapy and humanistic–existential therapies. You might want to mention that there are biological and alternative treatments available in addition to psychotherapy, and that they may be used in combination with other treatments as well. Finally, you might want to point out that treatment of psychological disorders is not a perfect science, rather a practice, like medicine, and that each treatment option carries a certain amount of risk. Overall, it would be good to end with the fact that there are more treatment options available today than ever before and that techniques have improved considerably from even 20 years ago.

- You could say that therapies are a lot like people, in that they have different personalities. Some types of therapy (e.g., humanistic) are optimistic, while others (e.g., psychoanalytic) are pessimistic and/or deterministic. Some therapies (e.g., behavioral) are strict and prescribed, while others (e.g., humanistic and Gestalt) are more laid back, leaving the direction of the treatment to the client to discover. With this analogy in mind, you can talk about how both you and your mom seem to get along better with some personalities than with others (although you and your mom may have different preferences here), and that is often how treatment works. Some people respond better to treatments that fit their personality and unique set of problems. And you could point out that some psychological organizations are even recommending certain kinds of treatments that go along with certain disorders on the basis of experience with those treatments and evaluations of their efficacy.

- Regarding your mom's friend who has not responded to treatment, you may want to start by pointing out that this isn't unheard of. Many people who suffer from depression do not respond to antidepressant medications or any kind of psychotherapy, regardless of the doses and types of medications or the combinations of therapies—but that there are several alternatives. Electroconvulsive shock works well for many who do not respond to other treatments of depression. Today, ECT is done under anesthetic, not in the *One Flew over the Cuckoo's Nest* style. You could talk about the advances in transcranial magnetic stimulation and psychosurgery that have been shown to be effective for treating severe depression.

14

Stress and Health

THE BIG PICTURE

"Hey, Eliot—you don't look so good." Eliot agrees: "Gus, I don't feel so hot. I think I'm coming down with something. I always feel kind of tired and worn out after finals, but this semester really got to me. Then I got this cold sore on my lip and this cut on my eye won't seem to heal, and I'm going home to see my family for Christmas." Gus asks, "Have you had any other stressors in your life lately? Different kinds of stress can shred your immune system and make you more likely to get sick." Eliot has quite a list: "Well, I didn't get enough time to study for my finals because of family and relationship drama. Janie and I are afraid she might be pregnant. My dad might be laid off by his real estate firm because of the mess in housing right now, which means I'd have to take a semester off to work for the money to come back to school. Plus, that makes my mom pretty upset. I got into a fight playing ultimate Frisbee—that's how I got this cut on my eye that won't seem to go away. I thought relaxing at the post-finals free-for-all kegger would lift my spirits. It was fun at the time, but then I felt worse." "Holy cow!" cries Gus. "You've experienced some pretty big stressors in the past few months. That certainly explains why you're feeling sick and why that cut is slow to heal. Your suppressed immune system probably explains that cold sore, too. Why don't you come with me and the guys to relax at the Hole in the Wall, skip the beer, and then maybe go get some exercise? All those things are supposed to help relieve stress. But you may want to pick something besides ultimate Frisbee, which seems to get you a little worked up."

Chapter 14 defines stress, discusses how it affects your physical and psychological health, and explores ways of reducing stress. It is clear that stress and the effects of stress relate to many other areas of psychology. You saw that chronic activation of the fight-or-flight response can lead to an abundance of glucocorticoids in the body that can slowly impair parts of the brain (Chapter 3) that, like the hippocampus, affect memory (Chapter 5) and other cognitive functions (Chapter 7). This chapter also describes the impact of risky behaviors, such as drinking and smoking (Chapter 8) and high-risk sexual behavior. There is a lot of evidence suggesting that high emotions (Chapter 9), particularly the anger associated with Type A behavior patterns, can be seriously detrimental to health. Worrying and being overly sensitive to problems with the body, however, can result in somatoform disorders (Chapter 12). The good news for those with optimistic personalities (Chapter 11) is that a bright outlook on life and having good social support (Chapter 15) can lessen some of the negative health effects caused by stress.

CHAPTER OBJECTIVES

After studying this chapter, you should be able to:

1. Describe how both major life events and minor hassles can serve as stressors.
2. Discuss how perceived control over events can contribute to the stressfulness of an event.
3. Describe the HPA axis and its functioning in reaction to *stress*.
4. Explain the three phases of the *general adaptation syndrome*.
5. Explain how and why stress affects responses of the *immune system*.
6. Describe the *Type A behavior pattern*, and link it to research on stress and cardiovascular function.
7. Discuss how primary appraisal and secondary appraisal operate in the interpretation of stress.
8. Describe the origins and features of *posttraumatic stress disorder (PTSD)*.
9. Summarize research on *burnout*, noting its causes and consequences.
10. Compare the mind management techniques of *repressive coping*, *rational coping*, and *reframing* in stress management.
11. Compare the body management techniques of *relaxation therapy*, *biofeedback*, and aerobic exercise in stress management.
12. Compare the situation management techniques of *social support* and humor in stress management.
13. Describe the *somatoform disorders*, such as *hypochondriasis*.
14. Explain the psychology of being a patient, focusing on the *sick role* and patient–practitioner interaction.
15. Explain how personality factors, such as optimism and hardiness, contribute to health.
16. Explain how sensible practices, such as *self-regulation*, eating wisely, avoiding sexual risks, and not smoking, contribute individually and collectively to health.

CHAPTER OVERVIEW

Use the terms below to fill in the following exercises. Terms may not be used more than once. The answers can be found at the end of this chapter.

adaptation	helping	role
adrenal	humor	secondary
biofeedback	hypothalamus	sensitivity
body	immune	sexual
brain	minds	situations
burnout	optimism	social
chronic	personality	somatoform
control	posttraumatic	stressors
emotional	providers	success
environments	psychosomatic	threat
exercise	quality	time
exhaustion	rational	treatment
faking	reframing	Type A
hardiness	regulation	
health	repressive	

Sources of Stress: What Gets to You

__________________ include both major life changes and minor hassles and can sometimes be traced to particular stressful __________________. Stressors add up over time, with more __________________ stressors producing more harmful effects. All stressors have in common the production of a __________________ to well-being that is perceived as difficult or impossible to __________________.

Stress Reactions: All Shook Up

The body and __________________ both react to stress. Acute stress initiates the fight-or-flight response, which activates the __________________–pituitary–__________________ axis. Chronic activation of this response generates what Hans Selye called the general __________________ syndrome, which progresses in stages from alarm to resistance and finally to __________________. Both the __________________ and cardiovascular systems can be affected by stress, and people with a __________________ behavior pattern, who respond to stress with hostility, are particularly likely to suffer from ill health. As the body begins reacting to stress, primary appraisal and __________________ appraisal interpret the stress. These psychological reactions may lead over time to disorders such as depression, __________________, or __________________ stress disorder, in which thoughts of the stressor continually plague the mind. The people who are most likely to suffer from burnout are those whose jobs involve __________________ turmoil and, for that reason, those in the __________________ professions.

Stress Management: Dealing with it

We manage stress in our lives by controlling our __________________, our bodies, and our __________________. __________________ coping is not particularly effective. Better alternatives include __________________ to see things differently and engaging in __________________ coping to overcome the stressor. __________________-oriented stress management strategies focus on reducing stress symptoms through relaxation, __________________, and aerobic __________________. Handling stress by managing the situation can also be effective, seeking out __________________ support and finding __________________ in stressful events.

The Psychology of Illness: When It's in Your Head

The psychology of illness concerns how __________________ to the body leads us to recognize illness and seek __________________. __________________ disorders, and __________________ illnesses, can stem from too much or too little sensitivity to the body. The psychology of illness also addresses why people adopt the sick __________________, sometimes resulting in the __________________ of an illness, and how patients and their health care __________________ interact in ways that ensure the __________________ of medical treatment.

The Psychology of Health: Feeling Good

__________________ psychology explores the connection between mind and body through the influence on health of __________________ and self-regulation of behavior. Personality traits such as ________________ can result in better response to physical illness, and traits that promote ________________ can provide resistance to stress-related illnesses. Controlling behaviors relevant to health can be difficult for many people because self-________________ is easily disrupted by stress. We tend to struggle most with controlling eating, ________________ behavior, and smoking. ________________ and thought devoted to strategies for maintaining self-control can result in significant improvements in health and ________________ of life.

QUICK QUIZ #1

1. ____________ are specific events or chronic pressures that place demands on a person or threaten a person's well-being.
   a. Traumas
   b. Annoyances
   c. Stressors
   d. Triggers
2. According to a 1980 study of airport noise, children attending schools under a flight path:
   a. were no different from children in schools in other areas.
   b. had higher blood pressure than did children in schools in other areas.
   c. solved puzzles faster than did children in schools in other areas.
   d. were required to wear headphones.
3. Where are the adrenal glands located?
   a. on the kidneys
   b. next to the hypothalamus
   c. in the pituitary
   d. on the pancreas
4. Who described the general adaptation syndrome and coined the term *stress*?
   a. Robert Sapolsky
   b. Walter Cannon
   c. Jamie Pennebaker
   d. Hans Selye
5. Which of the following is NOT caused by atherosclerosis?
   a. coronary heart disease
   b. a gradual narrowing of the arteries
   c. a buildup of plaque in the cardiovascular system
   d. a buildup of plaque in the cerebral cortex
6. The interpretation of a stimulus as stressful or not is called ____________; determining whether the stressor can or cannot be handled is called ____________.
   a. alarm; reaction
   b. fight; flight
   c. primary appraisal; secondary appraisal
   d. primary interpretation; secondary interpretation

7. Jean has been teaching for 23 years and now just goes through the motions every day. She stares blankly at her students, and she feels they stare blankly back at her. She recognizes that she is exhausted physically, mentally, and emotionally, but she cannot retire because she needs the money. It is likely that Jean is suffering from:
   a. burnout.
   b. PTSD.
   c. depression.
   d. claustrophobia.
8. ___________ is the use of an external monitoring device to obtain information about a bodily function and possibly enable control over that function.
   a. Body fusion
   b. Biotension reduction
   c. Biofeedback
   d. Biological mind meld
9. Shelly Taylor suggests that the female response to stress is to ___________, whereas the male response to stress is ___________.
   a. tend-and-befriend; fight-or-flight
   b. fight-or-flight; tend-and-befriend
   c. fight-or-flight; kill-or-mame
   d. tend-and-befriend; drink-and-dial

QUICK QUIZ #2

1. ___________ psychology is concerned with ways psychological factors influence the causes and treatment of physical illness and the maintenance of health.
   a. Neuroendrocrinological
   b. Health
   c. Abnormal
   d. Physiological
2. Several studies have shown that ___________ in a stressful situation can shield us from the negative effects of the stressor.
   a. perceived control
   b. actual control
   c. learned helplessness
   d. yoked control
3. ___________, released from the pituitary, activates the adrenal glands to energize the fight-or-flight response.
   a. Cortisol
   b. Corticotropin releasing factor
   c. Adrenocorticotropic hormone
   d. Oxytocin
4. ___________ are cells that produce antibodies that fight infection.
   a. Cytokines
   b. Endorphins
   c. Schwann cells
   d. Lymphocytes

5. Arriving at a job interview in his new car, André is cut off by an aggressive driver. He screams profanities as he screeches into the parking lot. He marches by the receptionist without stopping and offends the interviewer by looking at his watch repeatedly and talking about his new car. André's behavior could best be described as:
   a. friendly.
   b. Type A behavior.
   c. empathetic.
   d. Type C behavior.

6. A final exam that you studied for could be interpreted as a ____________; a final exam that you didn't study for could be interpreted as a ____________.
   a. challenge; threat
   b. threat; challenge
   c. challenge; trauma
   d. threat; fear

7. Lindsey's cat was recently hit by a car and killed. Her reply to colleagues who asked if she was doing all right was, "Have you seen the picture of my new boat?" How is Lindsey managing her stress?
   a. by rational coping
   b. by reframing the situation
   c. by repressive coping
   d. by being delusional

8. According to the text, aerobic exercise can reduce:
   a. depression.
   b. anger.
   c. cynical distrust.
   d. All of these answers are correct.

9. In the fMRI study by Coghill et al. (2003), which of the following areas of the brain was NOT particularly active in processing pain?
   a. anterior cingulated cortex
   b. somatosensory cortex
   c. thalamus
   d. prefrontal cortex

10. Which of the following conditions does NOT decrease compliance in treatment?
    a. The number of treatments decreases.
    b. The number of treatments increases.
    c. The treatment is inconvenient.
    d. The treatment is frequent.

QUICK QUIZ #3

1. Which of the following events has the highest stress rating on the College Undergraduate Stress Scale?
   a. flunking a class
   b. taking a class you hate
   c. taking finals
   d. falling asleep in class

2. What group of biochemicals is increased in response to the activation of emotional systems?
   a. indolamines
   b. monoamines
   c. cytokines
   d. catecholamines

3. What is the order of phases in the general adaptation syndrome?
   a. resistance, alarm, exhaustion
   b. alarm, resistance, exhaustion
   c. alarm, depletion, exhaustion
   d. focus, resistance, exhaustion

4. Which one of the following is NOT a risk factor for a diminished immune response to stress?
   a. smoking
   b. extended interpersonal problems
   c. low social status
   d. acute cut on the arm

5. Randy was living in New Orleans during Hurricane Katrina. He is still upset about his losses and relives those dreadful days over and over in his mind, regardless how hard he tries to stop the images that come into his mind. Randy has now moved to Idaho to escape the reminders of the hurricane. It is likely that Randy is suffering from:
   a. avoidant personality disorder.
   b. posttraumatic stress disorder.
   c. paranoid personality disorder.
   d. dissociative fugue.

6. Peter would like to propose to his girlfriend, but he does not deal well with stress and keeps postponing the big event. It is suggested to him that he rehearse thoughts like "You can do it," "She loves you a lot," and "She'll accept even if you're nervous." This training is an example of:
   a. stress inoculation training.
   b. reframing.
   c. stress incubation training.
   d. success visualization training.

7. Those who tend to be stress-resistant, or "hardy," exhibit all the following qualities EXCEPT:
   a. sense of commitment.
   b. liking for strange things.
   c. belief in control.
   d. willingness to accept a challenge.

"HEY, GUESS WHAT I LEARNED IN PSYCHOLOGY TODAY?" (AN ESSAY QUESTION)

We're guessing there's someone in your life who is interested in the quality of your educational experiences, is reasonably intelligent, but knows little about psychology. This might be your roommate, a previous teacher, your mom, or some other person you have access to and want to share your thoughts and feelings with. What would you tell that person about stress and health? What would you say about the different ways that we manage stress? If your mom had recently been diagnosed with high blood pressure, what advice would you give her to help reduce her stress and possibly her blood pressure?

THINGS TO PONDER

You've been provided a lot of information in this chapter about stress and health. When you put it all together, you may start to ponder how it all relates to other issues in this textbook. For example, you may ask yourself:

- How does the brain interpret something as complex and variable as stress?

  Recall the system in the brain that responds to fear (e.g., the amygdala and other related limbic structures). Many psychologists view stress as part of a continuum that includes fear.

  Consider the importance of correctly interpreting a threat and what that means in terms of evolution. The organism with the most efficient system for appraising danger lived to pass those genes on to its offspring.

- How can deception cause pain to subside?

  Reflect on the fact that the brain produces endorphins, which are very similar to exogenous painkillers like morphine, and they can be released when you are told that a treatment (unknown to you, is not known to have any effect and is therefore a placebo) will block an expected pain stimulus.

  Remember that believing is critical for the placebo effect. Believing that a placebo is the real treatment is very different from wanting the placebo to be the real treatment.

- How can connecting with other people be beneficial to physical health?

  Understand that social support (including marriage) has a significantly positive effect on overall health and longevity. It is more adaptive to tend-and-befriend than to fight-or-flee, and women tend to have the advantage over men in this area.

  Think about times when you forgot to take a medication, needed to get something off your chest, or felt like you were drowning in your work—and someone came along to help.

- Are pessimistic and cynical people doomed to have poorer health than cheery optimists?

  Consider that personality traits are stable. Much of the data presented in this chapter paint a bleak picture for those who are pessimistic and/or angry.

  Simply put, the answer to the question is yes. However, there is hope for training people with a gloomy outlook to be significantly more optimistic and hardy and therefore have a healthier overall prognosis.

WEB LINKS AND SUGGESTED READINGS

Stress Management from Mind Tools—
http://www.mindtools.com/smpage.html

- Tips and resources for managing stress, particularly job stress; includes MP3 downloads and links to career and life coaches.

The Web's Stress Management & Emotional Wellness Page hosted by Optimal Health Concepts—
http://www.OptimalHealthConcepts.com/Stress

- A page with a number of useful links for stress management. There are also links to consulting services, professional organizations regarding stress management, and a section called "Worthwhile Quotes."

Go to http://www.ehow.com/ and type "swedish massage" in the search box.

- A series of videos that introduces the basic techniques of Swedish massage. Help a friend to relax and reduce the stress in life.

Porter, E. H. (1913). *Pollyanna*. London: L.C. Page.

- The novel of an orphaned girl who lives with her grumpy and pessimistic Aunt Polly. Pollyanna's philosophy of life centers on what she calls "The Glad Game," an optimistic attitude she learned from her father. The game consists of finding something to be glad about in every situation. Her optimism may be a secret to physical and psychological health.

Sapolsky, R. M. (1992). *Stress, the Aging Brain, and the Mechanisms of Neuron Death*. Boston: MIT Press.

- Discussing the now widely recognized relationships between stress and physical illness, Robert Sapolsky suggests that stress and stress-related hormones can and do damage the brain. He proposes strategies to reduce stress and methods to protect neurons from further damage, and he clearly states the relevance for humans of animal research findings.

ANSWERS

Chapter Overview

Sources of Stress: What Gets to You

Stressors include both major life changes and minor hassles and can sometimes be traced to particular stressful **environments**. Stressors add up over time, with more **chronic** stressors producing more harmful effects. All stressors have in common the production of a **threat** to well-being that is perceived as difficult or impossible to **control**.

Stress Reactions: All Shook Up

The body and **brain** both react to stress. Acute stress initiates the fight-or-flight response, which activates the **hypothalamus**–pituitary–**adrenal** axis. Chronic activation of this response generates what Hans Selye called the general **adaptation** syndrome, which progresses in stages from alarm to resistance and finally to **exhaustion**. Both the **immune** and cardiovascular systems can be affected by stress, and people with a **Type A** behavior pattern, who respond to stress with hostility, are particularly likely to suffer ill health. As the body begins reacting to stress, primary appraisal and **secondary** appraisal interpret the stress. These psychological reactions may lead over time to disorders such as depression, **burnout**, or **posttraumatic** stress disorder, in which thoughts of the stressor continually plague the mind. The people most likely to suffer from burnout are those whose jobs involve **emotional** turmoil and, for that reason, those in the **helping** professions.

Stress Management: Dealing with it

We manage stress in our lives by controlling our **minds**, our bodies, and our **situations**. **Repressive** coping is not particularly effective. Better alternatives include **reframing** to see things differently and engaging in **rational** coping to overcome the stressor. **Body**-oriented stress management strategies focus on reducing stress symptoms through relaxation, **biofeedback**, and aerobic **exercise**. Handling stress by managing the situation can also be effective, seeking out **social** support and finding **humor** in stressful events.

The Psychology of Illness: When It's in Your Head

The psychology of illness concerns how **sensitivity** to the body leads us to recognize illness and seek **treatment**. **Somatoform** disorders, and **psychosomatic** illnesses, can stem from too much or too little sensitivity to the body. The psychology of illness also addresses why people adopt the sick **role**, sometimes resulting in the **faking** of an illness, and how patients and their health care **providers** interact in ways that ensure the **success** of medical treatment.

The Psychology of Health: Feeling Good

Health psychology explores the connection between mind and body through the influence on health of **personality** and self-regulation of behavior. Personality traits such as **optimism** can result in better response to physical illness, and traits that promote **hardiness** can provide resistance to stress-related illnesses. Controlling behaviors relevant to health can be difficult for many people because self-**regulation** is easily disrupted by stress. We tend to struggle most with controlling eating, **sexual** behavior, and smoking. **Time** and thought devoted to strategies for maintaining self-control can result in significant improvements in health and **quality** of life.

Quick Quiz #1

1. **C.** While traumas and annoyances can both be stressors, traumas are typically acute, and annoyances are less likely to threaten one's well-being.
2. **B.** These children also gave up sooner on difficult puzzles when compared to children at schools in other areas. Perhaps headphones would have helped.
3. **A.** The adrenal glands are part of the hypothalamus–pituitary–adrenal (HPA) axis, which elicits the body's sympathetic response. The adrenal glands direct the release of cortisol and catecholamines in humans.
4. **D.** In fact, all those named have been involved in studying the connection between

stress and health. Robert Sapolsky is a neuroendocrinologist; Walter Cannon was an influential early psychologist, known for the Cannon-Bard theory of emotion; and Jamie Pennebaker investigated the connection between inhibition and health.

5. **D.** Atherosclerosis leads to coronary heart disease by depositing fatty tissue, or plaque, onto the walls of arteries, thus narrowing them; this is the main cause of CHD. Plaques in the cortex are caused by a different protein and are a component of nervous system diseases like Alzheimer's disease.
6. C. Both primary and secondary appraisal are important in the interpretation of stimuli.
7. **A.** Jean's is a classic case of burnout. She is in a helping profession and is physically, mentally, and emotionally exhausted from her long-term and demanding work. (Burnout may also involve depression.)
8. **C.** The other choices are nonsense terms.
9. **A.** Taylor's work suggests that women are more likely than men to seek out social support in the face of stress.

Quick Quiz #2

1. **B.** Neuroendocrinology is the area of neuroscience that addresses the interactions of the nervous and endocrine systems. Abnormal psychology is concerned more with mental health than with physical illness. Physiological psychologists study the processes of the workings of the nervous system (e.g., the firing of neurons).
2. **A.** The actual control of the situation doesn't seem to be as necessary as perceived control in reducing the effects of a stressful situation. Learned helplessness may result from being in a painful or stressful situation with no perceived control. A yoked control subject has no perceived control of the stimulus that is controlled by its yoked counterpart.
3. **C.** Cortisone releasing factor (CRF) is sent from the hypothalamus to the pituitary gland, which releases adrenocorticotropic hormone (ACTH) to the adrenal glands, which in turn release cortisol and catecholamines; this is the cascading action known as the HPA axis. Oxytocin is a hormone, typically released by females, that encourages social relationships and is critical for reproduction.
4. **D.** Lymphocytes (including B and T cells) are a part of the general immune response to antigens. Cytokines are proteins that communicate with these cells and with the brain to direct the immune response. Schwann cells create myelin in the peripheral nervous system. Endorphins are endogenous painkillers.
5. **B.** Easily aroused hostility, impatience, sense of time urgency, and need for competitive achievement—all exhibited by André—fit the Type A behavior pattern.
6. **A.** A final that you are prepared for would be a challenge (assuming that it isn't too easy); the final you are unprepared for would be a threat. Trauma doesn't enter the picture unless you receive an unexpected, dreadful grade on the final. Fear is the emotional response to a threatening stimulus.
7. **C.** Lindsey is avoiding the thoughts of her dead pet by painting a rosy picture of her enjoyment of her new boat. She is not addressing the stress caused by the loss of her cat and is not trying to reframe the situation, but rather avoiding it all together. She is not delusional.
8. **D.** Several studies have shown that aerobic exercise reduces stress, depression, cynicism, and anger, even when participants are randomly assigned to the exercise group.
9. **C.** Imaging data from the study, in which participants responded to a thermal stimulus to the leg, showed that the cingulate, somatosensory, and prefrontal cortices are all important in pain processing.
10. **A.** Compliance decreases when treatment must be frequent, is inconvenient or painful, and as the number of treatments increases. These conditions are particularly difficult for older adults.

Quick Quiz #3

1. **C.** According to the College Undergraduate Stress Scale, finals week is the most stressful of the choices, with a rating of 90 (out of 100). Flunking is next, with 89, then a class you hate (62), and finally falling asleep in class (40).

2. **D.** Catecholamines include dopamine, norepinephrine, and epinephrine and are a class of monoamines, which also include indolamines (e.g., serotonin). Cytokines are proteins that initiate the immune response.
3. **B.** The alarm phase mobilizes resources, the resistance phase helps cope with the stressor, and in the exhaustion phase the reserves are depleted.
4. **D.** Acute stressors do not typically suppress the immune system. Continual smoking, prolonged social woes, and the perception of low social status are all chronic stressors that can diminish the immune response.
5. **B.** Randy, in constantly reliving the traumatic events of Hurricane Katrina and in being unable to escape mental images of the disaster, is a classic case of PTSD. He still knows who he is, so he does not have dissociative fugue. Both paranoid personality disorders and avoidant personality disorder are social in nature, so they do not apply in this case.
6. **A.** Stress inoculation training is related to reframing but is undertaken *before* the stressful event to enable successful coping with that event.
7. **B.** Those people who tend to be stress-resistant, or hardy, according to a study by Kobasa (1979), show a sense of commitment, a belief in control, and the willingness to accept a challenge. They may have also liked strange things, but it didn't contribute to their hardiness. These people also saw tasks that others perceived as insurmountable as manageable.

"Hey, Guess What I Learned In Psychology Today?" (An Essay Question)

What might you tell your mom about the psychology of stress and health?

- You might start by defining stress as both a physical and psychological response. You could talk about something that was an acute stressor (e.g., losing your keys) versus something chronic (e.g., a strained relationship with a boss) and how those things have a different impact on your mind and body. You could talk about the different concepts of fear ("So, a bear starts chasing you . . .") and how our bodies have evolved to deal with that kind of stress, but the kind of stress that lingers activates the same physical systems, and that is not adaptive. You might mention Selye's *Three Phases of Stress Response*. You could add that we all need to find ways to interpret and cope with stress in ways that reduce the negative effects that it can have on health.
- You could explain that there are different ways of managing stress, which include managing the mind, the body, and situations. Give examples of some of the main ways that we deal with stress in these different realms. You could pose a hypothetical example, like a bomb threat called in at work. There are three main ways for your mind to cope with the stressor: repressive coping ("If I keep working on this report this will all go away."), rational coping ("Where are the emergency exits and what is the number to call for updates on the situation?"), and reframing ("It's probably a prank."). There are also strategies for managing your bodily response to the threat. You could try relaxation techniques, like deep breathing, or biofeedback, but aerobic exercise is probably out of the question. Finally, there are ways to manage the situation. You could ask your colleagues what to do or talk about your—and their—worries.
- You could tell your mom that many of the same strategies in response to the bomb threat could be effective in reducing the stress that is most likely contributing to her high blood pressure. Repressive coping is probably not a good strategy for something this serious, and that facing things like this head on makes a lot more sense. That is a good way to begin discussing health-promoting behaviors and self-regulation. Self-regulation in eating is an important part of managing a medical condition. Things that are particularly difficult, like making healthy choices about food and maybe stopping smoking, may need to be addressed in a phased approach. Promoting healthy behaviors and practicing self-regulation could get your mom's blood pressure back into the safe range.

15

Social Psychology

THE BIG PICTURE

Joe, a relatively conservative, upper-middle-class white student from southern Colorado, is on the student government committee for recycling, which is considering a proposal levying a $20 per student per semester fee to run a campus recycling program. Joe sees the advantages of the program, but he doesn't believe that the university should institute another student fee. The rest of the five-member committee is for the fee and Joe is hesitant to buck the will of the group. The head of the committee, named Blue, is white, wears dreadlocks, and has a charismatic personality. His family in San Francisco is well off. Blue is passionate about recycling and other matters of social responsibility; he is what Joe thinks of as a "trustafarian." Liam is an Irish American from Boston whose family is rich. He is less concerned about the program, and he doesn't think that the fee is that steep. Juanita is a Mexican American from the Valley in Texas; she is a first-generation college student and the daughter of migrant workers. Although she doesn't welcome another fee, she is a strong advocate for the recycling program and cannot justify voting against the program on the basis of the financial cost to her. Kim, an Asian American from southern California, comes from a middle-class family and attends the university on a music scholarship. She was an original organizer of the recycling program; she is also the object of Joe's affection. Joe weighs the costs and benefits of his possible dissent. He might be able to sway Liam to his side of the argument, but the other three would be a tough sell. He would need at least one more person to kill the proposal, and his efforts would certainly jeopardize his relationship with the group and the likelihood of his getting a date with Kim. Despite the cognitive dissonance between his beliefs (on balance, against the proposal) and his contemplated action (voting for it), he votes with the group and the proposal is passed on to the university administration. Joe has a date with Kim on Thursday.

There are several social psychological issues at work in this story. Part of Joe's decision-making process is based on the categorization of his peers into groups. Some of his thoughts are affected by the stereotypes that he subscribes to them based on the information that he knows about each individual, and the larger group that he puts them in. For example, Blue fits almost every preconception of the group that Joe has affiliated him with, while Kim falls somewhat outside of the group that he affiliates her with. Joe's decision is clearly influenced by the beliefs and convictions of the group, and by his desire to be accepted by the group. But he is primarily driven by his attraction to Kim, and ultimately adjusts his behavior to gain access to an appealing mate.

Chapter 15 covers various concerns of social psychology: the influence of primary drives, the impact of other individuals and groups on behavior, and the ways in which we characterize other people. Given that people are social animals, and that psychology is the study of human behavior, it follows that social psychological principles are discussed in earlier chapters in the textbook. Some of the pioneers of psychology (Chapter 1) were interested in understanding social interactions and the ways in which different mechanisms, such as conditioning and observational learning (Chapter 6) and obedience to authority (Chapter 9) affect social behavior. Different structures and chemicals in the brain are activated in response to positive and negative social interactions (Chapter 3). Much of the way in which we remember events is colored by biases and misattributions (Chapter 5); some memories are repressed or avoided, which may contribute to abnormal and even pathological behaviors (Chapter 12). Language (Chapter 7) as communication is certainly social. Peer pressure and influences from others, both older and younger (Chapter 10), can provide encouragement or discouragement; they may also suggest different ways to alter conscious perception (Chapter 8) (by, for example, taking drugs). Personality (Chapter 11) is necessarily interwoven with social preferences and styles of interaction. Even the ways in which we seek relief from physical and psychological strain (Chapters 13 and 14) are primarily dependent on the quality of interactions with another person or group of people.

Social psychology is at work around every corner in your life and has powerful influences in other areas of psychology. Understanding some of the mindbugs involved in social psychology and how they contribute to our foibles may ultimately result in improved relationships with friends and lovers or even a financial windfall—the art of making a deal is to a great extent, a social art. Of course, there are times when it may be beneficial to push the understanding of subtle social influences aside and give in to one of the primary social drives. It worked out for Joe—so far.

CHAPTER OBJECTIVES

After studying this chapter, you should be able to:

1. Describe the processes of social behavior, *social influence*, and *social cognition*.
2. Define *aggression* and give examples of different forms of aggression.
3. Discuss some of the benefits and pitfalls of *cooperation*, and describe ways in which cooperation has been scientifically studied.
4. Define *altruism*, and discuss how evolution may have shaped altruistic behaviors.
5. Contrast *prejudice* and *discrimination*, and discuss how these processes grow from the formation of *ingroups* and *outgroups*.
6. Offer three reasons why the often dreadful behavior of *groups* would rarely be shown by individual members acting alone.
7. Define *deindividuation* and describe how it results from membership in a group.
8. Discuss how *diffusion of responsibility*, including *social loafing*, illustrates the diminished sense of responsibility we feel as members of a group.
9. Describe some of the pitfalls of group decision making and group behavior, especially the problem of *group polarization* and how it arises.
10. Explain how women and men differ in their selectivity of a mate, and describe what those differences are.
11. Identify the physical and psychological factors that contribute to attraction.
12. Explain the *mere exposure effect*, and provide an example of its operation in a real-world situation.
13. Discuss why physical attributes are of primary importance in interpersonal attraction, and describe characteristics of women and men that are generally considered attractive.
14. Distinguish *passionate love* and *companionate love*, and describe the development of each in a close relationship.
15. Explain how *social exchange*, cost–benefit ratios, and *equity* each play a role in maintaining a close relationship.
16. Compare the hedonic, approval, and accuracy motives and their relation to susceptibility to social influence.
17. Define *normative influence*, noting how the *norm of reciprocity* is involved in the *door-in-the-face technique* of social influence.

18. Compare *conformity* and *obedience*, and describe a classic experiment in each area.
19. Compare *systematic persuasion* and *heuristic persuasion*, and give an example of each.
20. Describe the desire for consistency most of us feel, noting how the *foot-in-the-door technique* and *cognitive dissonance* each stem from this desire.
21. Describe four ways in which stereotypes are a useful process that sometimes produces harmful consequences.
22. Explain *attribution*, and distinguish between situational attributions and dispositional attributions.
23. Define the *correspondence bias*, and discuss two reasons why it occurs.
24. Define the *actor–observer effect*, and show how it results from the overall processes of attribution.

CHAPTER OVERVIEW

Use the terms below to fill in the following exercises. Terms may not be used more than once. The answers can be found at the end of this chapter.

accepted	costs	norms
actions	culture	obeying
aggression	decisions	overused
appearance	dispositions	pleasure
attitudes	dissonance	prejudice
attraction	emotion	psychological
attributions	error	ratios
automatically	evolutionary	reason
backfire	expect	reproduce
behave	friendship	request
benefits	genetic	responsibility
better	groups	rewards
biased	impulsive	romantic
biology	inconsistencies	similar
categories	influence	situational
choosing	justify	social
common	loafing	status
communications	mate	stereotypical
conforming	misjudge	true
cooperation	motives	unique

Social Behavior: Interacting with People

Human beings are ________________ animals. Like all animals, human beings are designed to survive and ________________ in response to fundamental ________________ pressures. Survival requires scarce resources, and two mechanisms for obtaining those resources are ________________ and ________________. ________________ aggression is a reaction to a negative internal state, and males are particularly prone to use aggression to ensure their ________________. The primary risk of cooperation is that others may take ________________ without bearing costs. One way to reduce the risks associated with cooperation is to form ________________ whose members are ________________ in favor of one another. Groups of people often show __________ and discrimination toward those who are not members, collectively make poor __________, and sometimes take extreme actions that no individual member would take alone. Deindividuation, social __________, and diffusion of __________ are some of the causes of these extreme behaviors.

The ability to reproduce involves gaining access to a suitable __________. Both __________ and culture make the costs of reproduction higher for women than for men, so women typically do the __________ of potential mates. __________ is a feeling that draws one closer to a potential mate, and it has both __________ and personal determinants. Of the personal determinants, physical __________ plays a particularly important role because it can provide indicators of __________ endowment and willingness and ability to provide for offspring. __________ determinants are also important, and we seem to be most attracted to those who are __________ to us on a number of dimensions. Human reproduction is usually accomplished in the context of a long-term __________ relationship that is initially characterized by feelings of intense attraction and later by feelings of __________. We weigh the __________ and benefits of our relationships and tend to dissolve them when we think we can do __________, when we have different cost–benefit __________ from our partner, or when we have little invested in the relationship.

Social Influence: Controlling People

Social influence requires understanding basic __________, such as the motives to approach __________ and avoid pain. We are influenced by __________ and punishments. Something that makes humans __________ animals is that we can be influenced by observing others being influenced and can think about the causes of rewards and punishments that others receive, which can cause attempts at influence to __________. In general, we want to be __________ by others, so we try not to violate social __________. Most people feel that they should benefit from those who have benefited from them, and several __________ techniques put us in a position where we must either comply with a __________ or risk violating that norm. When we are unsure of the norms in a situation and look to the behavior of others to guide our behavior, we often end up __________ requests or __________ to the group's behavior. We are also motivated to have accurate __________ and beliefs, and we achieve this in three ways: by using the behavior of others; by using __________ from others; and by comparing new information to old information to help us decide what is __________. Some of the communications used to determine the truth appeal to __________, while others appeal to habit and __________. When we recognize __________ among our attitudes, beliefs, and actions, we may experience cognitive __________. To alleviate this unpleasant state, we may attempt to eliminate the inconsistency or __________ it.

Social Cognition: Understanding People

We make inferences about other people based on the ________________ to which they belong; this is the basis of stereotyping. Making such inferences can lead us to ________________ others for four reasons. First, stereotypes can be inaccurate, either because our ________________ has provided misinformation or because we have seen rare confirmatory examples of a person in a category exhibiting the ____________ behavior. Second, stereotypes can be ______________ because the mere act of categorization leads us to see category members as having more in ________________ than they actually do. Third, stereotypes can perpetuate themselves by causing us to see what we ________________ to see, to treat others in ways that lead them to ________________ as we had expected them to, and to explain away disconfirming evidence. Finally, stereotypes can operate unconsciously and ________________, making it difficult to avoid using them. We also make inferences about people based on their ________________, assuming that others act as they do because of the situations in which they find themselves or because of their own ________________. We are less prone to ________________ when making ________________ for our own behavior.

QUICK QUIZ #1

1. ____________ is the study of the causes and consequences of interpersonal behavior.
   a. Social influence
   b. Social psychology
   c. Social cognition
   d. Social behavior
2. The behavior whose purpose is to cause harm to someone else is known as:
   a. assertiveness.
   b. violence.
   c. premeditation.
   d. aggression.
3. When men commit acts of aggression, they are more likely than women to do so by:
   a. assertiveness.
   b. violence.
   c. premeditation.
   d. aggression.
4. Most college students like the other students who live on the same floor in their dormitory. This attitude is due to:
   a. physical factors.
   b. physical proximity.
   c. selectivity.
   d. psychological factors.

5. For several weeks Susanna has shopped for shoes to wear to her friend's wedding. According to the findings of social psychology, she will probably:
   a. like best the first ones she looked at.
   b. like least the ones she saw on the last day.
   c. like least those she could not afford.
   d. like best those that she has seen most often.
6. If you are having feelings of exhilaration and emotional intimacy with your partner, you are likely experiencing:
   a. compassionate love.
   b. first love.
   c. passionate love.
   d. consummate love.
7. ___________ are standards for behavior that are widely shared by members of a culture.
   a. Principles
   b. Norms
   c. Normative influences
   d. Laws
8. Most college students are socially comfortable wearing jeans and flip-flops to class. This attitude is likely due to ___________ influence.
   a. normative
   b. peer pressure
   c. attraction
   d. relative
9. ___________ are inferences about the causes of behavior.
   a. Attributions
   b. Stereotypes
   c. Norms
   d. Deductions

QUICK QUIZ #2

1. A financial secretary who embezzles is showing evidence of:
   a. restrained corruption.
   b. premeditated aggression.
   c. impulsive aggression.
   d. unbridled deviance.
2. Shaun, who demonstrates impulsive aggression, likely has high levels of:
   a. serotonin.
   b. testosterone.
   c. estrogen.
   d. epinephrine.

3. ___________ is behavior that benefits another without providing benefit to oneself.
   a. Cooperation
   b. Altruism
   c. Reciprocal altruism
   d. Bystander contribution
4. Behavior toward another person on the basis of his or her group membership is called:
   a. prejudice.
   b. discrimination.
   c. bias.
   d. polarization.
5. Ashley is a beautiful young woman with long blonde hair and blue eyes. Social psychology research would suggest that those who see her are likely to assume she:
   a. lacks social skills.
   b. enjoys fewer dates.
   c. has few friends.
   d. has many friends.
6. ___________ is doing what authorities tell us to do because they tell us to do it.
   a. Obedience
   b. Conformity
   c. Diminished cognitive function
   d. Resistance to authority
7. A candidate for president who frequently appears with various actors and popular singers is making use of:
   a. star power persuasion.
   b. systematic persuasion.
   c. hedonic persuasion.
   d. heuristic persuasion.
8. ___________ are assumptions about the causes of behavior.
   a. Attributions
   b. Stereotypes
   c. Norms
   d. Deductions
9. When one's actions don't match one's beliefs or attitudes, the likely result is an uncomfortable state known as:
   a. cognitive dissonance.
   b. the unbelieving effect.
   c. the sleeper effect.
   d. the perseverance effect.
10. Helen, who runs a carpet cleaning company, asks if a prospective customer would like a free estimate. Helen is using:
    a. the door-in-the-face technique.
    b. her knowledge of social acceptability.
    c. her knowledge of the self-fulfilling prophecy.
    d. the foot-in-the-door technique.

Quick Quiz #3

1. What is the perspective of psychology that suggests that much of social behavior is concerned with reproduction and survival?
   a. social
   b. evolutionary
   c. biological
   d. obstetrical

2. A robber stealing from a customer at an ATM is acting out:
   a. drug-related behavior.
   b. impulsive aggression.
   c. premeditated aggression.
   d. aggressive frustration.

3. When men commit acts of aggression, they are ____________ women to do so by causing social harm.
   a. more likely than
   b. less likely than
   c. equally likely as
   d. dramatically more likely than

4. ____________ is behavior by two or more individuals that leads to mutual benefit.
   a. Altruism
   b. Bystander contribution
   c. Reciprocal altruism
   d. Cooperation

5. Research has shown that the main reason fellow commuters may not step forward to help an elderly woman who falls in a subway car is that:
   a. there are many others on the subway who could help.
   b. they have been taught not to talk to strangers.
   c. they may feel she should have held on tighter.
   d. we are faced with bystander intervention.

6. Sarah feels that her life is good; she is happy teaching at a university where she works with valued colleagues and has a number of good friends. Social psychologists would say that one of the main reasons for her contentment is:
   a. her ability to deindividuate.
   b. the quality of her social relationships and group memberships.
   c. the absence of prejudice and discrimination in her relationships.
   d. her ability to form intimate relationships.

7. A researcher asked each of a group of high school students to list the three people in their algebra class to whom they were most attracted. Each student listed those students who sat at the nearest desks. This is an example of:
   a. the laws of physics.
   b. selectivity.
   c. the mere exposure effect.
   d. group attraction.

8. The primary reason that most men are attracted to particular women is:
   a. evidence of financial stability.
   b. physical beauty.
   c. good personality.
   d. sense of humor.
9. Which of the following is an example of a social behavior norm that a college student is likely to exhibit?
   a. running stop signs in isolated areas
   b. cutting in line in the cafeteria
   c. taking (or pretending to take) notes on the professor's class lecture
   d. paying for a leather jacket with a credit card
10. Social psychologists conducted an experiment in which two confederates entered an elevator immediately behind an unknowing student. The student generally faced the elevator doors, but the two confederates faced the back of the elevator. Research on informational influence suggests that the forward-facing student would be most likely to:
    a. ignore the confederates and continue to face the elevator doors.
    b. stare at the confederates.
    c. turn to face the back of the elevator.
    d. begin to feel anxious and possibly cry.

"HEY, GUESS WHAT I LEARNED IN PSYCHOLOGY TODAY?" (AN ESSAY QUESTION)

We're guessing there's someone in your life who is interested in the quality of your educational experiences, is reasonably intelligent, but knows little about psychology. This might be your roommate, a previous teacher, your mom, or some other person you have access to and want to share your thoughts and feelings with. What would you tell that person about social psychology? How would you describe the various ways that other people affect our own behavior? What would you tell your mom about the pitfalls of stereotyping people?

THINGS TO PONDER

You've been provided a lot of information in this chapter about social psychology. When you put it all together, you may start to ponder how it all relates to other issues in this textbook. For example, you may ask yourself:

- How can the same part of the brain respond both to physical pain and social affiliation?

  Recall the study showing that the anterior cingulate cortex is activated in response to physical pain and exclusion from a social group, and that the right ventral prefrontal cortex (i.e., activated for physical pain relief) is also activated in order to alleviate the pain of social exclusion.

  Consider that many of these social constructions are new in relative evolutionary terms, and that the brain has had to evolve existing or changing structures to deal with these new social stimuli.

- How are social influences affected by learning?

  Remember that, according to operant conditioning principles, rewards (reinforcers) and punishments control the likelihood that a given behavior will occur again.

  Reflect on the fact that humans can learn through contingencies; also, speculate about the causes of social influences, which can affect future learning.

- How does social interaction style affect personality?

  Understand that your perception of your personality and the way that others perceive it may be very different, depending on how you behave with people.

  Think about some of the dimensions of the Big Five that rely specifically on the nature of social relationships (e.g., extraversion, agreeableness).

- What are considered extreme violations of social norms?

  Realize that most personality disorders are chronic extremes, or exaggerations, of social norms, for example, preferring solitude (odd/eccentric cluster) or lack of empathy and reciprocation (antisocial/narcissistic).

  Some norms become laws, and violations of those norms are crimes (e.g., norm: wearing clothes in public; crime: indecent exposure).

WEB LINKS AND SUGGESTED READINGS

Social Psychology Network—http://www.socialpsychology.org/

- One of the largest Internet sites devoted to psychological research and teaching, with more than 15,000 links related to psychology, including links to key societies and journals (Society for Personality and Social Psychology, *Journal of Experiential Social Psychology*).

The Daily Show: Interview with Philip Zimbardo—http://www.thedailyshow.com/watch/thu-march-29-2007/phillip-zimbardo

- Jon Stewart interviews Philip Zimbardo about his book, *The Lucifer Effect*; Zimbardo discusses his famous 1971 Stanford prison experiment ("a simulation study of the psychology of imprisonment") in light of his most recent writings and ideas. http://www.prisonexp.org/

Inquisitive Mind, Social Psychology for You—http://www.in-mind.org/

- An online quarterly magazine that publishes articles on social psychology for a general audience; the articles are written by postgraduate researchers. Free registration is required. The site includes a bibliography and blog.

Fog, A. (1999). *Cultural Selection*. Dordrecht: Kluwer Academic Publishers.

- Agner Fog describes cultural selection theory, a relatively new interdisciplinary theory of cultural change applied to history, religion, art, peace and conflict, mass media, sexual behavior, and social control.

Poretz, M., and Sinrod, B. (1989). *The First Really Important Survey of American Habits*. Los Angeles: Price Stern Sloan.

- A collection of data about things like whether or not you prefer that the toilet tissue unwind over or under the spool. This brief book presents charts and graphs for data collected on everything from which side of the sandwich you like your peanut butter versus your jelly to whether or not you and your mate agree on political issues. The authors' tag line is, "Truth is stranger than fiction. And we've got the stats to prove it."

ANSWERS

Chapter Overview

Social Behavior: Interacting with People

Human beings are **social** animals. Like all animals, human beings are designed to survive and **reproduce** in response to fundamental **evolutionary** pressures. Survival requires scarce resources, and two mechanisms for obtaining those resources are **aggression** and **cooperation**. **Impulsive** aggression is a reaction to a negative internal state, and males are particularly prone to use aggression to ensure their **status**. The primary risk of cooperation is that others may take **benefits** without bearing costs. One way to reduce the risks associated with cooperation is to form **groups** whose members are **biased** in favor of one another. Groups of people often show **prejudice** and discrimination toward those who are not members, collectively make poor **decisions**, and sometimes take extreme actions that no individual member would take alone. Deindividuation, social **loafing**, and diffusion of **responsibility** are some of the causes of these extreme behaviors.

The ability to reproduce involves gaining access to a suitable **mate**. Both **biology** and culture make the costs of reproduction higher for women than for men, so women typically do the **choosing** of potential mates. **Attraction** is a feeling that draws one closer to a potential mate, and it has both **situational** and personal determinants. Of the personal determinants, physical **appearance** plays a particularly important role because it can provide indicators of **genetic** endowment and willingness and ability to provide for offspring. **Psychological** determinants are also important, and we seem to be most attracted to those who are **similar** to us on a number of dimensions. Human reproduction is usually accomplished in the context of a long-term **romantic** relationship that is initially characterized by feelings of intense attraction and later by feelings of **friendship**. We weigh the **costs** and benefits of our relationships and tend to dissolve them when we think we can do **better**, when we have different cost–benefit **ratios** from our partner, or when we have little invested in the relationship.

Social Influence: Controlling People

Social influence requires understanding basic **motives**, such as the motives to approach **pleasure** and avoid pain. We are influenced by **rewards** and punishments. Something that makes humans **unique** animals is that we can be influenced by observing others being influenced and can think about the causes of rewards and punishments that others receive, which can cause attempts at influence to **backfire**. In general, we want to be **accepted** by others, so we try not to violate social **norms**. Most people feel that they should benefit from those who have benefited from them, and several **influence** techniques put us in a position where we must either comply with a **request** or risk violating that norm. When we are unsure of the norms in a situation and look to the behavior of others to guide our behavior, we often end up **obeying** requests or **conforming** to the group's behavior. We are also motivated to have accurate **attitudes** and beliefs, and we achieve this in three ways: by using the behavior of others; by using **communications** from others; and by comparing new information to old information to help us decide what is **true**. Some of the communications used to determine the truth appeal to **reason**, while others appeal to habit and **emotion**. When we recognize **inconsistencies** among our attitudes, beliefs, and actions, we may experience cognitive **dissonance**. To alleviate this unpleasant state, we may attempt to eliminate the inconsistency or **justify** it.

Social Cognition: Understanding People

We make inferences about other people based on the **categories** to which they belong; this is the basis of stereotyping. Making such inferences can lead us to **misjudge** others for four reasons. First, stereotypes can be inaccurate, either because our **culture** has provided misinformation or because we have seen rare confirmatory examples of a person in a category exhibiting the **stereotypical** behavior. Second, stereotypes can be **overused** because the mere act of categorization leads us to see category members as having more in **common** than they actually do. Third, stereotypes can perpetuate themselves by causing us to see what we **expect** to see, to treat others in ways that lead them to **behave** as we had expected them to, and to explain away disconfirming evidence. Finally, stereotypes can operate unconsciously and **automatically**, making it difficult to avoid using them. We also make inferences about people based on their **actions**, assuming that others act as they do because of the situations in which they find themselves or because of their own **dispositions**. We are less prone to **error** when making **attributions** for our own behavior.

Quick Quiz #1

1. **B.** Social psychology focuses on how individuals relate to others, incorporating precipitating factors as well as the effects of the interactions on those involved. The other choices are areas within social psychology.
2. **D.** There are different forms of aggression, for example, impulsive and premeditated.
3. **B.** Women, when they commit acts of aggression, do so by causing social harm. Possibly because of their higher levels of testosterone, men are prone to impulsive aggression, whereas women's aggression is more premeditated.
4. **B.** Physical factors and psychological factors are important, but not as important as proximity.
5. **D.** This is an example of the mere exposure effect. The more times we see a person or object, the more familiar it feels to us, and that familiarity increases our liking.
6. **C.** Compassionate love takes time to get started and grows slowly. First love can be, and in fact usually is, passionate love, but the second, third, or even tenth love can also be passionate love.
7. **B.** Norms are usually not written down anywhere, but are standards of behavior that are generally accepted by all in a given culture who grow up with them. They are neither laws nor normative influences.
8. **A.** College students look at other students to learn appropriate styles of dress and behavior.
9. **A.** Most people are fairly accurate in their attributions, for example in judging whether a candidate takes a position because of belief or because it may be politically expedient.

Quick Quiz #2

1. **B.** Generally, embezzlement is not an impulsive act, but one that has been carefully considered, that is, premeditated.
2. **B.** Testosterone does not directly cause aggression; rather, it seems to prepare men for aggression by making them powerful and overconfident that they can prevail in a physical fight. In that sense, testosterone relates to impulsive aggression, which is found more often in males than in females.
3. **B.** When a person does something to help someone else without any thought to whether the action would benefit himself, this is called altruism.
4. **B.** Discrimination goes further than prejudice in that it is an act, not merely a belief. Discrimination is behavior based on a prejudiced belief.
5. **D.** Also, most people assume that beautiful women are more popular and more successful than other women.
6. **A.** Most people are sensitive to and accepting of social norms, and we are likely to obey when someone in authority gives a direction or order; we assume that the authority figure knows what behavior is necessary in a given situation.
7. **D.** Heuristic persuasion attempts to change attitudes or beliefs by appealing to emotion rather than reason, in this case playing on an association, however trivial, with a popular star.
8. **A.** Attributions are inferences about the underlying causes of others' words or actions. We often have to make decisions about other people and what they tell us. To do this accurately, we need to "turn off" our stereotypes and judge the person on their words or deeds. We make situational attributions if we think the person's behavior is caused by a particular setting or situation.
9. **A.** If our actions and attitudes do not match, we are quite uncomfortable. This is called cognitive dissonance, which can only be resolved by changing either our behavior or our beliefs so that they match.
10. **D.** All salespeople know that getting in the house to give an estimate dramatically increases their chances of making a sale. This occurs because we desire consistency. If we have a salesperson come into the house to look at a dirty carpet, we are admitting to ourselves that we need help with this problem. This belief would be consistent with getting the carpet cleaned. Thus, this is called the foot-in-the-door technique.

Quick Quiz #3

1. **B.** Reproduction and survival are two fundamental challenges for humans and other animals as well.
2. **C.** Premeditated aggression is aggression consciously employed to achieve a goal—such as holding up a bank, or a bank customer. Impulsive aggression occurs spontaneously, usually in a quarrel about a trivial matter.
3. **B.** Aggressive acts committed by women tend to involve social harm, for example spreading rumors and damaging another's reputation. Men's aggression tends to be more impulsive and physically violent.
4. **D.** Cooperation is behavior by two or more individuals that leads to mutual benefit.
5. **A.** This is an example of diffusion of responsibility. If there are many commuters in the subway car, each may assume that someone else will help, and therefore all are slow to accept responsibility to aid the woman.
6. **A.** We depend on others for safety, acceptance, love, and health (lonely people are susceptible to a wide variety of physical illnesses).
7. **C.** The mere exposure effect can be stated as the tendency for liking to increase with the frequency of exposure. In this case, there is more frequent exposure to nearer classroom neighbors than to those farther away.
8. **B.** From the evolutionary perspective, this may be the case because physical beauty implies fertility, health, and other benefits that may increase the chances for offspring and continued survival.
9. **C.** At many colleges, the social behavior norms include casual clothes in the dining hall or cafeteria, taking notes at lectures (or appearing to), and relatively upright posture in class (feet off the desks). Choice b would not be acceptable behavior; choices a and d are not relevant to the norms of a college environment.
10. **C.** Informational influence is based on our assumption that the behavior of others provides clues as to what is good and true. The forward-facing student in the elevator who turns around is assuming that the others in the elevator, facing the rear, have some influencing knowledge he or she is not privy to.

"Hey, Guess What I Learned in Psychology Today?" (An Essay Question)

What might you tell your mom about social psychology?

- You might start by describing how fundamental social psychology is to the rest of psychology and how our interactions with other people influence nearly everything that we do. You could ask her about the things that originally attracted her to your father and talk about how those things are influenced by basic reproductive motives stamped into our genes. You could ask her about the crowd that she hung out with when she was your age. Why was it important to be accepted by that group? Was it beneficial to her to be affiliated with those particular people? And, on a walk, you might ask her initial impressions of passersby on the street. Does she group people into categories without knowing them? Why? Then you could talk about the benefits and the potential errors in those types of quick judgments.

- You could ask your mom how she thinks she gets you to do things that you may not want to do. She may reflect on times when you were very young and she tried to bribe you with treats or scold you for naughty behavior. This could be an intro to talking about the aspects of hedonism—how we all try to avoid bad things and approach good things. She might have used a little passive aggression and told you that she was disappointed when you made a bad choice or came home with a low grade. You could explain that this technique relates to another major influence that we all respond to, the motivation to be accepted. Finally, she may mention trying to appeal to your sense of right and wrong when she tried to get you to do the dishes when you were 12. This is another opportunity to talk about the influence of the accuracy motive, and the fact that we all want to be right or try to do what is right. In fact, you could tell her that she was relying on cognitive dissonance to inspire you to "do the right thing" and get the dishes done.

- You might talk about someone your mom knows well, maybe a friend of yours, whom she may have misjudged initially but now regards very differently. Then you could describe the four reasons why we typically make incorrect inferences about people (inaccuracy, overuse of stereotypes, self-perpetuation, and automatic stereotyping) and try to determine if one or more of these reasons were at work when she formed her initial opinion of your friend. Your conversation might start like this: "Mom, do you remember when I brought Jerry over to the house for the first time and you thought that I needed to be careful when I was hanging out with him? Do you think it was because he was black, or from a poorer neighborhood than ours, or because his clothes were unfamiliar, or some combination of those things?" She may respond, "I was just concerned for your well-being," which is undoubtedly true, and also may be a doorway into a conversation about stereotypes. "Why would I be less safe with Jerry than my other friends? Is it because you see more male black criminals than white on the news? Did you automatically put Jerry into a category?" Now you could talk about some of the other four mindbugs. And knowing your mom's interests, you could point out, "Now who do you call for album recommendations and recipes? Sometimes I think you and Jerry have more in common than you and I do!"